D1565834

SULPICIUS SEVERUS

The Complete Works

Ancient Christian Writers

THE WORKS OF THE FATHERS IN TRANSLATION

ADVISORY BOARD

No. 70

SULPICIUS SEVERUS: THE COMPLETE WORKS

INTRODUCTION, TRANSLATION, AND NOTES

BY

RICHARD J. GOODRICH

THE NEWMAN PRESS
New York/Mahwah, NJ

Caseside design by Lynn Else
Book design by Lynn Else

Library of Congress Cataloging-in-Publication Data

Names: Severus, Sulpicius. | Goodrich, Richard J., 1962- translator.
Title: The complete works / Sulpicius Severus ; introduction, translation, and notes by Richard J. Goodrich.
Description: New York : Paulist Press, 2016. | Series: Ancient Christian Writers ; No. 70 | Includes bibliographical references and index.
Identifiers: LCCN 2015012840 (print) | LCCN 2015039974 (ebook) | ISBN 9780809106202 (hardcover : alk. paper) | ISBN 9781587685248 (ebook)
Classification: LCC BR65.S5 E5 2016 (print) | LCC BR65.S5 (ebook) | DDC 270.2—dc23
LC record available at http://lccn.loc.gov/2015012840

ISBN 978-0-8091-0620-2 (hardcover)
ISBN 978-1-58768-524-8 (e-book)

Published by The Newman Press
an imprint of Paulist Press
997 Macarthur Boulevard
Mahwah, New Jersey 07430

www.paulistpress.com

PRINTED AND BOUND IN THE UNITED STATES OF AMERICA

For Mary, forever.

CONTENTS

ACKNOWLEDGMENTS

No one writes a book alone. I have received a great deal of help from a number of people, including Chris Craun, Gillian Clark, and Sam Giere, as well as my colleagues in the history department at Gonzaga University. It has also been a great pleasure to work with the staff at Paulist Press, especially my excellent editor, Nancy de Flon.

The translations in this volume were reviewed by my former colleague and Latin master, David Miller. He caught a shocking number of mistakes, and without his rigorous scrutiny, this work would be much less than it is.

Finally, I owe much to the three women in my life: my wife, Mary, and daughters, Annie and Gracie. They have patiently suffered an absent husband and father, and their love and support makes all things possible.

INTRODUCTION

LIFE

Sulpicius Severus (ca. 355–420), a native of Aquitaine, lived in a world that was rapidly changing. It was an age of flux, of upheaval, a time when old certainties were passing away and no one could have predicted what the future held. He was alive when Emperor Valens lost his life and army at Hadrianople (378); he would have been stunned, along with Augustine and Jerome, when Alaric and the Visigoths sacked Rome (410). During his life, there were rumors of Germanic invasions (Sulp.-Sev. *Mart.* 18) and the Roman empire was beginning to cede control of its western provinces to Germanic generals; little more than fifty years after his death, the western Roman empire, which had controlled Gaul since the days of Julius Caesar, would cease to exist. Already the seeds of the end had been planted: a parade of usurpers vied for control of Gaul, and rumors of Germans spread mouth to mouth. Modern scholars might argue whether the empire ended with a bang or a whimper, an apocalyptic upheaval or simply a slow reversion to a preexisting state, but for Sulpicius, the end was near and his writings suggest that he knew it.

Sulpicius wrote little about himself: he claimed to be a sinful man, a wicked man, a man unworthy to write about the holy Saint Martin, but these assertions were rather conventional. His successors in Gaul also passed over him. It is not until Gennadius of Marseilles, writing almost a century later, that we learn more about Sulpicius. Gennadius stated that Sulpicius had been a priest who had written books about Saint Martin. As an old man, he had been led astray by the Pelagians. Realizing his error, Sulpicius had taken a vow of silence and stopped writing (Gennad. *Vir.* 19). While Gennadius does offer a correct list of Sulpicius's works, there is little else in the biography that is useful.

1

Tantalizing hints of a biography can be assembled by studying the letters of his friend, senator-turned-bishop Paulinus of Nola. Thirteen of Paulinus's letters to Sulpicius survive, and in this exchange, a portrait of the man emerges. The correspondence is one-sided—all of Sulpicius's letters to Paulinus have been lost. The two men enjoyed a close relationship, although Paulinus expressed frequent irritation over Sulpicius's refusal to visit Nola. Although Paulinus came from the superior senatorial class, the similarity in education, secular aspirations, and ultimate Christian goals make Paulinus's letters a reliable source for insights into Sulpicius's life and motivations.

Paulinus noted that Sulpicius was the younger of the two, and so his birth date may be placed in the middle of the fourth century.[1] Sulpicius was born into an upper-class family: his father owned property,[2] but there is no evidence to suggest that he came from the senatorial or patrician order.[3] Gennadius mentioned that he had a sister, but any letters Sulpicius wrote her no longer survive.[4]

Young Gallo-Roman men of good birth who displayed a talent for learning were expected to receive an education in the literary arts. The quality of Sulpicius's writing suggests that he had been an excellent student. Gaul had long been a center for the literary arts; its teachers included the famous Ausonius. Paulinus and Ausonius were friends and correspondents; it is possible that Sulpicius also knew the famous rhetor. The prestige and quality of these schools is obliquely asserted by the character Gallus: "When I think about myself, a Gallic man telling stories among men from Aquitaine, I become afraid that I might offend your sophisticated ears with my uneducated speech" (Sulp.-Sev. *Dial.* 1.27.2).

Like Jerome and Augustine, Sulpicius joined the young talented men who hoped to win the attention of the imperial court and carve out careers serving the emperors. At some point in his secular career, he met Paulinus, and the bishop would later fondly remember that the two had been friends before Christ had united them as brothers (P.-Nol. *Ep.* 11.5). Paulinus offered firsthand testimony of Sulpicius's secular achievements: "You were winning greater praise…you were still a prominent player in the theater of the world, the forum" (P.-Nol. *Ep.* 5.5). Although this claim should be interpreted cautiously—it was offered in the context of the great sacrifice that Sulpicius had made to become an ascetic; the greater the career, the greater the sacrifice—

there is no reason to doubt Sulpicius had enjoyed success. It should also be noted that later in his life, Sulpicius appeared to know a significant number of prominent men (see especially Sulp.-Sev. *Dial.*, book III), and this suggests that he moved easily in that circle.

At some point, Sulpicius married. The name of his wife is not recorded, but according to Paulinus, she came from a consular family (P.-Nol. *Ep.* 5.5). If true, this would attest to Sulpicius's less than humble origins as well as support the claim that his career was flourishing. Sulpicius also acquired a mother-in-law, Bassula, through this marriage. She was well-off and later would provide scribes and an estate to support Sulpicius's literary and ascetic endeavors.

There is nothing to suggest the duration of Sulpicius's marriage. There is no mention of children or signs of a family life. Sulpicius's wife died of unknown causes, and this loss plunged Sulpicius into an existential crisis. After meeting Martin of Tours, he decided to renounce his secular ambitions and adopt an ascetic lifestyle.

Asceticism was a burgeoning movement in the Roman empire. Although the movement had begun in the East, the success of Athanasius's *Life of Antony* had also inspired westerners. Augustine records the famous story of two young courtiers in Trier who had read the *Life of Antony* and been inspired to renounce the world and embrace a life centered on God (Aug. *Conf.* 8.6.15). Jerome was another example; after failing in his secular career, he spent time in the Syrian desert before returning to Rome to pose as an ascetic master. With all the force of a popular movement, the ascetic ideal swept across the empire, capturing the imagination of aristocratic men.

That is not to say that the movement was welcomed by all. Ascetics could be an alternate source of authority, one that challenged the "legitimate" power of the bishops and the ecclesiastical hierarchy. The monks and virgins, like the martyrs and confessors of a century earlier, emphasized their direct relationship with God, a relationship that could appear to circumvent the church. Personal charisma was often pitted against institutional authority. While Athanasius had demonstrated Antony's respect for, and subordination to, the hierarchical church, this was not true of all ascetics, and many bishops felt threatened by the burgeoning movement. In Alexandria, at the beginning of the fifth century, bishops and monks fought over the orthodoxy of Origen. The monks asserted they had the right to read the great theologian, while the bishops insisted that the monks needed to submit to episcopal authority and stop reading him. Ultimately, the bishops would appeal to the state to back up their authority (Sulp.-Sev. *Dial.* 1.6–7), forcing the monks to flee into exile.

As this incident suggests, many believed that the monastic movement needed to be under the control of the church, regulated to prevent the idiosyncratic ideas and practices of individual monks from leading them into heresy. During Sulpicius's lifetime, the Spanish ascetic Priscillian dabbled on the extreme edges of the faith and led others to share his unorthodox ideas. Many bishops would come to suspect all ascetics of heresy, and it was easy for the more mainstream ascetics to be lumped in with the less orthodox. When the Emperor Maximus threatened to send men into Spain to arrest and execute the Priscillianists, Martin agonized over the possibility that good ascetics would also be snared in the dragnet (Sulp.-Sev. *Dial.* 3.11.5).

Finally, as Jerome's career demonstrated, the secular world often opposed the more extreme elements of the ascetic movement. Many people in Rome viewed the ascetic excesses of Jerome's group of women with concern. When Blesilla, a young patrician girl, starved herself to death through fasting, voices were raised against Jerome: How long should we wait to drive these detestable monks out of Rome? (Hier. *Ep.* 39.6). The cultured Rutilius Namatianus sniffed disparagingly at those men who abandoned cultured life to rot away on offshore islands (Rut. Nam. *Red.* 441–450).

Sulpicius's father was not pleased by his son's decision to renounce the world. The plan was probably revealed in 394, as Paulinus congratulates him for this radical step in a letter written in early 395: "For in answer to my prayer…you revealed the increase of your inheritance among the saints. This you did by your wholesome disposal of the burdens of this world, for you have purchased heaven and Christ at the price of brittle worldly goods."[5] Paulinus framed Sulpicius's renunciation in terms of Christ's injunction: "You put your heavenly Father before your earthly one, and following the example of the apostles, you left him on the tossing and uncertain ship of this life. Leaving him with the nets of his possessions, enmeshed in his ancestral inheritance, you followed Christ."[6] Rather tellingly, Paulinus does not state that Sulpicius had severed all familial ties; to the contrary, his decision had won the support of his mother-in-law, Bassula (P.-Nol. *Ep.* 5.6). She approved of his decision to become an ascetic and offered valuable financial support to replace what he had lost through his break with his father.

Joining an established monastery was the obvious course for a young man renouncing the world. Both Sulpicius and Paulinus had visited Saint Martin; both professed great respect and admiration for the bishop of Tours; neither joined his monastery at Marmoutier. Paulinus moved to Nola, where he used his wealth to build a shrine and monastery in honor of Saint Felix; Sulpicius withdrew to his estate at Primuliacum and began an ascetic experiment there. Two decades later, the ascetic expert John Cassian criticized those Gallic monks who chose to set themselves up as abbots of monasteries without first serving under experienced men themselves (Cassian *Inst.* 2.3), but neither Sulpicius nor Paulinus demonstrate any awareness that this might be a problem. In fact, they were simply Christianizing the ancient Roman ideal of *otium ruris*, a leisured, literary retreat to the country, where, cut off from secular concerns (*negotium*), a man could engage in philosophy and the camaraderie of like-minded friends.

This lifestyle little resembled the more austere Egyptian practices memorialized in sources such as the *Rule of Pachomius*. Paulinus built buildings, wrote poetry, and maintained a lively correspondence with the leading secular and theological figures of his day. He wrote of his own life,

> Finally...unbusied by public affairs and far from the din of the marketplace, I enjoyed the leisure of country life and my religious duties, surrounded by pleasant peace in my withdrawn household. Gradually my mind became disengaged from my worldly troubles, adapting itself to the divine commands, so that I strove more easily towards contempt for the world and comradeship with Christ, since my way of life already bordered on this intention.[7]

Sulpicius's ascetic life also took a literary turn as he began to produce the works that make up this volume, along with a number of letters that are now lost. Couriers carried letters back and forth between the foundation at Nola and Primuliacum.

While this renunciation of the world might seem less than spectacular to a modern reader, both Paulinus and Sulpicius did turn their backs on public life and commit themselves to a more serious pursuit of Christianity. Nevertheless, as was true for many educated western ascetics, renunciation did not necessarily mean rejecting wealth and status. In most respects, their lifestyle did not change much after renouncing the world. While a normative pattern for the monastic life had yet to emerge, the lives of the westerners might have seemed a bit odd to the more rustic monks of Egypt. Sulpicius and Paulinus both practiced a Christianized form of *otium ruris*; rather than turning to philosophy, as Roman gentlemen did,[8] both began to carve out careers as Christian authors.

LITERARY CAREER

Most men and women who renounced the world and devoted themselves to the ascetic life were never heard from again. Many thousands flocked to the deserts of Egypt, or later enrolled in the great medieval monasteries of the West. As would be expected, these people died in obscurity, out of the public eye. They had abandoned the world, and the world abandoned them.

Obscurity, however, had never been a goal of the reputation-conscious Roman elite. Nor, despite Cassian's later assertion to the contrary, was there a normative model for monasticism in effect at this time.[9] Certainly some would be tempted to travel east and embrace the forms of ascetic life found there, but it should come as no surprise that aristocrats like Paulinus and Sulpicius would favor a model that harmonized with traditional Roman practices.

Jerome and Rufinus were precedents for Paulinus and Sulpicius. Jerome had served the ecclesiastical hierarchy for a season in Rome, but after having been driven out of the city after the death of Pope Damasus, he had withdrawn to Bethlehem. There, supported by the wealthy Paula, he had devoted himself to his literary career. Rufinus, likewise, was living off of the wealth of the famous Melania the Elder in Jerusalem. Both men established themselves as freelance Christian authors, using their monasticism as a platform and source of authority for their writings.

Jerome was gaining popularity in the West when Sulpicius made his renunciation. His *Life of Hilarion* was written in 390, and it may have provided a model for Sulpicius's *Life of Martin*.[10] The similarities between the two works suggest that Sulpicius had read it, and perhaps the *Life of Hilarion* was the stimulus that Sulpicius needed to goad him into writing a competing account about Martin. In addition to suggesting a genre for the celebration of Martin's life and accomplishments, the *Life of Hilarion* also emphasized the miraculous in the life of the saint. Like Martin, Hilarion was a miracle worker, and this might explain why Sulpicius, following Jerome's lead, included the miracle stories that proved so controversial.

Emulation of Jerome and a desire to produce literary works were possible motivators, but it would appear that Sulpicius also had a desire to explain his renunciation of the world, an apologetic motivation that might also have contributed to his literary debut. Paulinus hints at this: "You write that you are taking pains to explain my course and your own" (P.-Nol. *Ep.* 1.4). This, suggested Paulinus, was a dangerous course: in arguing with his adversaries, he might fail to persuade them, and, in the course of the debate, might lose confidence in the choice that he had made. In fact, wrote Paulinus, Sulpicius needed to think carefully about his objective in offering an account to these people; was he trying to win the favor of the world? That was not a proper goal for the monk, who should only be worried about pleasing Christ (P.-Nol. *Ep.* 1.6). Paulinus hinted that Sulpicius had been contemplating a written work that would explain the choice he had made to cultured skeptics. Consequently, his literary debut, the *Life of Martin*, can also be read as a sophisticated *apologia*. Written to charm and entertain Roman aristocrats, the *Life* offered a counterweight to those bishops concerned about the growth of asceticism in the West, while also explaining why men like Paulinus and Sulpicius would choose to renounce the world.

Competition with established authors and an apology for the ascetic lifestyle were important motivators. Nevertheless, the religious imperative should not be discounted. Paulinus developed this idea at length after receiving a copy of the *Life:*

> Your words, as eloquent as they are chaste, bear witness that you have conquered the law of the members and the outer corrupt man, that you are preparing a pure paste, and that unleavened bread without yeast is being prepared for Christ. You would not have been privileged to tell of Martin if you had not made your mouth worthy of such sacred praise by means of a pure heart. So you are a man

blessed before the Lord, since you have recounted, in language as apposite as your love is righteous, the history of this
great priest who is most clearly a Confessor of the church.
He, too, is blessed as he deserves, for he has merited an historian worthy of his faith and life; he is destined for heavenly
glory by his merits, and for fame among men by your writing. And these words of yours are a fleece, helping to cover
with a most welcome garment our Lord Jesus, whose limbs
they cover with fine adornment, and they deck out with the
bloom of your talent. The Lamb will in His turn clothe you
with His fleece on the day of retribution, investing your mortal frame with His own immortality.[11]

Paulinus argued that Sulpicius could not have produced such a
morally excellent work had not the author perfected his soul by turning it toward Christ. Not only did the *Life* enhance Martin's reputation
among men (an apologetic motif), but it also added to Christ's glory,
and in turn, Christ would reward Sulpicius. Sulpicius had signaled the
same hope in his introductory paragraphs, writing, "I do not expect a
pointless memorial from men, but an eternal reward from God"
(Sulp.-Sev. *Mart.* 1.6). By setting out a profoundly Christian model for
others to follow, Sulpicius could hope to reap a reward in the Lord's
vineyards.

THE *LIFE OF MARTIN*

The *Life of Martin* was Sulpicius's literary debut. Published in the
summer of 396,[12] it was not the first life of an ascetic, but it is innova-
tive in being the first in a series about western bishops.[13] The *Life of
Martin* was followed by Paulinus of Milan's *Life of Saint Ambrose.* In this
work, Paulinus credited Sulpicius with providing a model for his work.
Athanasius and Jerome had written about desert monks, but "Severus,
God's servant eulogized the life of the venerable Martin, bishop of the
church at Tours" (Paulin. *Vit. Ambr.* 1). Paulinus of Milan made a clear
distinction between the writings about eastern monks and Sulpicius's
account of a western monk-bishop. The *Life of Ambrose* was followed by
Possidius's *Life of Augustine.* In this work, Possidius noted the great
writers before him who had written about those whom the Lord had

enabled to live among men and still persevere in the faith (i.e., Martin and Ambrose; Possid. *Vit. Aug.* pref.). Sulpicius's work provided a model and a precedent for later works devoted to lives and deeds of western bishops.

Sulpicius wrote a complete biography of Martin, from infancy to his own day. The work, he claimed, was based primarily on personal interviews with the bishop. Whereas others might have heard stories about Martin, Sulpicius had firsthand knowledge, acquired from Martin himself. This was an achievement because Martin was notorious for hiding his works out of a concern for modesty (Sulp.-Sev. *Mart.* 1.7; Sulp.-Sev. *Dial.* 2.1.1–9). Near the end of the *Life*, Sulpicius described how he acquired his source material: having heard of Martin, he made a trip to Tours in order to meet him. There he learned about the bishop, partly from Martin himself and partly from questioning those who knew him (Sulp.-Sev. *Mart.* 25.1). It is difficult to assess how many times Sulpicius met with Martin; Paulinus asserted that Sulpicius traveled to Tours often (P.-Nol. *Ep.* 17.4), but this claim must be evaluated in its context: Paulinus was accusing Sulpicius of frequently visiting Martin, but having no time to visit him in Nola. Consequently, the frequency of Sulpicius's trips to Tours may have been exaggerated in order to lend more force to Paulinus's complaint.

The *Life* was never intended to be a step-by-step guide to the ascetic life. A reader who wants to learn how to become a monk will find little help in the book. It does not offer a schedule for the daily offices of prayer, nor does it give guidelines for fasting. Rather, it holds Martin up as a finished product. He is the goal, the culmination of the ascetic life, an example of what the truly committed could hope to become. Sulpicius wrote "to fully describe the life of that most holy man to serve as an example for others later. This work will spur my readers on to true wisdom, to service in the heavenly army, and divine excellence" (Sulp.-Sev. *Mart.* 1.6). Martin exemplified what was possible in the Christian life, and Sulpicius hoped to "preserve from obscurity a man who should be imitated" (Sulp.-Sev. *Mart.* 1.6). There was no good to be derived from reading about Hector fighting or Socrates philosophizing, because their achievements were restricted to the secular age. By establishing Martin as a standard and working to emulate him, a person could make a contribution to the eternal kingdom of God, an everlasting achievement. Consequently, the *Life*, like Jerome's *Life of Hilarion*, offers a series of vignettes designed to show Martin in action, living a Christlike life in the world.

There is a qualitative difference between this work and the later treatises of John Cassian. Cassian alluded to this difference when he wrote that he was not going to produce an account of miracles "that offer the reader nothing but astonishment and no instruction in the perfect life" (Cassian *Inst.* pref.7). Cassian offered a program, guidelines designed to help a person make progress in the ascetic life. Sulpicius and Jerome offered the finished product and wrote very little about how their subjects had acquired their excellence.

The censure of miracle stories in Cassian's *Institutes* is most certainly a reference to the *Life of Saint Martin*. One of the work's most distinctive characteristics is its emphasis on the miracles of Martin. Chapters 6 through 24 offer an unending parade of miracles: the resuscitation of the dead, the expulsion of demons, and preaching the gospel to Satan. Cassian's critique does not suggest disbelief in the miraculous—he was quick to assert that he knew of many miracles that had occurred among the Egyptian Desert Fathers (Cassian *Inst.* pref.7)—but rather he doubted whether stories about miracles contributed anything to the educational process. What was the point of this obsession with the miraculous? How did these stories teach the reader to become a better disciple of Christ?

For Sulpicius, the miracles demonstrated that Martin was a modern apostle, performing the exact deeds that Christ and his disciples had done nearly four hundred years earlier. The miracles located Martin on the Christian spectrum, placing him among the greatest of the Christians: Sulpicius wrote that after he had restored his catechumen to life, "from this point on the name of the blessed man was beginning to spread. All of the people were regarding him as holy, powerful, and even, truly, as an apostle" (Sulp.-Sev. *Mart.* 7.7). The link between miracle and apostolic nature would be clearly articulated in the *Dialogues*, when Postumianus, responding in exasperation to the claims that some people doubted the miracles discussed in the *Life*, said, "When the Lord Himself has attested that those types of works that Martin performed were to be done by all the faithful, the person who fails to believe that Martin did these things also disbelieves that Christ said they would be done" (Sulp.-Sev. *Dial.* 1.26.5). The Bible documented the miracles performed by Jesus and the apostles; consequently, if Martin was living a comparable life, if Martin truly was on the same level as the apostles, then it was self-evident that he would match their miracles.

Martin was held up as a pattern of virtue, and part of the testimony to his virtue was the fact that he was able to wield the same power that had characterized the early princes of the church. The miracles were not intended to edify the reader as much as to demonstrate that God's power rested fully in Martin, power that had been absent since the end of the apostolic age.

Themes in the Life of Martin

Martin's stature as a fourth-century apostle is an obvious theme of the work. There were also some smaller themes developing that would gain greater prominence in Sulpicius's later works. The reluctance of Martin's fellow bishops to ordain him (9.1–7) inaugurated a contrast between the true, apostolic bishop (Martin) and his contemporaries who were more interested in seeking wealth, power, and prestige. The decision of these men to refuse Martin's ordination because of his squalid appearance signaled their superficiality and lack of spiritual insight. Fortunately, the people, in accordance with the will of God, overrode the bishops, and Martin joined their ranks. Sulpicius's critique of these secular bishops (who are usually portrayed as hostile toward Martin) will link all three of his major works.

Martin's struggle against Satan and his demons is another major theme in this work. Chapters 17 and 21–24 depict Martin as locked into a struggle with the forces of darkness. In all instances, he prevails over his adversaries, but the reader is left with the impression that Satan was roaming the earth, stirring up constant trouble. With the church triumphant and the Roman empire rapidly adopting Christianity (and the stories of Martin destroying pagan sites and winning converts for Christ demonstrated the pace of change), it might be expected that Satan was fighting a rearguard action. In fact, Satan appeared to be growing more active, and this was intended to signal the imminent return of the antichrist and the tribulations of the apocalypse.

Reception

Direct evidence of audience reaction to this work may be found in the letters of Paulinus. At P.-Nol. *Ep.* 11.11, the aristocrat recorded his delight with the work, praising it lavishly. Paulinus argued that

Sulpicius had essentially won his place in heaven by producing a work that honored Christ to such a degree. Paulinus is also said to have been relentless in promoting the book in Italy and Rome, winning a large readership for it there (Sulp.-Sev. *Dial.* 1.23.4). In a later letter, Paulinus mentioned that he had read the book to the famous Melania the Elder when she had visited him at Nola. She, along with the Bishop Nicetas, both admired the work (P.-Nol. *Ep.* 29.14).

That is not to say that his work was received without criticism upon its release. "I dread repeating what I heard recently," said Postumianus in the *Dialogues*; "Someone said that you had written many lies in that book of yours" (Sulp.-Sev. *Dial.* 1.26.4). Then, as now, Sulpicius's relentless sequence of miracles led many to question the veracity of the author. Internal evidence suggests that those who knew Martin firsthand, the monks who had lived with him, also raised doubts about the miracles attributed to Martin in the *Life* (see Sulp.-Sev. *Dial.* 2.2.1–2, in which a miracle that occurred in a crowded church was seen by only a few worthy onlookers). To counter this negative reaction, Sulpicius would later be forced to return to his subject and defend his version of Martin's life.

EPISTLES

Only three of Sulpicius's letters have survived. Like Paulinus, Sulpicius was a very active writer of letters, employing a team of couriers who carried his missives across western Europe. It is a great loss that so little remains of this corpus, although hints about the contents of his letters can be teased out of Paulinus's response to them.

Of the three letters extant, one predates Martin's death, and the other two follow that event. Since *Epistle* I was designed to offer a defense of the *Life of Martin*, which had been published in 396, it is certain that this letter must be dated between the summer of 396 and November 397. Since it would have taken some time for the *Life* to spread to its readers and generate criticism, 397 seems the likelier option. This letter represents Sulpicius's first response to criticism of the *Life*. One reader had wondered why, if Martin had authority over flames (as argued at Sulp.-Sev. *Mart.* 14.1–2), he had been scorched in a recent fire in a church.

Sulpicius took a very Jerome-like approach to this problem: he went on the offensive, attacking his adversary's faith (his adversary was like the Jews who mocked Christ on the cross) as well as his biblical knowledge (if the apostles, especially Paul, had suffered, why wouldn't the apostolic Martin also suffer?). He then recounted the story of the fire in the church, emphasizing that although Martin lost his head when he had first awoken to the danger, he quickly resorted to his familiar weapons of prayer and was saved. Although Martin had been tested, this incident only confirmed what had been written in the *Life*.

Epistles II and III are responses to Martin's death, and both must have been written shortly after November 397, although some time might have elapsed before *Epistle* III was written. *Epistle* III sets up a dramatic situation in which Sulpicius's mother-in-law has pilfered a copy of *Epistle* II and then written to complain about a lack of detail in that letter. Consequently, this letter should probably be dated to early 398.

Epistle II is a letter of consolation written to the deacon Aurelius, and it exploits most of the themes common to the consolatory genre.[14] Sulpicius had just learned of Martin's death, news that had been fore-shadowed by a dream in which he saw Martin, followed by Clarus, ascending into heaven. While Sulpicius weeps and grieves over his loss, he knows that Martin has now gone to join the company of heaven, assured of a preeminent place among the saints. A brief defense of this view is developed in which Sulpicius argues for that preferential placement. Even though Martin had not been physically martyred, he would have been first in line had he lived through the great persecutions. Life will be much poorer for those left behind, but Aurelius can be assured that they have won a powerful patron in the heavenly court.

The final letter, *Epistle* III, is a response to his mother-in-law, Bassula, who had complained about the lack of detail about Martin's death in Sulpicius's *Epistle* II. After making some mock complaints about the fact that Bassula's agent's house had purloined this letter, Sulpicius then offers an account of Martin's last days. The letter concludes with a description of Martin's funeral, in which all of the holy men and women of Gaul turned out to honor the dead bishop, creating a procession that rivaled the triumphs awarded to victorious Roman generals.

CHRONICLES

After the publication of the *Life of Martin*, Sulpicius confined himself to letter writing for a few years. In addition to the surviving letters described above, Paulinus's responses attest to a thriving correspondence between the two men, and it is likely that Sulpicius favored others with his epistles as well.

In a letter written in 402,[15] Paulinus referred to Sulpicius's new endeavor: "But I have given some thought to your project, which as you told me, has engaged you in analyzing and comparing the account of past ages in the interests of our faith."[16] Paulinus claimed that he had been a poor history student in school, but he would pass on Sulpicius's request for help to Rufinus, who also was a history writer. If Rufinus could not help Sulpicius, wrote Paulinus, no one in the West would be able to.

Shortly after this letter was written, Sulpicius published his *Chronicles*, two books that recounted the history of the world from Creation to the Priscillianist controversy of his own day. The last dated event mentioned in the work was the consulship of Stilicho, who held the post in 400. Sulpicius incorporated material from Paulinus's *Epistle* XXXI (on Helena's role in the discovery of the One True Cross) in the *Chronicles*. This letter was written in late 402 or early 403.[17] While it is impossible to provide a certain publication date, the *Chronicles* were probably released between 404 and 406.[18]

The *Chronicles* were a significant departure from the *Life of Martin*. The most startling change is the secular nature of the work. Readers who were accustomed to Sulpicius's emphasis on the miraculous were in for a disappointment in the *Chronicles*. With the exception of his account of the discovery of the One True Cross, Sulpicius managed to strip most miracles out of the biblical narrative. The *Chronicles* are straightforward narrative history, as if written by Sallust, Tacitus, or Ammianus Marcellinus. Sulpicius signaled his intent to write straight history in the preface to this work, where he noted that his readers should not adopt his account in preference to the Bible, "because the mysteries of divine events may only be drawn from those fountains" (1.pref.3). Sulpicius turned determinedly away from unpacking or expounding the "mysteries," by which he meant the hidden allegorical or anagogical significance of events.[19] His work was to be a straightforward, sequential recollection of events, stripped of miracle and spiritual significance.

Sulpicius's division of events is also rather fascinating: seventy-nine chapters were written about the period leading up to the birth of Christ; one chapter deals with the life of Christ and the acts of the apostles; five chapters are dedicated to the persecutions of the early church; a paragraph to Constantine; two chapters to Helena's discoveries in Israel; and then the work closes with eleven chapters on the Arian controversy followed by six on the Priscillianist controversy.

According to Van Andel, Sulpicius devoted so many pages of his work to the Hebrew Bible, while eschewing typological exegesis of that text, because he felt that the stories of God's interactions with the Jews were designed to provide warnings for the church. Despite repeated warnings, the Jewish people refused to obey God's commandments, which ultimately led to their rejection. This was a lesson that Christians needed to assimilate, and there was little time to master this lesson. As noted above, one of the themes in Sulpicius's writings is the imminent end of the world: the apocalypse and the return of the antichrist was at hand. Consequently, the Hebrew Bible could be mined for *exempla* that might serve as a warning for the church in its end-times.[20] Just as Sallust had used his *exempla* to warn his contemporaries living through the Second Triumvirate, Sulpicius chose to use stories from the Hebrew Bible to sound a warning for his own age.[21]

Another theme carried over from the *Life of Martin* was the injunction that priests and bishops should not mix with secular power (kings and emperors). This theme was implied by Martin's reluctance to share dinner with Maximus, contra those bishops who could often be found sharing meals with the lowliest officials (Sulp.-Sev. *Mart.* 20.1–7). With the exception of David, kings are portrayed in a negative light in the *Chronicles*:[22] they are either wicked or easily led astray. The danger of imperial power is fully articulated in the final chapters of the work, in which Sulpicius discusses the role of the state in ecclesiastical controversies.

Constantine had set the precedent for imperial involvement in church disputes when he used secular power to enforce decisions against the Donatists and (initially) the Arians. While Christian historians like Eusebius saw this as the actualization of a Christian Roman empire, the fusing of church and state, Sulpicius had a much darker view. Consequently, his account of both the Arian and Priscillianist controversies emphasized the dangers of this unholy union. A king or emperor could not be expected to be conversant with theological matters, and so the tendency was to support whichever party in a debate was the most eloquent (Sulp.-Sev. *Chron.* 2.41.4), those who were the most obsequious (2.38.1), or (darkly) whichever side was prepared to pay for imperial support (2.48.2). Even good kings or emperors were easily led astray (2.35.1) or became wicked over time (1.45.1).

Once deployed, the power of the emperor to exile or execute had disastrous consequences for the church. Emperors believed that they were doing the right thing in wielding their power on behalf of the church, but this was not always the case (2.35.1). Orthodox bishops like Athanasius and Hilary of Poitiers were stripped of their posts and sent into exile by the Emperor Constantius (2.39.1–5). Constantius would also use his power to attempt to force a resolution of the Arian controversy by essentially imprisoning the western bishops at Rimini, refusing to allow them to leave until they signed a pro-Arian statement of faith. When necessary, the emperor could also order the execution of dissidents such as Priscillian and his followers, men who, although certainly wrong (in Sulpicius's judgment), did not deserve to lose their lives over a theological dispute (2.51.1–3). This unholy use of power was counterproductive, noted Sulpicius, as it stimulated the growth and spread of the Priscillian heresy in Spain (2.51.4).

Emperors represented a significant danger to the church; worldly bishops were another. This apologetic theme, first suggested in the *Life of Martin,* also ran through the *Chronicles.* According to Sulpicius, the Jewish high priesthood had begun to unravel when it fell under the control of men who aspired to the job out of lust, avarice, and the desire to dominate others (2.17.3). This Sallustian catalog of vices was also applied to the bishops of the church, a place in which men could exercise power, gather money, and win renown for themselves. The shameful behavior of the Jewish high priests during the intertestamental period, men who purchased the office by bribing the Seleucid king (2.18.1–2), foreshadowed the poor conduct of bishops in the later books of the *Chronicles.* This criticism will become rather more pointed in the *Dialogues,* which censured the folly of those more interested in secular power and imperial favor than in serving the church as Martin had done. Or, as Sulpicius wrote when discussing the zeal of the martyrs, "Now [men] are more accustomed to compete for bishoprics because of their depraved ambitions" (2.32.2).

This was entirely inappropriate in view of the other great theme that ran through this work: the end of the age. Many people believed that the history of the earth was to be played out in "six days," or six one-thousand year periods. The *Chronicles* pick up a theme initiated in the *Life*, the proposition that the return of the antichrist is near. This apocalyptic emphasis helps explain Sulpicius's interest in chronology—he needed to ascertain the number of years that had already passed—as well as his decision to count only nine persecutions in the period before Constantine—one great persecution, marked by the advent of the antichrist, remained.[23] According to Van Andel's calculations, 5,500 years had passed before Christ was born; this meant that Christ's return was scheduled for the year 500.[24] Nero and the antichrist would return before that date (and indeed, at Sulp.-Sev. *Dial.* 2.14.4, Sulpicius hinted that the two were already alive). The increased incidence of demonic activity and the appearance of false prophets signaled at Sulp.-Sev. *Mart.* 24.1–3 were signs of the time. The *Chronicles* were to be read as a warning: the end was near and the wise would do well to heed the true prophetic voices and examples found in men like Martin of Tours.[25]

DIALOGUES

Sulpicius's Martinian themes were largely implicit in the *Chronicles*; a critique of bishops and imperial power evoked comparisons with Sulpicius's favorite bishop, but in fact, Martin only made a brief appearance at Sulp.-Sev. *Chron.* 2.50.1–2. Sulpicius's final work, the *Dialogues*, however, was an unabashed return to a defense of Martin. Ostensibly the *Dialogues* are the transcripts of a conversation that took place over a two-day period at Primuliacum. One of Sulpicius's couriers, Postumianus, had just returned from a three-year trip to the East, where he had gone to assess the state of Egyptian asceticism. Arriving at Primuliacum, he is taken aside by Sulpicius and Gallus (said to be one of Martin's disciples) and made to tell stories about the holy men he had encountered on his journey. His stories are then trumped by the stories Gallus relates about Martin. Any pretense that Postumianus was a real advocate for the merits of the eastern monks was quickly discarded; Postumianus reveals that he has always acknowledged the superiority of Martin over all challengers, and in fact, his chief desire is to learn more about Martin.

The first day ends with the setting sun and a promise extracted from Gallus to continue his stories the following morning. When daybreak arrives, the monastery at Primuliacum is inundated with visitors—priests, monks, leading secular magistrates, and a crowd of laypeople—who have traveled through the night in anticipation of hearing stories about Martin. The clerics and nobility are admitted into the audience, the lower-class members of the laity are dismissed, and Gallus resumes his storytelling. When the second day of stories draws to a close, Postumianus is charged to carry the transcripts of the discussions eastward, that all may know, throughout the entire empire, that Gaul's holy man is second to none.

The *Dialogues* were the most sophisticated and clever of Sulpicius's writings. Composed in parallel with, or shortly after, the *Chronicles*, they were probably published around 406.[26] The dating is fairly imprecise, bounded by an account of the Egyptian Origenist controversy, which occurred in 400, and a reference to the work in Jerome's *Commentary on Ezekiel*, which was published 410–412.[27] The work was undoubtedly published in two parts: books I and II were followed by book III at a later time. This is clear from Gennadius's reference to the work, in which he stated that it existed in two books (Gennad. *Vir.* 19), as well as from the early manuscript tradition. It is also substantiated by internal evidence. In discussing the necessity of justifying his stories through an appeal to witnesses, Sulpicius noted that people had begun to question the sources of the previous day's discussion, which clearly would not have been possible unless books I and II had been made available to a wider public (3.5.3). Consequently, it would appear that certain members of the reading public had leveled the same accusations against the first two books as they had against the *Life of Martin*, and a third attempt to shore up Sulpicius's version of Martin was made.

Sulpicius claimed that he was employing the dialogue form, rather than writing a straightforward treatise, in order to avoid tedium among his readers. The *Dialogues* are entertaining, but the greater advantage of this form may have been that it created the illusion that

Sulpicius was not the source of these stories. By utilizing a dialogue, Sulpicius placed his views about Martin in the mouths of others: Postumianus and Gallus make the case for Martin, while Sulpicius can appear in the role of a neutral onlooker. This had unique advantages for the author, although it could not be expected to fool everyone. A similar use of the dialogue format was targeted by Augustine when he wrote that Cicero "did not say it [that there is no God] through his own voice; he saw that such a claim was disturbing and troublesome, and so he made Cotta argue the point against the Stoics in his book on the *Nature of the Gods*" (Aug. *Ciu.* 5.9). An author could advance controversial claims by placing them in the mouths of the characters in the debate. Nevertheless, Augustine clearly realizes that any appearance of true debate, or the possibility that through discussion a dialogue might reach a conclusion the author did not intend, was simply a literary artifice.

As a literary construct, however, the dialogue form at least appeared to grant an airing of opposing views on a question. Consequently, a reader might come to a conclusion other than what the author intended. Cicero, when justifying his use of dialogue in *On the Nature of the Gods*, wrote that it was an effective way to separate the author from argument: it was the authoritative argument, rather than the authority of the author, that should prevail (Cic. *N.D.* 1.5.10). Sulpicius used the *Dialogues* as a distancing device, separating his authorial persona from the task of justifying his version of Martin. One reader, at least, seems to have been taken in by this device. Gennadius wrote about the work, "He also wrote a Conference between Postumianus and Gallus, in which he acted as mediator and judge of the debate" (Gennad. *Vir.* 19). Sulpicius emerges as no more than an interested onlooker rather than the creator of more lies about Martin.

Over the course of the three books, witnesses are produced to attest to the veracity of what Sulpicius had written in the *Life*. Martin was as amazing as Sulpicius had claimed. If he had erred, it was probably only in his failure to go far enough in celebrating the greatness of Martin. Utilizing the vehicle of the dialogue form, a cloud of witnesses is assembled to support Sulpicius's claims. The main protagonist is Gallus, the disciple of Martin, but ultimately, it is going to become clear that the entire world recognizes the superiority of Martin. The Egyptian monks who fill the first book acknowledge the fact; Postumianus and Gallus recognize it; Rome, which has become embroiled in fierce competition as readers struggle to snap up copies of the *Life*, knows it; the clerics, monks, and magistrates who assemble for the second day of discussions attest to it. In fact, like a prophet without honor, it is only in Martin's homeland, only in Gaul, that the people refuse to admit what the entire rest of world freely confesses: that Martin was exactly as Sulpicius had described him, an apostolic man who was in no way inferior to the companions of Christ.

The major themes begun in the *Life* and continued in the *Chronicles* reach fruition in the *Dialogues*. Martin is established as the monk-bishop par excellence. Whereas all the other bishops and priests of Gaul were time servers bent on the acquisition of wealth, luxury, and power, Martin continued to serve as Gaul's only truly apostolic man. While other bishops jockeyed for imperial attention, Martin shepherded his flock, protecting them from rapacious imperial officials, demons, and natural disasters. Pressed by backbiting, jealous colleagues, he nevertheless shared and frequently exceeded the great qualities of the eastern ascetics, even though he did not enjoy the luxury of desert solitude. In this final work, as with the *Life*, Martin was held up as a model, a pattern of virtue for all to emulate.

AFTERMATH

Sulpicius released the *Dialogues* and then fell mysteriously silent. It is odd that a writer at the height of his literary career would suddenly set aside his pen and write no more. Gennadius attributes this to Sulpicius's unfortunate decision to adopt Pelagianism. Once he had realized his mistake, he had taken a vow of silence and wrote no more (Gennad. *Vir.* 19). This seems wildly speculative: his works are no more Pelagian than other monastic writings of this period. It seems unlikely that Gennadius had any real knowledge about Sulpicius's later years. I have always wondered if Sulpicius's positive statements about the usurper Maximus (see Sulp.-Sev. *Mart.* 20.1–3; Sulp.-Sev. *Dial.* 2.6.1–2) or the thinly veiled suggestion that Emperors Honorius and Arcadius were the new Nero and antichrist (or at least were about to be supplanted by the two men who had now returned to earth; see Sulp.-Sev. *Dial.* 2.14.1–4) had finally come to the notice of the empire, leading to his proscription. The usurpers Constantine III (407–411) and Jovinus (411–413) were active in Gaul shortly after the *Dialogues* were published. After the suppression of Jovinus's revolt, many Gallic noblemen were executed;[28] an author of questionable loyalty might also have been swept up in a purge of this kind.

I advance this proposal with considerable hesitation and acknowledge that it is entirely speculative, with very little evidence to support it. What is indisputable, however, is that if Sulpicius did continue to live and write, none of his subsequent works was preserved. From our perspective, this is a tremendous loss, as one of the greatest writers of the late antique world here falls silent. The legacy he forged on behalf of his hero, Saint Martin, continues to endure. In France today, nearly every village and town has a church dedicated to Saint Martin; school children know the story of Martin sharing his cloak with a beggar. The version of Martin that Sulpicius created and defended ultimately prevailed, a testament to the skill of Sulpicius Severus.

Notes on the Translations

Sulpicius's works are translated from the critical editions found in the Sources Chrétiennes series. Specifically:

The Life of Martin *and the* Epistles

Sulpice Sévère: Vie de Saint Martin. Tome I: Commentaire. Introduction, critical text, and French translation by Jacques Fontaine. Sources Chrétiennes 133. Paris: Les Éditions du Cerf, 1968.

The Chronicles

Sulpice Sévère: Chroniques. Introduction, critical text, French translation, and commentary by Ghislaine de Senneville-Grave. Sources Chrétiennes 441. Paris: Les Éditions du Cerf, 1999.

Dialogues

Sulpice Sévère: Gallus. Dialogues sur les "vertus" de Saint Martin. Introduction, critical text, French translation, and notes by Jacques Fontaine. Assisted by Nicole Dupré. Sources Chrétiennes 510. Paris: Les Éditions du Cerf, 2006.

To make the text easier to navigate, I have added a brief synopsis to the beginning of each chapter throughout this work; these synopses are not found in the original manuscripts.

THE LIFE OF SAINT MARTIN

PREFACE

The dedication to Desiderius

1. Severus to my dearest brother Desiderius.[1] I had decided, my brother, to shut up the pages of the book that I wrote about the life of the holy Martin in its own papyrus, and to confine it within these walls of my house.[2] I chose this because, as I am very weak by nature, I wanted to avoid human judgment, lest, as I expected, the lack of sophistication in my writing might displease my readers and I would be deemed most worthy of everyone's censure. They would say that I had presumptuously taken on a subject that should have been reserved for writers who were known for their eloquence. But you kept begging me and I was unable to refuse what you requested so frequently. What would I not spend for your love, even if it diminished my self-respect?

2. Therefore, I produced this book with confidence in the promise you made; I believe that you will show it to no one, because you have promised this. Nevertheless, I feel uneasy that you might serve as a doorway for it, and once it has been released, I won't be able to call it back. 3. If this should happen, and you show it to others to read, please, if you don't mind me asking, instruct the readers to weigh the deeds contained in it more than the words that convey them. Let them extend forbearance if, perhaps, my defective style makes their ears ring, because the kingdom of God stands firm, not through eloquence, but through faith. 4. Let them also remember that salvation was not preached to the world through orators—although certainly, had it had been profitable, the Lord could have adopted this course too—but through fishermen.

5. When I first applied myself to writing, because I judged it a crime to conceal the virtues of so great a man, I decided that I would not be ashamed of my mistakes. I had never acquired much knowledge of these matters, and if, perhaps, there had been a time when I had taken a little something from literary studies, I would have lost my knowledge through disuse over such a long time. 6. Nevertheless, to protect myself against criticism, let the book be published with my name omitted, if that seems right to you. Scrape the title off the front so that the page is silent, and let it be enough that the page speaks of the material and says nothing about the author.

CHAPTER 1

Eternal glory, won by living a Christian life, is to be preferred to the fleeting, transitory glory awarded by the world

1. Many men, having devoted their lives uselessly to study and secular glory, have attempted to leave an everlasting (as they believe) memorial to their name by illuminating the lives of prominent men with their pen.[3] 2. Their work, in fact, is never everlasting,[4] but does bear a small portion of the fruit that hope had imagined, since the authors were trying to perpetuate their own memory, although clearly in vain; and with examples of the greatest men before them, their readers are inspired to emulate the great men in a significant manner.[5]

Nevertheless, nothing in the works of these writers pertains to the blessed and eternal life. 3. For how has the glory of their works, glory that will perish alongside this age, been profitable to them? What reward is produced for posterity by reading about Hector fighting or Socrates philosophizing? It is foolishness, not only to imitate them but also to refuse to reject their madness in the strongest terms: clearly those who judge human life only by their actions in the present have placed their hope in fables and surrendered their souls to the grave. 4. This is because they devoted themselves solely to the purpose of perpetuating their memory among humans, although it is the duty of humans to seek everlasting life rather than an everlasting remembrance. This is obtained, not by writing, fighting, or philoso-phizing, but rather by living with holy piety and religion. 5. Among those men indeed, what human error (passed on through literature) has achieved is to show that there are many who are clearly striving after either empty philosophy or the foolishness of that virtue.

6. From this I perceive that it will be worthwhile for me to fully describe the life of that most holy man to serve as an example for oth-ers later. This work will spur my readers on to true wisdom, to service in the heavenly army, and divine excellence.[6] I regard this work as being, to a certain extent, to my advantage, inasmuch as I do not expect a pointless memorial from men, but an eternal reward from God.[7] Even if I have not lived in a manner that would serve as an example for others,[8] I have taken pains in this work to preserve from obscurity a man who should be imitated.

7. And so in writing about Saint Martin, I will begin with what bears upon what he did either before he became a bishop or during his bishopric, although I will never be able to relate everything he did, since many of his deeds are not known—only he knew about them. This is because he did not require praise from men, and conse-quently, he wanted, as far as he could, to conceal all of his excellent powers.[9] 8. In fact, many of the stories I investigated have been omit-ted, because I believed it would suffice if only his greatest deeds were recorded. At the same time, I was also thinking about my readers, wor-ried that too many examples might turn them off. 9. Finally, I appeal to those who will read this work, that they should believe what has been written, and that they remember that I have not written anything except what is truthful and proven.[10] In any case, I would prefer to keep quiet than to write lies.

⌘

CHAPTER 2

Martin's childhood and early military service

1. Martin was born in the town of Sabaria, in Pannonia,[11] but he was raised within Italy, in Pavia. His parents were somewhat distin-guished in secular terms, but they were pagans. 2. His father was a

soldier at first and then later became a tribune of the army. Martin, pursuing the military life as a young man, served among the imperial guards under emperor Constantius,[12] and then under the Caesar, Julian.[13] He did not do this voluntarily, however, since practically from his earliest years, the holy childhood of the illustrious boy had aimed at divine service.[14] 3. For when he was ten years old, against his parents' will, he took refuge in the church and begged to be made a catechumen. 4. Soon, when he was twelve, he was completely converted to the work of God in a most remarkable manner; he longed for the desert, and he would have satisfied his desires if his young age had not prevented him. Nevertheless, while still of a young age, his mind was always thinking carefully about either the monasteries or the church, an intention that he later devoutly carried out.

5. But when the rulers issued an edict that the sons of veterans must be drafted into the army, Martin was handed over by his father, who envied the fruitful deeds of his son. Consequently, when Martin was fifteen, he was captured, chained, and bound with military oaths.[15] He was content to be accompanied by only a single servant, whom he, as master, served in a reversal of roles to such a degree that often he removed his servant's shoes and washed his feet;[16] the pair took their meals together, although Martin quite frequently waited on his servant.

6. For nearly three years, before his baptism, he was in the army, although he kept himself untouched by the vices that commonly ensnared that kind of men. 7. How great was the kindness of that man among his fellow soldiers! How amazing was his charity, patience, and even the humility that went far beyond the human norm. It is unnecessary to praise his frugality, which he practiced so devotedly that others regarded him not as a soldier, but as a monk. Because of these qualities, he had bound all of his fellow soldiers so tightly to himself that they respected him with amazing affection.

8. Although he had not yet been regenerated in Christ, he was acting like a baptismal candidate with his good works: assisting those who were in difficulties, giving help to the suffering, feeding the needy, clothing the naked,[17] and retaining nothing for himself from his military stipend except what was needed for his daily sustenance. Although he had not yet become a hearer of the Gospels, he was not worrying about tomorrow.

༺ↄ൜൜ↄ༻

CHAPTER 3

Martin divides his cloak with a beggar;
Martin is baptized but continues his military service

1. And so at a certain time, when he possessed nothing more than his weapons and a single military uniform, in the middle of a winter that had raged more cruelly than usual, with the result that the power of the cold had extinguished many lives, he met a naked beggar at the gate of the city of Amiens. This man begged those who were passing by to pity him, but everyone was passing by his misery in silence.

Martin, full of God, understood that the beggar had been reserved for him, as the others were not extending mercy. 2. What could he do? He had nothing more than the military cape that he was wearing, for everything else had been used up in similar works.[18] And so, taking the sword that he wore, he divided his cloak in half and gave part of it to the beggar. He put the other half back on. Some began to laugh about this deed because he looked unsightly with half of his uniform cut off. Nevertheless, many whose minds were more sensible moaned deeply[19] because they had not done something similar, especially when they possessed more than enough to clothe a poor man without incurring their own nudity.

3. The following night, after he had fallen asleep, he saw Christ in the cloak, the part of the garment that he had used to cover the beggar. He was commanded to look most diligently at the Lord and to acknowledge the garment he had given as his own. Then he heard Jesus speaking in a clear voice to the multitude of angels who were standing around him, "Martin, while still a catechumen, clothed me with this garment." 4. Truly the Lord was mindful of his own words that he had spoken before: "Whatever you have done for one of the least of these, you have done for me."[20] He declared that through Martin's action toward the poor man, he had been clothed, and in order to offer testimony to confirm such a good work, he deigned to display himself dressed in the garment that the poor man had received.

5. The most blessed man was not carried away by this vision into human boastfulness,[21] but rather he was becoming acquainted with

the excellence of God in his work. When he turned eighteen, he took the step of baptism. Nevertheless, he was not able to renounce the military immediately,[22] having been encouraged to stay by the entreaties of his tribune, whom he was serving as a junior officer. For in fact the tribune promised that once his own term of service had been completed, he also would renounce the world. 6. In anticipation of this, Martin hesitated for nearly two years after he had been baptized, although clearly he served in name only.

☙

CHAPTER 4

Martin seeks a discharge from the army;
God arranges a miracle on Martin's behalf

1. Meanwhile, the barbarians had invaded Gaul, and the Caesar Julian, having gathered the army together near the city of the Vangiones,[23] began to distribute a donative to the soldiers. As was customary, the soldiers were being called forward individually until the distribution came to Martin. 2. Then, judging this to be an opportune time in which he could win his release—for he believed that he would lack integrity if he took the donative but then did not fight—he said to Caesar, "So far I have served you. 3. Allow me now to be a soldier for God. Let those accept your donative who will fight, but I am a soldier of Christ. I am not permitted to fight."

4. But then the tyrant raged against these words, saying that Martin wanted to withdraw from the army out of a fear of the battle that was to occur on the next day, and not from a religious reason.[24] 5. Then Martin, intrepid, or rather a man made even stronger by the terror unleashed against him, said, "If my desire is attributed to cowardice rather than faith, then tomorrow I will stand unarmed in front of the battle line. In the name of the Lord Jesus, by the sign of the cross, protected by neither sword nor helmet, I will walk through the enemy formation unharmed."

6. Julian ordered that Martin be taken into custody in order to force him to carry out his words by being exposed unarmed before the barbarians. 7. But on the following day, the enemy sent envoys to seek peace; they surrendered themselves and all their possessions.

Who can doubt from this that the blessed man gained a victory? God arranged it so that he would not be sent into battle unarmed. 8. Although the Holy Lord could have guarded his own soldier among the swords and spears of the enemies, nevertheless so that the eyes of the saint should not be violated by looking upon the deaths of others, God removed the need to fight. 9. Christ did not have to demonstrate any victory on behalf of his soldier, other than one in which no one was killed; the enemy was conquered without bloodshed.

༺ೲༀ

CHAPTER 5

Hilary of Poitiers ordains Martin an exorcist; he travels home to convert his parents; en route he converts a band of robbers

1. Next, after abandoning the army,[25] Martin headed for the holy bishop Hilary of the city of Poitiers,[26] whose trustworthiness in the matters of God were well-known and acknowledged, and for a considerable time, Martin stayed with Hilary.[27] 2. Now Hilary attempted, after making Martin a deacon, to entwine him more tightly and bind him to divine ministry.[28] But after Martin resisted repeatedly and proclaimed that he was unworthy of the office, Hilary, a man of greater discernment, understood that Martin would only be able to be tied down in one way, namely, if he imposed the type of office upon him that would be seen as something of a detrimental position. Consequently, he ordained Martin an exorcist. Martin did not refuse this ordination, in case it might appear that he had despised such a humble post.

3. Shortly thereafter, he was warned in a dream that he should visit, out of religious concern, his homeland and parents, who were still occupied with paganism.[29] He departed with the support of Saint Hilary, who with many prayers and tears had extracted a promise from Martin that he would return. Martin was gloomy, they say, as he began that pilgrimage, having attested to the brothers that many adverse things would come against him, which later events proved.

4. First, while following a track through the Alps, he came upon a band of robbers. When one of them raised his axe and aimed a stroke

at Martin's head, another robber grabbed the right arm of the man wielding the axe. Nevertheless, Martin's hands were bound behind his back, and he was handed over to one man to guard and plunder. After this man led Martin to a more remote region, he began to question him, asking who he was. Martin replied that he was a Christian.

5. The robber asked if he was afraid.[30] Then Martin, with great confidence, professed that he had never been so safe, for he knew that the mercy of God would appear especially in times of trial. In fact, he felt greater grief for that man, who was, as one might expect, unworthy of the mercy of Christ, because he was living as a robber.

6. And entering into a gospel discussion, he proclaimed the word of God to the thief.[31] To make a long story short, the thief believed and, escorting Martin, returned him to his path, asking Martin to pray to God on his behalf. In later years, this same man appeared, leading a religious life, so that these events that we have related above might be heard from that man himself.

◐▧◑

CHAPTER 6

Martin meets Satan on the road; Martin's mother becomes a Christian; Martin opposes the Arians in Milan; he embraces the eremitic life; Hilary returns from exile

1. And so Martin went on from there. When he passed Milan, the devil en route assumed the appearance of a man and came to meet him, asking where he was heading. And when that one had received a response from Martin, namely that he was destined for where the Lord called him, the devil said to him, 2. "Wherever you go, whatever you attempt, the devil will oppose you."

Then Martin, responding to the devil with the voice of a prophet, said, "The Lord is my helper. I will not fear what men can do to me."[32] At once the enemy vanished from his sight. 3. Ultimately, as he had conceived in his heart and mind, he set his mother free from the error of paganism; nevertheless, his father persisted in these evils. However, he saved many in that region by his own example.

4. Now this was when the Arian heresy had spread through the entire world and was especially prevalent in Illyricum. Martin, nearly alone, fought back vigorously against the perfidy of the priests, and he had many punishments inflicted upon him. He was publicly flogged and finally compelled to leave the city.[33]

While Martin was in Gaul, on his way back to Italy, he discovered that Saint Hilary had left, sent into exile by the power of the heretics, and that the church was in an uproar. Consequently, he established a monastery for himself in Milan. In that place also, Auxentius,[34] the instigator and leader of the Arians, attacked Martin most harshly, and after inflicting many injuries on him, chased him out of Milan.

5. And so he decided to yield to circumstance, and he withdrew to an island named Gallinaria with a companion, a certain priest who was a man of great virtues. Here he lived for some time on the roots of herbs; at this time, he ate hellebore as food, which, they say, is a poisonous grass. 6. When he perceived that the power of the poison working in him was bringing death near, he drove off the threatening danger with prayer, and immediately all of his pain was put to flight. 7. Not long after this, when he discovered that Saint Hilary had been granted permission to return through the king's penitence,[35] Martin attempted to meet him in Rome, and he set out for the city.

ᕤᎨᕥᎨᕤ

Chapter 7

Martin establishes a monastery near Poitiers;
Martin raises a catechumen from the dead

1. At that time, Hilary had continued on, and Martin followed in his footsteps. After Hilary received Martin with much rejoicing, Martin established a monastery for himself not far from Hilary's town.[36] At this time, a certain catechumen joined him, a man who wanted to be trained in the disciplines of this most holy man. A few days later, seized by weakness, his disciple began suffering from the onset of a fever. 2. By chance, Martin was away at that time, and after he had been gone three days, he returned and discovered the lifeless body. The death had been so sudden that the catechumen had departed the human world

without baptism. The body had been laid out in the middle of a room, and it was being attended—the sad duty of the mourning brothers—when Martin ran in, weeping and lamenting.

3. But then, perceiving the Holy Spirit with his entire mind, Martin ordered the others to leave the cell in which the body was lying, and then he locked the doors and threw himself down on the lifeless body of the brother.[37] When he had been praying hard for some time and perceived through the Spirit that the power of God was present, he calmly straightened up a little and concentrated on the face of the dead man, expecting a result from his prayers and the mercy of the Lord. After nearly two hours had passed, he saw the limbs of the dead brother move a little, and his eyes quivered as they began to see again.

4. Then, speaking with a loud voice to the Lord and giving thanks, Martin filled the cell with a shout. When this noise was heard, those who were standing outside the doors rushed in. They saw an amazing sight: the man whom they had left for dead lived. 5. Having been restored to life, the catechumen received baptism at once, and he lived for many more years. He was the first subject or evidence of Martin's virtues among us.

6. The same man often told how, when he had been separated from his body and led before the judgment seat, he had received the harsh sentence of being assigned to dark places with the common crowds. Then, through the message of two angels, the judge learned that Martin was praying on behalf of this man.[38] At this, two angels were ordered to guide him back, that he be restored to Martin and returned to his former life. 7. From this point on, the name of the blessed man was beginning to spread. All of the people were regarding him as holy, powerful, and even, truly, as an apostle.

⁂

Chapter 8

Martin raises a slave from the dead

1. Not long after, while he was passing the land of a certain Lupicinus, a man esteemed in the eyes of the world, he was met by the

noise and sorrow of a crowd of mourners. 2. Troubled by this, he drew near and asked them whom they cried for. They told him that one of the family's young slaves had hanged himself. After learning this, Martin entered the cell in which they had laid the body, and shutting out the entire crowd, he stretched out on the corpse and prayed for a while. 3. Soon, giving the appearance of one returning to life, the dead man raised himself, with his downcast eyes fixed on Martin's face. Then, slowly, struggling to rise with a great effort, he grasped the right hand of the blessed man and clambered to his feet. Then he went out with Martin to the entrance of the house, where the entire crowd saw him.[39]

CHAPTER 9

Martin elected bishop of Tours; the bishops oppose Martin's election

1. About the same time, Martin was sought to become the bishop of the church at Tours.[40] When it proved difficult to extract him from his monastery, a certain Rusticius, one of the citizens, had his wife pretend to be sick, and then by throwing himself down before Martin's knees, he convinced him to come out.

2. Crowds of people from the city had been arranged along the route; he was escorted under a certain kind of custody into the city. Most amazing was that the crowds had gathered not only from Tours, but from neighboring cities as well, in order to cast their ballots. 3. By the single will of all the people, by the same wish and the same decision, Martin was deemed most worthy of the bishopric; how lucky would be the church that would have such a priest!

Nevertheless, a few men and some from among the bishops who had been summoned to ordain the high priest were stirred up and they impiously fought against this selection. They were saying that Martin was a contemptible person who was unworthy of the bishopric: his appearance was despicable, his clothes were filthy, and his hair was unkempt.[41]

4. The folly of their words, which only declared him an illustrious man even though they wanted to censure him, was mocked by the saner decision of the people. These men were not permitted to disrupt what the people were planning by the will of God. Nevertheless, it is said that some among the bishops, especially a certain Defensor, resisted. On account of his reluctance, he was severely censured by the reading from the prophet.

5. By chance, the lector who had the duty of reading the passage for the day had not arrived since he was blocked by the people. The assistant priests grew agitated as they waited for the lector, who had not come. Finally, one of those who were standing around took the Psalter and seized upon the first verse that he found.

6. Now this was the psalm, "From the mouths of infants and suckling babes you have produced praise on account of your enemies, so that you may demolish the enemy and their Defender."[42] At this reading, a cry arose from the people, and the segment that opposed Martin was discomfited. 7. The people believed that this psalm had been read through divine will, so that Defensor would hear a testimony against his own actions. From the mouths of infants and suckling babes, the praise of the Lord was perfected in Martin, and the enemy had been both revealed and destroyed.

Chapter 10

Martin, though a bishop, still lives like a monk; a description of the monastery at Marmoutier

1. But now, having assumed the episcopacy, Martin showed such quality and greatness that it is beyond my abilities to capture his excellence. For he persevered most steadfastly in the qualities that he had displayed before his election: 2. the same humility resided in his heart, the same economy marked his choice of clothing.[43] Thus, full of power and grace, he executed the office of bishop, but not as one who had abandoned the purpose and virtue of the monk. 3. For some time, he lived in a cell that was attached to the church; then, when he was unable to bear the disturbances of those who were crowding

around, he established a monastery for himself nearly two miles away from the city.

4. This was a place that was so secret and remote that he had no desire for the solitude of the desert.[44] For on one side, it was encircled by a cliff that had been cut out from a high mountain; the River Loire had enclosed the remaining level ground in a loop that was drawn back a little. It was only possible to reach the monastery by one road, which was long and very narrow.

He had a cell built from wood, and many of the brothers built their cells in a similar manner. 5. Others made refuges for themselves by hollowing out the rock of the overhanging mountain. There were nearly eighty disciples who were being trained in accord with the example of their blessed teacher. 6. No one there was allowed to have anything of his own; all things were held in common.[45] It was not permitted to buy or sell, as is the custom of many monks, for there was to be no art practiced there[46] except that of the copyists, and this work was relegated to the youngest of the monks. The elder monks were kept free for prayer.[47]

7. It was very unusual for any of them to go outside their own cell, except when they came together at the place of prayer.[48] All the monks received their food together after the hour of fasting.[49] No one drank wine, unless compelled by sickness.[50] 8. Many were clothed in garments of camel hair; softer cloth was regarded as criminal there. What might seem a great marvel was necessary, because there were many noblemen among the monks who, having been brought up in a very different way, had forced themselves to embrace patience and humility. We see that many of these men later became bishops; 9. for what city or church would not desire for itself a priest who had been trained by Martin?

ↄ៣ฌ๑

CHAPTER 11

Martin debunks a site thought
to have been associated with martyrs

1. But let me now address his remaining achievements, those he carried out during his episcopacy. There was, not far from town, near

the monastery, a site that had been consecrated by the false opinion of men as being a spot in which martyrs had been interred. 2. It was also believed that earlier bishops had established an altar there. But Martin, never hasty to grant belief to uncertain things, was demanding that those priests and clerics who were older than him reveal the name of the martyr, or the date of his passion. He told them that he had grave reservations about this site, because there was nothing certain in the memories that the elders had handed down to him.

3. For some time, he had stayed away from the place. He did not want to take anything away from its sanctity, because he was uncertain, but he also did not want to lend his authority to the rabble for fear of strengthening a superstition. 4. Finally, on a certain day, Martin went to the place, accompanied by a few brothers. Standing over the sepulcher itself, he prayed to the Lord that he might display who it was in the tomb or what merit the corpse possessed.

Then, turning to the left, he saw a savage ghost, dressed in mourning clothes, standing nearby. Martin ordered the ghost to speak its name and merits. The ghost proclaimed its name and revealed its guilt: he had been a thief who had been executed on account of his wicked acts, and was now honored in error by the rabble; there was nothing in his life that he had held in common with the martyrs; they enjoyed glory while he was held in punishment. 5. Rather marvelously, those who had accompanied Martin heard the voice as it spoke, but they were unable to see the person. Then Martin related what he had seen. He commanded that the altar that had been built there be removed from the site, and thus he freed the people from the error of that superstition.

Chapter 12

Martin disrupts a pagan funeral

1. It later came to pass,[51] while Martin was on a journey, that he saw a certain pagan's corpse coming toward him as it was being carried to the grave during a pagan funeral rite. Martin saw the accompanying crowd of people from a distance and, not sure what they were

doing, he stopped for a little bit. There was a gap between them of nearly five hundred yards and it was difficult to make out what he was looking at. 2. Nevertheless, because he discerned a rustic company, and because, through the action of the wind, the linen windings of the corpse were fluttering about, he concluded that the people were engaged in a profane rite of sacrifice.[52] This was the custom of Gallic countrymen: in wretched folly the people would circle their fields, with idols of the demons hidden under a shining white shroud.

3. And so, having made the sign of the cross against them, he commanded the crowd not to move from where they were and to put down their burden. At this, you would have seen that those wretches amazingly became as stiff as stone[53] at first. 4. Then, when they were not strong enough to move forward, even when they struggled mightily, they started rotating in a ridiculous circle. Finally, defeated, they put down the burden of the corpse. Thunderstruck and looking at each other in turn, they were quietly wondering what had happened to them. 5. But when the blessed man discovered that the procession was for a funeral and not a sacrifice, he raised his hand again, and restored their ability to leave and take the corpse with them. Thus, when he willed, he compelled them to stay, and when it pleased him, he permitted them to depart.[54]

CHAPTER 13

Martin and the pine tree

1. Likewise, when he had destroyed a most ancient temple in a certain village, and he had begun to cut down a pine tree that was near the temple, the high priest of that place and the rest of the crowd of pagans began to oppose him. 2. Although they had remained calm through the command of the Lord while he had overthrown the temple, they were not going to permit him to cut down the tree. He carefully reminded them that there was no sanctity in the tree; they must instead follow the God whom he himself served. The tree must be cut down because it had been dedicated to a demon.

3. Then one of the pagans who was more daring than the others said, "If you have any faith in your God, whom you claim you worship, we ourselves will cut down this tree, and you will stand beneath it as it falls. If, as you say, your God is with you, then you will avoid injury."

4. Then calmly, confident in the Lord, Martin promised that he would do this. At this, the entire crowd of pagans agreed to the condition framed in this manner, and regarded the loss of the tree as of little consequence should they destroy the enemy of their sacred rites through its fall. 5. The pine leaned in one direction, so that there was no doubt about which direction it would fall. They bound Martin and put him in the place where, in the judgment of the country people, they all believed the tree would land.

6. They began to cut down their own pine tree with great joy and exuberance. A crowd of marvelers stood at a distance. And now, little by little, the pine began to sway and to threaten its own destruction through falling. 7. The monks, standing at a distance, were worrying, terrified by the approaching danger. Having lost all hope and faith, they expected only the death of Martin. 8. But Martin, confident in the Lord, was waiting intrepidly. First the pine, collapsing, emitted a crashing noise. Then it was falling, rushing down upon him. Raising one hand in opposition, Martin interposed the sign of salvation.[55] Then you would have thought it had been repelled by a kind of tornado. The tree fell in a different direction, so that it almost flattened the country men who had been standing all around the place.

9. Then a great shout was offered up to heaven. The pagans were stunned by the miracle, the monks wept with joy, and the name of Christ was praised by all the people together. It was agreed that on that day, salvation had come to those regions. For there was almost no one from that immense multitude of pagans who did not believe in the Lord Jesus, and who did not renounce the impiety of their error and desire the laying on of hands. In truth, before Martin, very few, or more precisely, nearly no one had accepted the name of Christ in those lands. This name has thrived through the powers and example of Martin, with the result that now there are very few places in that region that are not filled with busy churches or monasteries. For wherever Martin destroyed temples, he immediately began constructing either churches or monasteries.

⟨⟩

CHAPTER 14

Martin drives back the power of fire;
two angels help Martin destroy the temple at Lévroux

1. He displayed the same amount of power[56] in a similar work performed at about the same time. For after he had set fire to a certain powerful temple that was very ancient and well-known, balls of flame were carried by the blowing wind against an adjacent, or should I say, adjoining house. 2. When Martin observed this, he climbed rapidly onto the roof of the house, placing himself in the course of the advancing flames. Then, amazingly, you would have seen a great wind arise to bend back the power of the fire, so that it might appear that there was a conflict of elements as they were struggling between themselves. Thus, by the power of Martin, the fire worked only in the place where he commanded.

3. In the village named Lévroux, when Martin wanted to destroy a temple in the same way, a building that had been richly endowed by the pagan religion, a crowd of pagans resisted him, with the result that he was injured and driven off. 4. Consequently, he withdrew to a nearby district and there, for three days, having covered himself with sackcloth and ashes, praying and fasting constantly,[57] he called upon the Lord. Since human hands were unable to overthrow that temple, divine power was needed to destroy it. 5. Then two angels armed with spears and shields, the equivalent of a heavenly army, suddenly appeared to him. They said that the Lord had sent them to him. They would put the rustic crowd to flight and offer protection to Martin, in case anyone tried to resist while he destroyed the temple. Therefore Martin was to return and devoutly carry out the work that he had begun.

6. Martin returned to the village; the pagan mob watched but took no action as he destroyed the profane temple. He tore it right down to its foundation and reduced all of the altars and idols to dust. 7. At this sight, when the rustics realized that they had been held spellbound and petrified by the divine will to keep them from resisting the bishop, nearly all of them believed in the Lord Jesus, claiming openly

and confidently that they should worship the God of Martin and forsake the idols that had been unable to assist either them or others.

❧

Chapter 15

Martin attacked by pagans while destroying temples

1. I must also relate what was done in the village of the Aedui.[58] While he was destroying a similar temple, an angry throng of pagans attacked him. And when one of their bolder men made for him with a drawn sword, Martin threw his cloak back from his shoulders and offered his naked neck to his would-be assassin. 2. The pagan did not hesitate to strike, but when he had raised his right hand high, he toppled over on his back. Overcome with fear of the divine, he began praying for forgiveness.

3. Something else happened that was similar to this: a certain man wanted to strike Martin with a butcher's knife while Martin was destroying idols, but in the act of striking, the blade was knocked out of his hands and disappeared. 4. Frequently, however, when the country people were speaking against him to prevent him from destroying their temples, he attempted to soften the pagan spirits through holy preaching, so that, once the light of truth was revealed to them, they themselves destroyed their temples.

❧

Chapter 16

Martin heals a paralyzed girl in Trier

1. Because of his power of healing, it was rare for a sick person to come to him who did not receive an immediate cure; this will be made evident in the following example. 2. A certain girl of Trier was in the grip of a dreadful paralytic sickness, with the result that for a long time she had been unable to perform normal, human bodily

functions. She seemed dead in every part of her body, and her faint breath barely moved her. 3. Her grieving relatives were on hand, expecting only her death, when suddenly it was announced that Martin had come to that city. When the girl's father heard this, he ran breathlessly to ask Martin's aid for his daughter. 4. By chance, Martin had already entered the church. There, with the people and many of the other bishops who were present watching, the wailing old man clasped Martin's knees, saying, "My daughter is dying from a miserable kind of paralysis, and what is worse than even death, only her spirit is living as her body has died. I ask that you go to her and bless her, for I am confident that through you, she will be restored to health."

5. Martin, bewildered by this speech, backed away in astonishment, saying that such a thing was not in his power, that the old man had erred in his judgments, and that he was unworthy that the Lord should demonstrate such a sign of power through him. Crying more vigorously, the father held firm and prayed that Martin would visit his unconscious daughter. 6. Finally, the bishops who were standing around compelled him to go, and Martin went down to the girl's house. A great crowd was watching from their doorways to see what the servant of God would do.

7. First, he took up the arms that were familiar to him in this kind of situation: stretching out on the ground, he prayed. Next, he looked at the girl and asked for oil to be brought to him. He blessed the oil, and when he poured the powerful holy fluid into the girl's mouth, her voice was immediately restored. 8. Then, little by little, individual parts of her body began to come back to life as he touched them. Ultimately, as the people attest, she rose and began walking with firm steps.

CHAPTER 17

Martin casts out two demons

1. At the same time, a servant of a certain proconsul named Tetradius[59] had been possessed by a demon and was suffering a painful

death. Martin was called so that he might lay a hand upon him, but he ordered that the servant be brought out to him. Unfortunately, it was impossible by any means to draw the evil spirit out of the little room it occupied; it attacked those who approached with rabid teeth. 2. Then Tetradius fell prostrate before the blessed man, praying that Martin would go down to the house that held the demoniac. Martin said that he was not allowed to pollute himself by going into the house of a heathen, a pagan. 3. Tetradius, at that time, was still wrapped in the grip of pagan error. Tetradius responded that if Martin was able to drive the demon out of the boy, he would become a Christian. 4. Consequently, Martin laid his hands on the boy and drove the unclean spirit from him. Having seen this, Tetradius believed in the Lord Jesus and immediately enrolled himself as a catechumen. Shortly thereafter, he was baptized, and he always honored Martin, the author of his salvation, with amazing affection.

5. Around the same time, in the same town, Martin, having entered the house of a certain father, stopped at the threshold, saying that he saw a horrible demon in the atrium of the house. When he commanded the demon to depart, it seized the father, who was waiting inside the house. The poor man began to gnash his teeth and wound those who were nearby. Chaos descended upon the house, the household was roiled up, and people fled the scene.

Martin confronted the raving man, and first he commanded him to stand still. 6. But when the man roared, with teeth bared, and threatened to bite him, Martin slipped his fingers into his mouth. "If you have any power," said Martin, "then devour these."

7. Then, as if he had received a white hot sword in his throat, he drew back his teeth to avoid contact with the fingers of the blessed man. These punishments and torments forced the demon to flee from the possessed man's body, but it was not allowed to exit through the man's mouth; in fact, it was excreted as diarrhea, leaving a foul remnant behind.[60]

෨ᩤᩤᩫ

Chapter 18

Martin thwarts a demonic plot to scare the Gallic people;
Martin kisses and heals a man with leprosy;
threads from Martin's robes heal people

1. Meanwhile, when an unexpected report about the movement and incursions of the barbarians had stirred up the city, Martin ordered that a demoniac be brought to him. He ordered the demon to declare whether the report was true. 2. Then it acknowledged that there were ten demons with him who were responsible for spreading this rumor among the people, so that Martin might be driven out of the city by fear; in fact, the barbarians were not even considering an invasion. When the unclean spirit acknowledged this in the middle of the church, the city was freed from the fear and discord that had prevailed at that time.

3. But in Paris, while passing through the gate of that city in the company of a large crowd, he kissed and blessed a miserable leper,[61] to the horror of those around him. Immediately the man was completely cured of his illness. 4. The next day, that man came to the church, his skin shining, and offered thanks for the health that he had received.

We should not overlook another fact: threads plucked from Martin's robe and cloak produced numerous miracles[62] among the sick. 5. For when the threads were tied to fingers or placed on the neck, they often drove diseases out of the sick.

෨ᩤᩤᩫ

Chapter 19

A letter from Martin heals Arborius's daughter;
Martin heals Paulinus of Nola's eye ailment; Martin healed by
an angel after he falls down a flight of stairs

1. There was also the case of Arborius, a man of prefect's rank,[63] very holy and of a faithful mind. When his daughter was burning up

with serious quartan fevers,[64] he placed a letter that, by chance, had just come from Martin on the girl's chest, just when her temperature went up. Immediately the fevers were expelled. 2. This matter made such a deep impression upon Arborius that he immediately vowed his daughter to God and dedicated her to a life of perpetual virginity. He then took the girl to Martin and offered her presence as a testimony to his power, which, even though he had not been on hand, had effected a cure. He also would not allow any man other than Martin to consecrate her through the imposition of the virgin's habit.

3. Paulinus,[65] a great man, as would be shown later, contracted a serious eye disease and a very thick veil had been drawn across the eye and covered his pupil. When Martin touched his eye with a little brush, he restored it to its earlier health with all the pain eliminated.

4. In an unfortunate accident, Martin fell down the stairs from an upper room, and he was cut up with many wounds because of the rough steps he struck while falling. He was lying near death in his cell, racked with terrible pains, when he saw an angel in the night who cleaned his wounds and smeared a healing ointment on the bruises of his body. Consequently, on the following day, his health had been restored to such an extent that no one would have believed that he had ever suffered any misfortune.

5. It takes too long to go through every single case; let these examples, only a few from the many possibilities, suffice. And let it be enough that we have neither deviated from the truth in these excellent stories nor become tedious by relating too many.

⚭

CHAPTER 20

Martin has dinner with Emperor Maximus;
a prophecy about Maximus's death

1. Next, in order to interleave some of his lesser deeds among the great—although such is the quality of our times in which all things have already become depraved and corrupted that it would be most peculiar to discover a priestly steadfastness that did not yield to the flattery of a king—when many bishops from various parts of the world

had come to Emperor Maximus,[66] a man possessing a fierce temperament, whose ego had been inflated by his victory in the civil wars, and when the disgraceful fawning of all the bishops around the emperor was noted, and when, with contemptible fickleness, they had subordinated priestly dignity to royal patronage,[67] apostolic authority remained in Martin alone.[68]

2. For if it became necessary to seek favors from the king for individuals, Martin commanded rather than asked. Although he was frequently invited, he stayed away from the king's dinner parties, saying that he was unable to participate in the meal of one who had expelled two emperors—one from his throne and the other from his life.[69] 3. Maximus asserted that he had not assumed power willingly, but that the obligation to defend the kingdom had been imposed upon him by his soldiers, with divine assent, and consequently, it would appear that his actions were not inconsistent with the will of God. Supported by the power of God, a victory had been won, an incredible outcome, and he had killed none of his adversaries except in battle. Finally, overcome by either these reasons or Maximus's entreaties, Martin came to dinner. The king was extraordinarily delighted that Martin accepted his invitation.

4. The best and most noble men came to dinner, as if they had been summoned to a feast day: Euodius, the prefect and also consul,[70] a man who was always more just[71] than anyone else; two counts endowed with the greatest power; the brother of the king; and his uncle. Martin's priest took his place in the middle of these men, while Martin himself sat on a stool placed beside the king.

5. Near the middle of the banquet, as was the custom, a servant offered a bowl to the king. He ordered that the bowl should be given instead to the holy bishop, expecting and arranging it so that he might receive the cup from the right hand of that man. 6. But Martin, after he drank, passed the bowl to his priest, judging that no one present was worthier to drink after himself. If he handed the cup to either the king, or to one of those men sitting near the king, his integrity might not have been preserved, so he offered it to his priest.

7. The emperor, and all of those who were present, admired what he did; he pleased them greatly with the very deed through which they had been disregarded. The news that Martin had done at the king's lunch what none of the other bishops had ever done at banquets with the lowest officials was well publicized throughout the entire palace.

8. Martin predicted Maximus's fate long before it happened: if he proceeded to Italy, where he wanted to go, bringing war to the Emperor Valentinian, he should know that in the first attack, he would emerge victorious, but a little later, he would perish. 9. This is exactly what transpired. With his initial incursion, Valentinian was forced to flee.[72] But then, after about a year, Valentinian marshaled his forces, captured Maximus within the walls of Aquileia, and killed him.[73]

⟳

CHAPTER 21

*Satan and Martin; Satan kills one of the peasants
who worked for the monastery*

1. It is a fact that he often saw angels as they were speaking together, joining in conversation in his presence. But the devil was always visible and apparent to his eyes, so that, whether he confined himself to his proper substance or whether he transformed himself into various figures of spiritual wickedness, Martin always perceived him, no matter what form he took.[74] 2. When the devil learned that he was unable to escape notice, he pressured Martin frequently with abusive chatter, because he was unable to ensnare him in his traps.

Once, holding the bloody horn of a cow in his hand, he burst into Martin's cell with a great roar, and displaying a bloody right hand and rejoicing in his admission of recent wickedness, he boasted, "Where is your power, Martin? I have just killed one of your men."

3. Then Martin, after gathering the brothers, related what the devil had said. He told them to go through each of the cells carefully, in order to determine who had been affected by this destruction. No one appeared to be missing from among the monks, but they reported that a peasant, hired for a salary, had gone to the forest in order to haul back wood in a cart. Martin ordered some of the monks to go meet him. 4. They discovered the peasant, not far from the monastery, nearly dead. Drawing his last breath, he managed to indicate the cause of his wounds and death to the brothers: evidently the oxen had been yoked together and, while he was tightening the

reins that had become slack, one of the cows tossed its head and plunged its horn into his groin. Shortly after this, he died.

You must decide why the Lord had decided to give this power to the devil. 5. What was marvelous about Martin is that not only in this instance that I have related, but in many others of this kind, whenever things happened, he foresaw them far in advance or indicated to the brothers what had been revealed to him.

⟨ornament⟩

CHAPTER 22

Satan attempts to deceive and mislead Martin; Martin preaches to Satan

1. Frequently, however, the devil, while he was trying to ridicule that holy man with the thousand ways he had of harming someone, used to present himself to Martin, visible, in radically different forms. He displayed himself in an altered appearance, sometimes in the person of Jupiter, frequently as Mercury,[75] and often even as Venus or Minerva. 2. Against these manifestations, Martin, ever undaunted, used to protect himself with the sign of the cross and the aid of prayer. Jeers were frequently heard as the throngs of demons were heckling him with their brash voices. But realizing that all their words were false and empty, he was unmoved by the phenomena.

3. Some of the brothers used to attest that they had heard a demon rebuking Martin in a brazen voice, asking why Martin received among the brothers in his monastery certain monks who had been baptized at one time, had squandered this sacrament through various errors, but then later had repented. The devil recounted the crimes of each man. 4. Martin, contradicting the devil, had firmly responded that past transgressions were cleansed through conversion to a better life, and those who stopped sinning would be absolved from their sins through the mercy of the Lord. The devil spoke against this sentiment, claiming that criminals had no right to forgiveness; the Lord could grant no mercy to those who once had fallen. Then, it was reported, Martin exclaimed against this remark, 5. "If you, yourself, most miserable demon, were to desist from the pursuit of humans and

repent of your deeds, even at this late date when the day of judgment is near, then I, trusting in the Lord Jesus Christ, could truthfully promise mercy to you."[76]

O what a holy presumption, driven by his devotion to the Lord, in which, even if he was unable to take this authority on himself, he displayed his disposition.[77] 6. And because this discussion about the devil and his arts has cropped up, it does not seem out of place, although it is tangential, to relate something that happened. There is a certain share of Martin's powers in it, and the noteworthy affair will rightly be committed to the record as a miracle and an example of what to avoid, if anything of the kind should occur anywhere in the future.

※

CHAPTER 23

Anatolius attempts to deceive Clarus and the brothers

1. There was a certain Clarus, a most noble young man, then a priest and now blessed because of his happy death.[78] After he had abandoned all things and come to Martin, it took very little time for him to reach the height of faith and the pinnacle of all virtue, and thus became distinguished. 2. And so, when he had established a dwelling for himself not far from the bishop's monastery, and many brothers were staying with him, a certain young man named Anatolius, feigning all humility and innocence under the guise of being a monk, approached and lived for some time with the others.

3. After some time had passed, Anatolius began to say that angels customarily spoke in his presence. When no one believed him, he attempted to convince them to believe through certain signs and many other things. Finally, he went so far as to assert that messages passed between himself and God, and that he wanted to be regarded as one of the prophets.

4. Clarus, however, could not be persuaded to believe. Anatolius, when he was not believed by the holy man, threatened that the

anger of the Lord and an impending beating was about to descend upon him. 5. Finally, it is said, he burst out in these words, saying, "Behold, during this night, the Lord will give me a white garment from heaven; when I put it on, I will appear among you. This will be the sign that the power of the Lord is in me: that I have been given the garment of God."

6. There arose a sense of great expectation among the brothers, who were stirred up by this statement. And so, around the middle of the night, the entire monastery seemed to be on the move, roused by the noise of people stomping around. You might have perceived that the cell that contained the young man flashed repeatedly with lights, and a noise made by those moving around in it, along with the murmur of many voices, was heard.

7. Then silence fell and Anatolius came out; he called one of the brothers, whose name was Sabatius, to his side. He showed him the tunic in which he had been clothed. 8. Astounded, Sabatius called the other brothers, and even Clarus himself ran up. A light was obtained, and all of them inspected the garment diligently. It was incredibly soft, of exceptional whiteness, sparkling with purple dye, and no one was able to recognize the kind of garment or of what skin it had been made. Nevertheless, it appeared to the careful eyes and the fingers that handled it to be nothing more than clothing.

Meanwhile, Clarus warned the brothers to keep at their prayers, so that the Lord would show them more clearly just what this garment was. 9. Consequently, they spent the rest of the night in hymns and psalms. When morning dawned, Clarus grabbed Anatolius's right hand because he wanted to take him to Martin. He was well aware that Martin could not be deceived by the arts of the devil. 10. But then the miserable young man began to struggle and shout objections, saying that he had been forbidden to show himself to Martin. While they were compelling him to go against his will, the garment vanished under the hands of those who were pulling him along. Who will be able to doubt the power of Martin after this story? The devil was unable to conceal or protect his own fantasy any longer when it was going to be forcibly brought before Martin's eyes.

෴

CHAPTER 24

False prophets begin to appear signaling the advent of the Antichrist; Satan again attempts to deceive Martin

1. Moreover, it was noticed that at about the same time there was a young man in Spain who, after he had demonstrated his authority through many signs, had become so filled with pride that he began claiming that he was Elijah. 2. When many people had rashly believed this, he added the claim that he was Christ. He succeeded in this deception to such an extent that a certain bishop named Rufus worshiped him as God.[79] Later, because of this, we see that Rufus was ejected from his bishopric. 3. Also, many of the brothers reported back to us that at the same time in the East, a certain man presented himself and declared that he was John.[80] From this, we are able to conclude, since these types of false prophets are beginning to emerge, that the return of the antichrist is near, the being who is already working the mystery of iniquity through these events.

4. I should not appear to pass over how the devil tempted Martin with great skill during those days. For on a certain day, he appeared in Martin's cell while Martin was praying. Radiant light went out in front of him and wrapped around him to make it easier to deceive people, as he had taken on the brightness of lightning. He also had wrapped himself in a royal gown, had crowned himself with a diadem of gems and gold, and had covered his feet with gold. His face was so calm and his appearance so cheerful that no one would believe he was the devil.

5. Martin had been stupefied by the initial sight of him, and the two maintained a great silence for a long time. Then the devil spoke first and said, "Recognize whom you see, Martin! I am Christ! I am about to descend to earth, but I wanted to display myself to you first." 6. When Martin remained silent and offered no response of any kind to these words, the devil dared to repeat his audacious claim, saying, "O Martin, why do you fail to believe when you can see that I am Christ?"

7. When the Spirit revealed that he should know that this was the devil and not the Lord, Martin said, "The Lord Jesus did not pre-

dict that he would return dressed in purple or wearing a shining crown. I will not believe that Christ has come unless I see him in the same clothing and form in which he suffered, and unless he displays the marks of the cross." 8. With these words, the devil immediately vanished like smoke, and the cell was filled with a great stink, a certain sign left behind that he had been the devil. I learned about the incident that I have just related from the mouth of Martin himself, just in case anyone suspects that this is only a fable.

Chapter 25

Sulpicius meets Martin

1. After I had heard of his faith, life, and virtue, I burned with a desire to meet him and made a pleasant journey in order to see him. At this time, because my heart was aflame to write about his life, I learned about him—partly from his own testimony, as much as I was able to discover by questioning him, and partly from those who had been present or knew about him. 2. Even then it was hard to believe the humility and kindness with which he received me. He congratulated me often, and rejoiced in the Lord that I held him in such esteem that I would make a pilgrimage to see him. 3. I was so wretched—I hardly dare confess it—yet he had deemed me worthy to share his holy meal. He offered the water to wash my hands, and in the evening, he washed my feet. I did not have the willpower to struggle or to demur. I was overpowered by his great authority to the extent that I would have regarded it as wicked if I had not acquiesced.[81]

4. The primary focus of his discussion with us was that we should reject the seductions of the world and the burdens of this age, so that we might follow the Lord Jesus freely and without hindrance. And he often mentioned to us the most superior example of the present times, that most illustrious man Paulinus, whom I mentioned above.[82] Paulinus, after casting aside the greatest wealth, was following Christ and, nearly alone in these times, had fulfilled the gospel injunctions. 5. Martin proclaimed that Paulinus was worth following, worth imitating, and that the present age was blessed by his great faith and

the pattern of his virtue. Following the precept of the Lord, although wealthy and possessing much, he had sold all of his things and given his money to the poor. What had been deemed an impossible action had been made possible through his example.

6. But there was such gravity, such dignity in Martin's words and conversation! How shrewd, how effective he was, how readily inclined to solve questions from the Scriptures, and how easily he did this! 7. And because I know that there are many doubters on this point, since I have encountered those who did not believe this when I was telling them, I call Jesus and our common hope to attest that I have never heard from any other mouth such knowledge, such ability, so much discussion that was so good and so pure. 8. This panegyric is altogether insufficient to encompass the virtues of Martin; it is amazing that such an uneducated man had even that much eloquence at his disposal.

∽

Chapter 26

The difficulty of capturing the greatness of Martin

1. But now this book requires an end, and my discussion must be closed. This is not because I have exhausted the stories that might be told about Martin, but because I, like inexperienced poets who become negligent near the end of the work, am succumbing to defeat before such a mass of material. 2. For even if it was possible to lay out the deeds and words of that man in one way or another, I claim, truthfully, that no speech will ever explain his inner life, his daily life among the people, and his heart that was always focused on heaven.

3. Even if Homer himself rose,[83] as they say, from the underworld, no speech could document his perseverance and temperance in abstinence and in fasting; his power in vigils and prayers; his nights spent in just the same way as his days, with no time free from God's work to spend in either leisure or business, nor even food or sleep, except to the extent that they represent a natural necessity. Indeed, everything is greater in Martin than what words can express.

For never did any hour or moment pass in which he was not deep in prayer or busy with reading, although, even when reading or perhaps doing something else, his heart never wandered away from prayer. 4. It is customary among blacksmiths to strike their anvils as a form of relaxation while working. Martin also followed this practice, as, while it appeared that he was doing something else, he would always be praying.

5. O truly blessed man, in whom there was no deceit. He judged no one, condemned no one, and never returned evil in the face of all of his injuries. When he was the high priest and was hurt with impunity by the lesser priests, he never, for this reason, removed them, either from their position or from his presence.[84] To the best of his ability, he handled them with charity.

CHAPTER 27

More good qualities of Martin; a final attack on the bishops; the Life of Martin *will be treasured by holy people*

1. No one ever saw him angry, disturbed, grieving, or laughing. He was always the same, displaying a manner of heavenly cheerfulness on his face that seemed beyond the nature of humankind. 2. There was never anything in his mouth except Christ, never anything in his heart except piety, except peace, except mercy. He was generally in the habit of weeping over the sins of those who were seen to mistreat him, those who appeared to be his detractors; while he was withdrawn and quiet, they were carping at him with poisonous words and the mouths of vipers.

3. And in truth, I encountered some who were jealous of his virtues and life, who disliked in him the qualities they did not find in themselves, those virtues they were unable to imitate. O wickedness, to be mourned and lamented! His persecutors were none other than the bishops (although clearly only a few of them). 4. It is unnecessary to name any of them, even though some of them are still yapping around us today. It will suffice if they are ashamed, should any of them read this and recognize themselves. For if this work provokes

anger, the reader will be admitting that it has been written about him-self, although perhaps I have been thinking about other people. 5. Nevertheless, I will not flee from my task; if there are any readers who are of this kind, let them hate me along with such a great man.

6. I readily place my trust in the belief that this little work will be welcomed by all holy people. For the rest, if anyone reads this work in a disbelieving spirit, it is he who will sin. 7. I myself am aware that I was impelled to write by faith in the facts and by the love of Christ. I have set forth what is undoubted and spoken what is true. I hope that the person who believes these words, rather than simply reading them, will receive the reward that God has prepared.

EPISTLES

Epistle I—To Eusebius

Sulpicius answers the doubt of one man who wants to know
why Martin was scorched in a recent fire

1. Yesterday, when several monks came to me, someone, during the inexhaustible stories and long discussion, mentioned my book that I wrote about the life of that blessed man Martin. I heard with very great pleasure that many people were reading it carefully. 2. Then someone told me that a certain man, prompted by an evil spirit, had asked why Martin, who had revived the dead and repulsed flames from houses,[1] had himself been recently scorched by a dangerous fire and exposed to suffering.

3. O miserable man, whoever you are! We recognize the perfidy of the Jews in his words and statements; they scolded the Lord with these words when he was placed on the cross: "He saved others, but he is unable to save himself."[2] 4. But truly, if this man, whoever he is, had been born in those times, he would also have spoken against the Lord with the voice that now, in a similar manner, he employs to blaspheme the holy saint of the Lord.

5. And so, what of it, whoever you are? Is Martin therefore not powerful? Does it follow that he is not a holy man because he was tested by fire? O blessed man, in every way similar to the apostles, even in these jeers from men! Naturally, the pagans were said to have felt this also about Paul when a snake bit him: "This man must be a murderer; he was saved from the sea, but the fates do not allow him to live."[3] But Paul, shaking the snake into the fire, suffered no harm. The people believed he would immediately fall down and die unexpectedly. When they saw that nothing bad happened to him, they changed their minds and began to say that he was a god. But now you, O most

55

unfortunate of all mortal men, following their example, ought to have censured yourself for your own treachery; if the fact that Martin seemed to have been singed by the flames of the fire presented a stumbling block to you, then you ought to have attributed this mere singeing to his merits and power; he was surrounded by flames and did not die.

6. Admit, O miserable man, admit what you do not know: nearly all the saints were distinguished more for the dangers they faced than for their powers. For instance, I see Peter, a man of powerful faith, opposed by the nature of the elements, walking with his feet upon the sea and pressing the unstable waters with his corporeal footstep. But it does not seem any less impressive to me that the preacher to the nations[4] who was devoured by the waves also, after three days and the same number of nights, emerged restored from the deep water. In fact, I do not know whether it was more impressive to have survived in the deeps, or to have walked above the depths of the sea.

7. I believe, you fool, that you have either not read these stories, or if you have read them, you did not listen. For it was with divine counsel that the blessed evangelist inserted an example of this kind in the holy books. This was not simply so that the human mind could learn about the dangers of shipwrecks and serpents from these stories, but rather, as the Apostle, who gloried in his nakedness, hunger, and the dangers of robbers, relates, because all of these troubles must commonly be endured by holy men.[5] It has always been the primary virtue of the righteous to endure and overcome these adversities. As they suffer a variety of trials and always remain undefeated, it becomes apparent that the more they are afflicted, the stronger they become by overcoming their tribulations. 8. Hence that event, which he attributes to a weakness in Martin, is full of dignity and glory, since he was assailed by this most dangerous incident and yet prevailed.

Furthermore, no one should be amazed that this story was omitted from that book that I wrote about his life; after all, I stated in that same book that I had not included every single thing that Martin did, because, if I had wanted to follow up on every story, I would have produced an immense volume for my readers.[6] He did so many things that it would have been impossible to include them all. 9. Nevertheless, I will not permit this story, which has provoked a question, to lurk out of sight; I will relate the entire matter as it happened. I do

this so it will not seem that I had deliberately neglected to relate something that could be used to criticize that blessed man.

10. When Martin had come in the middle of winter to a certain
diocese, following the regular custom in which it is the practice of
bishops to visit their churches, the clergy had prepared a place for
him in a private room inside the church. They had also lit a fire
beneath the extremely thin, rough floor and piled a large quantity of
straw to make a bed for him. Later, when Martin reclined on the bed,
he was horrified by the unusual softness of the bedding, which was
more tempting than it should have been. He was, naturally, accustomed to lying on the bare ground with only his robe thrown over
him. 11. Disturbed, as if he had received an injury, he threw aside all
of the straw. It happened, by chance, that part of the chaff he
removed landed on a small stove. He, as was his custom, slept on the
bare ground, exhausted by the day's journey.

In the middle of the night, as I said above, the dry straw was kindled by the heat of the fire seeping through the cracks in the floor.
12. Martin was woken from his sleep by the unexpected emergency. As
he admitted later, delayed by the extreme danger and especially by
the devil who was laying traps and urging him onward, he turned to
prayer later than he should have. His first instinct was to burst outside, and after struggling in vain with the bolt that fastened the door,
he realized that the fire was growing most dangerously around him.
It had reached the point where the robe he was wearing caught fire.
13. Finally, coming back to his senses, looking to the Lord and knowing that his protection was in God rather than flight, he eagerly seized
the shield of faith and prayer and lay down in the middle of the flames,
entrusting himself completely to the Lord. And then, with the fire
driven back by divine intervention, he continued to pray in the middle
of a circle of flames that did not harm him.

The monks, who were outside the doors as the noise of the fire
raged and roared within, broke down the locked doors and, after
extinguishing the fire, carried Martin out of the middle of the flames,
although they believed that he had been completely consumed by a
fire of such long duration. 14. Nevertheless (and the Lord is a witness
of my words), Martin himself told me—and he confessed this with
great groaning—that the devil's art had deceived him in this incident.
When he woke from sleep, he did not have the sense to fight back
against the danger through faith and prayer. The fire raged around

him for precisely as long as he, with a disturbed mind, struggled to break down the door. 15. But when he had taken recourse in the standard of the cross and the weapons of prayer, the middle of the flames diminished and then he sensed that those flames that had been burning him were sprinkling him with dew.[7] From this, let anyone who reads this letter understand that Martin was indeed tested by this danger, but he also was found truly worthy.

EPISTLE II—TO AURELIUS

A letter to the Deacon Aurelius on the death of Martin

1. After you[8] left me early in the morning, I was sitting alone in a cell, and the thought that often occupies me had entered my mind: a hope for future things, a disdain for the present world, a fear of judgment, a dread of punishments; following that, and actually the source of every other thought, the recollection of my sins had made me unhappy and tired. 2. Next, when I was exhausted by the anguish of my mind and I had laid my body on my narrow cot, sleep overcame me as often happens from sadness. Sleep is always lighter and more uncertain in the morning hours, with the result that hesitancy and doubt is spread throughout one's body and produces a state that is missing in the other kind of sleep, when, while almost awake, you think you are asleep.

3. Suddenly, I seemed to see Saint Martin, clothed in a white toga, with a fiery appearance, eyes shining, and glowing hair. It seemed to me that he appeared in the same bodily condition and form that I had known, with the result that—this is difficult to explain—it was impossible to look at him, although I was able to recognize him. Smiling at me a little, he held up in his right hand the book that I had written about his life.[9] 4. I grasped his holy knees and demanded a blessing as was the custom. I felt him place his hand on my head with the most charming touch, and among the solemn words of blessing, he was repeating that name of the cross that was so familiar to his lips. Suddenly, with my eyes fixed upon him, although I was unable to get enough of his appearance or the sight of him, he was ripped away from me and carried through the air. He crossed the emptiness of the sky as I watched him with sharp eyes. He was carried

by a fast-moving cloud, received into the heaven that stood open for him, and then could no longer be seen. 5. Not long after this, I saw the holy priest Clarus,[10] who had recently died, take the same path that his master had ascended.

I woke up, straining and struggling, rashly wanting to follow him as he entered the high places. Now that I was awake, I was beginning to express joy over the vision I had seen, when a servant came to me[11] with an expression that was gloomier than usual, speaking and lamenting at the same time. 6. "What are you so sad about, that you are anxious to tell me?" I asked.

And he replied, "Two monks have arrived from Tours, and they are reporting that our lord Martin has died."

I must acknowledge that I fell over and, with tears rising, wept freely. Even now, as I write these things to you, brother, my tears are flowing and my overwhelming grief does not admit any consolation. But when this was reported to me, I wanted you to become a participant in my sorrow, you who were a companion in my love. 7. And so come to me immediately, so that together we may mourn the man we loved together, although I know that he should not be mourned; he has conquered the world, triumphed over our age, and now at last has received his crown of righteousness. Nevertheless, I am unable to command myself to stop grieving. 8. I have sent ahead a patron but have lost a comfort in this present life; if grief would tolerate reason, I ought to rejoice.

For he is now joined with the apostles and prophets, and if I may say this without any offense to all the saints, he is second to none in that company of the righteous. Consequently, I hope, believe, and have confidence that he is, above all, numbered among those who washed their gowns in blood. Free from every blemish, he is accompanying his leader, the Lamb. 9. For although, by reason of the age in which he lived, he was unable to experience martyrdom, nevertheless, he will not be denied a martyr's glory because through his desire and virtue, he wanted, and was able, to become a martyr. Clearly, if he had been permitted to struggle alongside the company that existed in the times of Nero or Decius, I call as my witness the God of heaven and earth that he would have freely climbed onto the torture rack; he would have placed himself voluntarily in the fires and, like those Hebrew youths in the middle of the balls of flame, would have sung a hymn to the Lord while in the furnace.[12]

10. And if perhaps it had pleased the persecutor to inflict that punishment of Isaiah, he would surely never have proven unequal to the prophet and feared to have his limbs amputated with saws and red hot blades.[13] If impious anger had chosen to drive him, undismayed, off sheer cliffs or rugged mountains, then I assert, confident of the veracity of this claim, that he would have fallen to his death voluntarily. But if, considering the example of the teacher of the Gentiles when facing the sword, he was being led out among the other victims, as often happened, he would have compelled the executioner to allow him to take the first place among them all in the carnage. 11. But, in truth, even facing all the punishments and tortures under which, for the most part, humans yield because of their weakness, even under these circumstances he would not have withdrawn from the confession of the Lord. Unmoved, he would have resisted to such an extent that he would have laughed happily at his wounds and rejoiced in his torments while he was being tortured.

12. But although he was not forced to face these torments, nevertheless he did achieve martyrdom without shedding his blood. For did he not bear all the sufferings that cause human grief out of his hope for eternity, namely hunger, vigils, nakedness, fasting, the scorn of enemies, the reproaches of the wicked, his care for the sick, and his concern for those in danger? 13. For who suffered without this man suffering? Who was tempted without him being stung? Who perished without him weeping? Quite apart from his various daily struggles against the power of human and spiritual wickedness, while various temptations were always reaching out for him, he always was conspicuous for his bravery in conquering, his patience as he waited, and his equanimity as he endured trouble.

14. O that man who was truly indescribable in piety, mercy, and the love that, though it daily grows cold even among the holy men, nevertheless lasted in him to the end, growing stronger with every day. I enjoyed a very special place in his love and goodness; he was particularly fond of me although I was unworthy and did not deserve it.[14]

15. Hey, my tears flow again and sobbing breaks loose from the bottom of my heart. Who will offer me a similar rest after this? In whose love will there be comfort? Poor me, unlucky me! If I live longer, will I ever be able to stop mourning the fact that I have outlived Martin? Will there be a pleasant life after this? Will there be a day or even an hour without tears? Will I be able to mention him to you,

my beloved brother, without tears? Will I ever, speaking to you, be able
to talk about anything other than him?

16. But why am I stirring you up to tears and weeping? Look, I
want to console you now, I who cannot console myself. Believe me: he
will not abandon us, he will not abandon us! He will be present as we
discuss him; he will stand near us as we pray. And just as he deigned
to show his presence today, he will appear often, to be seen in his
glory. Always present, he will protect us with his blessing, just as he did
not long ago. 17. From this, according to the sequence of the vision,
he demonstrated that heaven stands open for those who follow him,
and in the vision, he taught what should be followed. In it he
instructed which way we should direct our hope and mind. But what
shall I do, brother? I am aware that I will be unable to climb that difficult path and enter heaven. My burden of troubles weighs me down
and a great mass of sin holds me down. It denies me the ascent to the
stars and leads me to a miserable afterlife in the brutal underworld.
18. There is only this hope remaining, this final hope, namely, that
what we are unable to obtain for ourselves, we may deserve through
Martin's prayers. But why do I occupy you any longer with a letter that
is so loquacious and stops you from coming to me? This page is full
and has no more room. 19. Nevertheless, the reason I offered such a
long discourse was that since this epistle was bringing sorrowful news,
the same letter, as a type of discussion between us, should also offer
you consolation.

EPISTLE III—TO BASSULA

A letter to Bassula on the death of Martin

1. If it was permissible to summon parents to court,[15] I would certainly haul you before the judgment seat of the praetor, in the matter
of looting and of theft, with justifiable resentment. For why should I
not complain bitterly about the injury I have suffered from you? You
have left no sheet of papyrus paper in my home, no book, no letter.
You have stolen everything, and you have also published this material
widely. 2. Words I wrote informally to a friend,[16] what, perhaps, I dictated while we were playing—although it was to remain secret—all of
these works seem to reach you before they are written or dictated. You

have, no doubt, subverted my scribes, with whose help you publish my inept works. Nevertheless, I am unable to take action against them if they obey you, as they came under my control through your most liberal generosity; moreover they remember that they are still more yours than mine. 3. You alone are the guilty party, you alone are to blame. You plot against me and you ensnare them with trickery, so that without any selection, what was written informally or negligently is released, and it is sent to you when it is not yet fully elaborated and is unpolished.

As for the rest, I shall remain silent. I ask only how it is possible for that letter that I recently wrote to the deacon Aurelius to reach you so quickly. I am located in Toulouse and you are in Trier, far removed from your homeland on account of your concern for your son. So what opportunity did you have to steal that private letter? 4. For I received your letter in which you wrote that, in the same letter in which I had mentioned the death of that holy Martin, I should have explained in more detail about the passing of that blessed man. This makes it appear as if I had published that letter to be read by people other than the man to whom I had sent it, or that I was appointed for such a great work, so that everything that ought to be known about Martin should only be recorded in my writing. 5. Consequently, if you desire to hear anything about the death of the holy bishop, seek knowledge from those who were present. I have resolved to write nothing to you out of fear that you will disseminate my words widely. Nevertheless, if you promise that you will not read this to anyone, I will satisfy your desire a little and I will offer a share of those things that I have learned.

6. Martin had known of his death long before it arrived, and he told the brothers that the end of his body was near. Meanwhile, an occasion arose for him to visit the diocese of Condes. The clergy of that church were fighting among themselves, and Martin wanted to restore peace, although he clearly could not ignore the approaching end of his days. Nevertheless, he would not excuse himself from traveling for this reason, and he decided that this final act of his powers would be good if he died after restoring the peace of the church.

7. So, setting out, accompanied as always by his very large and holy crowd of disciples, he observed seagulls in the river chasing after fish and using their greedy beaks to constantly pressure their prey. "This is the method of the demons," he said. "They lay traps for the

unwary, they capture the oblivious, and they devour those who have been ensnared. Moreover, they cannot be satisfied with those they have devoured." 8. Then he issued a powerful order that the birds should leave the pool in which they were swimming, and seek dry and deserted regions. Evidently, he used the same authority over the birds that he customarily employed to put the demons to flight. A flock formed and, when all the birds had gathered together as one, they abandoned the river and set off for the mountains and forests. This produced admiration in the crowd, which witnessed that the power was so great in Martin that he could even command the birds.

9. He was detained in that village or church to which he had gone for a considerable length of time. He restored peace among the clergy, and when he thought about returning to his monastery, he began to feel the strength suddenly ebbing out of his body; summoning the brothers, he indicated that he had reached his end. 10. They all began to mourn and grieve, and in lamenting voices, they said, "Why are you deserting us, Father? Or to whom are you relinquishing and abandoning us? Ravening wolves will invade your flock; who, with the shepherd struck down, will stop them from biting us?[17] We know that you desire to be with Christ, but your rewards are safe and will not be diminished if they are postponed. Instead, have pity on us, whom you abandon."

11. Then Martin, moved by these tears, always overflowing with the mercy of the Lord in his heart, was said to have wept. Then, turning to the Lord, his only reply to those who were weeping was, "Lord, if I am still necessary for your people, I do not object to the work. Let your will be done."

12. Clearly, positioned between hope and grief, he had nearly doubted which he ought to prefer. He did not want to desert his people, nor did he want to be separated from Christ any longer. Nevertheless, placing no importance in his will and leaving nothing to his desire, he committed himself entirely to the decision and power of the Lord. 13. Thus he prayed, "Continuing to fight in this body is onerous, Lord, and it is enough now that I have fought for so long; but if you command me to continue in this labor on behalf of the soldiers in your camp, I will raise no objections nor offer the exhaustion of old age as an excuse. Devotedly, I will carry out your tasks, and I will serve as your soldier under your banner for as long as you command; no matter how much I may desire a discharge after my labor on

account of age, the spirit is the conqueror of the years, and it does not know how to yield to old age. But if you spare me more toil at this age, your will, Lord, is what is best for me. You yourself will watch over these people for whom I fear."

14. O ineffable man, undefeated in toil, and not to be defeated by death, who never inclined toward either side, who did not fear dying nor raise objections to a continuing life. Although he was in the grip of a fever for several days, he did not turn aside from the work of God. Spending the nights in prayers and vigils, he compelled his weary limbs to serve his spirit, reclining on that famous couch in ashes and sackcloth. 15. And when his disciples asked whether at least some vile straw should be placed under him, he replied, "It is not becoming for a Christian to die, except in ashes. If I leave any other example to you, I have sinned."

Consequently, with his eyes and hands always fixed on heaven, he did not permit his undefeated spirit to relax from prayer. When the priests, who had gathered around him at that time, asked if he could relieve his body by rolling on his side, he said, "Permit, permit me, brothers to gaze upon heaven rather than earth, so that my spirit will be directed toward the way it must take in order to travel to the Lord." 16. After speaking these words, he saw the devil standing nearby. "Why do you stand there, cruelest of beasts?" he said. "You will discover nothing in me, unclean beast. I am being received into Abraham's bosom."

17. With these words, he offered his spirit to heaven. Those who were there have testified to us that they saw his face appear as the face of an angel. His limbs looked as white as snow, so that they said, "Who would ever believe that this man was covered in sackcloth and enveloped in ashes?" For he already appeared there as he would appear in the coming glory of the resurrection, in the changed nature of his flesh.

18. It is unbelievable how great a multitude of people gathered for his funeral rites. The entire city rushed out to meet the body; all the people from the farms and villages came, as did many from neighboring cities. O how great the mourning of all the people, how great, especially the laments of the grieving monks! It is said that on that day, two thousand of them came together—the special glory of Martin. So many offspring, following his example, had borne fruit in the service of the Lord.

19. Undoubtedly, the shepherd was guiding his flock before him: the pale crowds of this holy throng and the cloaked masses both of old men who had served out their labor and of the novices, newly vowed to the sworn service of Christ. Next, came the choirs of nuns, holding back their tears on account of their modesty; what holy joy they were pretending, although secretly they were mourning. Even though faith prohibited their tears, their emotion forced out an occasional groan. As a matter of fact, the holy exultation for his glory was as great as the pious grief for his death. 20. You would have pardoned those who wept and congratulated those who rejoiced; every single person showed grief for themselves and joy for Martin. And so these crowds escorted the body of the blessed man to the site of his tomb with hymns sung to the heavens.

21. If I may be permitted, I will not compare this worldly procession to a funeral, but rather to a triumph. Who would compare Martin's procession to a funeral service? Let the generals ride in their chariots behind their chained captives; those who had conquered the world under Martin's leadership escorted his body. Let the madness of the people honor the generals with disordered applause; Martin was applauded with divine psalms and honored with celestial hymns. Those men, after their triumphs, will be shoved into brutal hell; Martin rejoiced because he was welcomed into Abraham's bosom. Poor and unassuming, Martin entered heaven as a wealthy man. From there, I hope, he is guarding us, and he will notice me, as I write these words, and you, as you read them.

CHRONICLES

BOOK I

PREFACE

1. I have taken on the task of briefly condensing the events that have been disclosed in the Sacred Scriptures, starting from the beginning of the world, and, having divided the periods, speaking selectively about events right up to our own time. Many people who were desperate to learn about divine things through reading matter in an abridged form were eagerly demanding this work from me.[1] Consequently, I did not spare myself the hard work of enclosing in two books all of those events that have been written out in multiple volumes. I have aimed for brevity but have omitted virtually none of the important events.

2. It did not seem illogical to me, when I had run through sacred history up to the crucifixion of Christ and the acts of the apostles, also to link the events that came after: the destruction of Jerusalem, the harassment of the Christian people, and later on, the times of peace; then again I shall discuss all the troubles that arose from the internal trials of the churches. Nevertheless, it does not pain me to acknowledge that, wherever reason has compelled me, I have found secular histories[2] useful for distinguishing times and sequences of events and have extracted missing information from those works in order to supplement our understanding. In this way, I will teach the inexperienced and convince the learned.

3. Nevertheless, these passages that I have arranged, condensed from the sacred volumes, should not be considered authoritative by those reading them as if they might adopt them and skip over those books from which they were derived. It is not until someone comes to know the former works thoroughly that he will recognize here what

was collected from there. For all the mysteries of divine events may only be drawn from those fountains. Now I will begin my narration.

CHAPTER 1

The creation of the world through the Nephilim (Gen 1:1—6:4)

1. God established the world nearly six thousand years ago,[3] as we will explain in the course of this volume. Nevertheless, those who have published their investigations of the length of time agree little about this among themselves. Since this disagreement happens either by the will of God or the failure of antiquity,[4] my view should escape censure.

Once the world was established, God made humans. The man's name was Adam and the woman's was Eve. Although they had been placed in paradise, when they tasted the fruit from the tree that had been forbidden to them, they were driven into our land as exiles. After this, they gave birth to Cain and Abel, but wicked Cain killed his brother. Cain had a son, Enoch, who, for the first time, founded a city;[5] this city was named after its founder. Irad was the son of Enoch, and Mehujael the son of Irad. Mehujael had a son, Methushael, and Methushael produced Lamech, who, it is said, killed a young man. The name of the murdered young man is not related; the prudent believe that this is an indication of a future mystery.

2. Adam, after the death of his younger son, produced a third son, Seth; Adam was 230 years old[6] at the time. Ultimately, he lived 930 years. Seth produced Enosh; Enosh, Kenan; Kenan, Mahalalel; Mahalalel, Jared; and Jared, Enoch. It is said that God took Enoch away because of his righteousness. Enoch's son was named Methuselah, and he produced Lamech. Lamech was the father of Noah, who was distinguished by his righteousness; God valued and accepted Noah above all other mortals.

3. At this time, when the human race was already flourishing, the angels,[7] whose abode was in heaven, eagerly indulged their illicit appetites because they had been ensnared by the appearance of beautiful maidens. They relinquished their own natures and origins, abandoning the higher realms where they resided, and entered into mortal marriages. These angels, gradually spreading harmful morals, corrupted the human offspring, and from their intercourse, the

giants are said to have been brought forth. The intermingling of two different natures produced monsters.[8]

CHAPTER 2

The flood (Gen 6:5—8:19)

1. God was offended by these deeds, and especially by the bad behavior of humans, which had progressed beyond measure. Consequently, he had decided to destroy the human race completely. But he exempted Noah, a just man who lived blamelessly, from the ordained judgment. God warned Noah that a flood was imminent, and so Noah built an immense ark of wood and made it watertight by smearing it with bitumen. Noah shut himself up in this ark with his wife, their three sons, and their daughters-in-law. He brought matched pairs of birds and, in the same way, pairs of different types of beasts, into the ark—the rest were destroyed in the flood.

2. Then Noah, when he perceived that the power of the rain had diminished and that the ark was floating quietly on the sea,[9] deduced—as was the case—that the waters were receding. He dispatched a raven to investigate the situation. When the bird did not return, having been detained (as I believe) by the corpses, he sent out a dove. When the dove found no place to land, it returned. Sent out a second time, the bird brought back an olive branch, a clear sign that the tops of the trees had been exposed.[10] Finally, when sent out a third time, the dove did not return. From this it was apparent that the waters had receded. Therefore, Noah left the ark. That event, I calculate, took place 2,242 years after the beginning of the world.

CHAPTER 3

The sons of Noah; the tower of Babel (Gen 8:20—11:9)

1. Noah's first action was to build an altar to God, and he burned sacrifices from among the birds. Shortly thereafter, God blessed him and his sons, and he received the command not to feed on blood or shed the blood of humans, because Cain, who had been free of this

command, had defiled the earliest days of the world. And so then, in that desolate age, Noah's sons produced offspring. Noah had three sons: Shem, Ham, and Japheth. But Ham, because he had ridiculed his intoxicated father, was cursed by his father.[11]

2. His son, named Cush, produced a giant man, Nimrod; it is said that Nimrod built the city of Babylon.[12] I have no desire to list here the many cities that are said to have been established at that time. Although the human race was multiplying and mortals inhabited various places and islands, everyone still employed one language as long as the multitude, which would be dispersed throughout the entire world, drew itself together in one place. These people made a decision, in accordance with the nature of the human mind, to secure renown through a certain extraordinary project, before they should be separated from one another.

3. Consequently, they came together to build a tower that would rise to heaven. However, by the will of God, in order to hinder the tasks of the workers, much of what they were saying began to be expressed differently from usual and in a form of language that was mutually unintelligible. After this, they were more easily dispersed, and they started abandoning one another, as foreigners. The world was divided among the sons of Noah in such a way that the descendants of Shem were in the east, Japeth in the west, and Ham in the lands between them. From then until the emergence of Abraham, the genealogy contained nothing noteworthy in it that is worth mentioning.

CHAPTER 4

Abram and Lot; the battle with the eastern kings
(Gen 11:31—14:24)

1. Abraham[13] was the son of Terah, born 1,070 years after the flood. His wife was named Sara, and initially his home was in the region of the Chaldeans.[14] Later, he stayed, together with his father, near Haran. At that time, he received a command from God and relinquished paternal home and father. Taking Lot, his brother's son, as a companion, he made his way to the land of Canaan, to the place that is called Shechem, and there he settled. Soon, because of a shortage of grain, he entered Egypt and later returned to Canaan. 2. Lot,

because the family was large, separated from his uncle so that they might more easily exploit the open expanses of the land that were then empty. He settled in Sodom.[15] The reputation of that town had suffered because of its inhabitants; men forced themselves upon men, and because of this, it is said that God hated Sodom.

3. At the same time, the kings of the neighboring clans had taken up arms, although previously there had been no combat among the humans. The kings of Sodom, Gomorrah, and the neighboring regions engaged in battle against those who were attacking the nearby lands, and in the first campaign, they were defeated. Then Sodom was pillaged by the victors, a prize for its enemies, and Lot was led away into captivity. When Abraham learned of this, he quickly armed 318 of his own servants, and he put the kings, made arrogant by their victory, to flight and took away their loot and weapons. After this victory, he was blessed by the priest Melchizedek, and Abraham gave the priest a tenth of the spoils. He then returned the rest of the goods to those from whom they had been stolen.

CHAPTER 5

The covenant with Abraham;
the destruction of Sodom and Gomorrah (Gen 15:1—19:38)

1. God spoke to Abraham during this time, and he promised to multiply Abraham's offspring, matching the sands of the seas and the stars of heaven. It was also foretold that Abraham's future descendants would live as foreigners, and subsequent generations would endure four hundred years of slavery in an enemy land, but afterward they would be restored to freedom. Then his name and the name of his wife were changed by the addition of one letter:[16] from Abram to Abraham, and Sarai to Sarah. The divine mystery of this action is not without significance, but it is not the purpose of this work to explain it. 2. At the same time, the law of circumcision was imposed upon Abraham, and he had a son, Ishmael, from a maidservant. Then, when he was one hundred years old and his wife was ninety, God, who had come to him with two angels, promised that they would have a son, Isaac.

3. Then the angels sent to Sodom found Lot sitting at the gate. Lot, believing them to be men, invited them into his home to receive

hospitality and eat dinner. Then wicked young men from the town demanded the newly arrived foreigners to rape. Lot offered his daughters to those men in place of his guests, but they did not accept them because illicit pleasures were more to their taste. They then dragged Lot himself off to be raped. The angels, quickly protecting him from insult, blinded the eyes of the shameless men. They then told Lot of the coming destruction of the town, and he quickly departed with his wife and daughters. The group was forbidden to look back, but his wife, disregarding the command—in accordance with the human defect that abstains with difficulty from those things that have been forbidden—turned her eyes back. Immediately, it is said, she was transformed into a pillar. Sodom was destroyed by divine fires. After this, Lot's daughters, believing that the human race had been destroyed, engaged in sexual intercourse with their inebriated father; these unions produced Moab and Ammon.

CHAPTER 6

The birth of Isaac through the death of Abraham
(Gen 21:1—25:11)

1. At virtually the same time, when Abraham was already one hundred years old, his son, Isaac, was born. Then Sarah drove out the maidservant who had given Abraham a son. It is said that the maidservant lived in the desert with her son and was protected by God. Not long after, God, testing the faith of Abraham, demanded that Abraham sacrifice his son, Isaac, to him. Abraham did not hesitate to offer his son. When he had placed the boy on the altar and was raising the sword, a command came from heaven that he should spare the boy. A nearby ram served as the sacrificial victim. When the sacrifice was complete, God spoke to Abraham, reaffirming those things that he had already promised. Sarah died while in her 127th year. Her body was interred, through her husband's solicitude, in Hebron, a town of the Canaanites, for Abraham was living there at that time.

2. Then Abraham—when he saw that his son Isaac had become a young man, inasmuch as he had reached his fortieth year—commanded his servant to search for a wife for Isaac from the same tribe and land from which he himself was thought to be descended.

He also stipulated that the servant should conduct the young woman he found to the land of the Canaanites, and not believe that, for the sake of marriage, Isaac would return to the land of his ancestors. To ensure that his servant would carry out these orders briskly, Abraham bound him with an oath, the servant's hand placed upon his master's thigh. Subsequently, the servant traveled to Mesopotamia, where he reached the town of Nahor, Abraham's brother. He entered the house of Bethuel of Syria, Nahor's son. Bethuel's daughter was Rebekah, a beautiful virgin. Having seen the girl, the servant asked for her and brought her back to his master. 3. After that, Abraham took another wife who was named Keturah; she is said to have been a concubine in the Chronicles.[17] She gave Abraham sons. He gave his wealth to Isaac, son of Sarah, but nevertheless he gave gifts to those sons he had by his concubines. In this way, they were distinguished from Isaac. Abraham died after living for 175 years, and his body was laid to rest in the tomb alongside his wife Sarah.

Chapter 7

The conflict between Jacob and Esau; Laban and Jacob (Gen 25:21—30:14)

1. Rebekah was barren for a long time, but through her husband's persistent prayers to the Lord, she bore twins almost twenty years after her wedding day. The twins are said to have often run riot in their mother's womb, and it was proclaimed in an oracle of God that two races were foretold in them: from the beginning, the elder child would be subjected to the younger. The firstborn child, covered with rough hair, was called Esau, while the younger was named Jacob. 2. At that time, a severe grain shortage had arisen. Because of this shortfall, Isaac withdrew to Gerar, to King Abimelech,[18] having been warned by the Lord not to go down into Egypt. And God promised possession of all that land to Isaac and blessed him there. When he had grown wealthy in terms of his herd and all the worldly goods he pursued, he was driven out of the land by the envy of the residents. After his expulsion, Isaac sat down near the well of the oath. 3. And so when Isaac, now laden with years and his eyes veiled, was preparing to bless his son Esau, Jacob, following his mother

Rebekah's counsel, put himself forward for the blessing in place of his brother. As a result of this, Jacob was placed over his brother, to be honored by leaders and nations. Esau, infuriated by this action, was preparing to murder his brother. Fearing this, and urged on by his mother, Jacob fled into Mesopotamia. His father suggested that he take a wife from the house of Laban, Rebekah's brother. This demonstrates how much care they took; even though they lived in foreign lands, they propagated their line from among their own family.[19]

On his way into Mesopotamia, Jacob is said to have seen the Lord while asleep; on account of this, believing the site of his dream to be holy, he took a stone from there, and he vowed that if he should return in prosperous circumstances, he would give the place the name *House of God*, and a tenth of all the goods that he acquired would be given to God. Then he went to Laban, his mother's brother. Laban generously extended hospitality to him as the acknowledged son of his sister.

CHAPTER 8

Jacob, Leah, and Rachel; Jacob wrestles with God
(Gen 30:15—32:32)

1. Laban had two daughters, Leah and Rachel. It is said that Leah had bad eyes, while Rachel was beautiful. Jacob, having been captivated by the sight of Rachel, was inflamed with love for the maiden. He asked her father to give her to him in marriage, selling himself into seven years of service. But when the time had finished, Leah was substituted for Rachel, and he was forced to undergo a second seven-year term of service. Then Rachel was given to him. But we learn that for a long time, Rachel was barren while Leah was fertile. 2. These are the names of the children Jacob had with Leah: Reuben, Simeon, Levi, Judah, Issachar, Zebulun, and Dinah. Gad and Asher, however, were from Leah's maid. Dan and Naphtali were born from Rachel's maidservant. Rachel, by then having lost hope of bearing a child, gave birth to Joseph.

3. Then Jacob wanted to return to his father. Although his father-in-law, Laban, had given him a portion of the herds as pay for his service, the share was not enough. Jacob, the son-in-law, had

thought Laban would be fair to him, but suspected him of deception and secretly departed approximately twenty years after his arrival. Rachel, without Jacob's knowledge, stole her father's idols. Because of this loss, Laban pursued his son-in-law, and when the idols were not discovered, he made peace with Jacob and returned to his own country. He begged his son-in-law not to take wives in addition to his own daughters. 4. Next, it is said that after Jacob separated from Laban, he saw angels and the camp of God. But when his trip passed near the region of Edom, where his brother, Esau, was living, he probed his brother's mistrust toward himself by sending messengers and gifts. Then he advanced to meet his brother. Jacob did not yet completely trust himself to his brother. It is reported that on the day before the brothers met each other, God, having assumed human appearance, wrestled with Jacob. Although he had prevailed against God, nevertheless he did not fail to recognize that his adversary was not mortal, and he demanded a blessing for himself from his opponent. At that point, God altered his name, so that he was called Israel rather than Jacob. When in turn he sought to learn the name of God from God, God replied that he was not to ask that because his name was too wonderful. As a result of the struggle, Jacob's hip became lame.

CHAPTER 9

Jacob settles in Shechem; Dinah raped by Shechem;
the vengeance of the sons of Israel; Joseph sold into slavery
(Gen 33:18—37:36)

1. Israel avoided the house of his brother and moved his herd to Salem, a town of the Shechemites. There he settled on a price for a piece of land and pitched his tent. Hamor, prince of Chorraeus, was the leader of that town. His son, Shechem, raped Dinah, the daughter Jacob had with Leah. When this was discovered, Simeon and Levi, Dinah's brothers, employed a trick to kill all the men in the town, and they energetically avenged the injury done to their sister. Jacob's sons pillaged the town and carried away the goods of all the people. Jacob is said to have been very distressed by what transpired in that town.

Shortly thereafter, warned by God, he moved to Bethel and established an altar to God in that place. After that he set up his tent in the region of the tower of Gader.[20] Rachel died during childbirth; her son was named Benjamin. Isaac died at the age of 180 years.

2. Now Esau was very wealthy, and he had also taken wives from among the Canaanite people. I do not believe it necessary to list his off-spring in such an abbreviated work as this. If anyone is eager to know this information, let that person consult the source. After his father died, Jacob remained in that land where Isaac had lived. For the sake of pastures, his sons occasionally separated from him with the flocks, but Joseph and little Benjamin stayed at home. 3. Joseph was very precious to his father, and because of this, his brothers were jealous. At the same time, he also had frequent dreams that seemed to foretell that he would be greater than all of them. Consequently, when his father sent him to inspect the flocks and visit his brothers, they saw an opportunity to harm him; when they saw their brother, they plotted his murder. When Reuben opposed them (his mind shrinking back from so vile a criminal deed), Joseph was lowered into a cistern. Later, through Judah's per-suasion, the brothers were diverted to a gentler plan, and they sold Joseph to traders who were en route to Egypt. These traders passed Joseph on to Potiphar, the Pharaoh's commander.

CHAPTER 10

Judah and Tamar; Joseph in Egypt (Gen 38:1—41:47)

1. At the same time, Judah, the son of Jacob, took Shua of Canaan in marriage. Judah had three sons with Shua: Er, Onan, and Shelah. Er was joined through intercourse to Tamar. When Er died, Onan received his brother's wife. It is said that God killed Onan because he poured his semen onto the ground. Then Tamar was joined to her father-in-law after she had taken on the guise of a pros-titute, and she bore twins for him. Now during the birth, this amazing event occurred: when the boy was coming forth, in order to discern which child was born first, the midwife had tied a scarlet thread on his wrist, and then, having drawn his arm back into the womb of his mother, the boy was born after his brother. The babies were given the names Perez and Zerah.

2. Now the king's superintendent regarded Joseph with kindness. He had purchased Joseph for a price, and Joseph was administering to

the superintendent's house and family. He was good looking and had drawn the eyes of his master's wife to himself because of his remarkable appearance. Overcome with an improper love, she made advances toward him several times, and when he did not acquiesce, she smeared him with a baseless charge, complaining to her husband that she had been threatened with rape. Consequently, Joseph was thrown into prison. Two of the king's attendants were in the same prison. When they related their dreams to Joseph, he announced that these dreams were predicting their futures: one of them would pay his penalty with his head, while the other would be set free. And that is what happened.

3. After two years, a dream troubled the king. When Egypt's wise men were unable to alleviate the king's concern about his dream, that attendant of the king who had been released from prison told his king that Joseph was an amazing interpreter of dreams. Consequently, Joseph was released and he interpreted the dream for the king: the next seven years were to have the most abundant crops, with scarcity in the following years. The king was struck with fear. Perceiving that Joseph had a divine spirit in him, he put him in charge of the grain supply, making Joseph equal in power to himself. Then Joseph gathered together a great stockpile from the abundant crops throughout all Egypt and, increasing the number of granaries, took measures against the coming famine. At this time, the hope and welfare of Egypt rested on this man. During this time, he had two sons from Asenath, Manasseh and Ephraim. He was thirty years old when he received the highest power from the king. He had been seventeen years old when he was sold by his brothers.

CHAPTER 11

Joseph's brothers in Egypt; Jacob travels to Egypt;
Joseph's death (Gen 42:1—50:26)

1. Meanwhile, although sound measures against the famine had been taken in Egypt, a serious shortage of grain was battering the entire world. Compelled by necessity, Jacob sent his sons into Egypt, keeping only Benjamin at home with him. And so the brothers came to Joseph, the administrator of affairs, who made decisions about the

grain supply, and they worshiped him as they would a king. He cunningly pretended not to recognize them when he saw them, and he accused them of coming with hostile intent in order to secretly spy on the lands. Moreover, he was troubled because he did not see his brother Benjamin. And so the matter was settled in this way: they promised to produce Benjamin so that he might be questioned about whether they had entered Egypt in order to spy. To keep them faithful to the promise, Simeon was handed over as a hostage and grain was given to them freely. When they returned a second time, they brought Benjamin as agreed.

2. Then Joseph revealed himself to his brothers, not without shame on the part of those who deserved worse. Thus he sent them home, loaded with grain and many gifts, predicting that five years of famine still remained; because of this, they should migrate with the patriarch and with every child and household. Accordingly, Jacob descended into Egypt. He was received by the very happy Egyptians, the rejoicing king, and courteously by his son.[21]

This occurred when Jacob was 130 years old, 1,360 years after the flood. To put it another way, 215 years elapsed from the time when Abraham settled in the land of the Canaanites to the time when Jacob entered Egypt. Finally Jacob, in the seventeenth year after his arrival in Egypt, with disease pressuring him, begged his son Joseph to take his body back to his tomb.

3. Then Joseph offered his sons for a blessing. When they were blessed, Jacob placed his blessing on the younger son to the detriment of the older. He then blessed all of his sons in turn. He was 147 years old when he died. His funeral was conducted with magnificence. Joseph laid his body in the tomb of his fathers. After their father's death, he treated his brothers, who were terrified on account of their consciences, with kindness. Joseph died when he was 110 years old.

CHAPTER 12

The Israelites oppressed in Egypt; the birth, boyhood, and flight of Moses; the story of Job (Exod 1:1—2:25; Job)

1. It is amazing to relate how quickly the Hebrews, who had arrived in Egypt, increased in number, and how they filled Egypt with

their multiplying progeny. But after the king died who was supporting them generously because of Joseph's merits, they were oppressed under the rule of the successive kings. They were given the hard work of building cities, and because by then the Egyptians feared their growing numbers (it was thought that someday they might demand their freedom through a military uprising), an imperial edict was issued that compelled them to drown their newborn children. It was impossible to evade this bloodthirsty order. At this time, the daughter of the Pharaoh cared for an infant found in the river, raising him as her son. She gave the boy the name Moses. This Moses, when he had attained adulthood, spotted a Hebrew man who was being battered by an Egyptian, and he was moved to indignation by this sight. He rescued this brother from injury and killed the Egyptian by striking him with a stone.[22] Later, fearing punishment for this deed, he fled into the land of Midian. He stayed with Jethro, a priest of that land, married his daughter Zipporah, and they had two sons, Gershom and Eliezer.[23]

2. During the same period of time,[24] there was Job, who, through natural law,[25] embraced both a recognition of God and all justice. He was extremely wealthy in material terms and even more noble in that he was not corrupted by his wealth[26] while it was intact nor was he made worse by its loss. For when he was stripped of all his possessions through the agency of the devil, deprived of his children, and afflicted with awful ulcers to the point of death, it was not possible to defeat him or lead him to sin in any manner because of his inability to endure grief. Ultimately, Job attained the reward of divine attestation, was restored to health, and received twice what he had lost.

CHAPTER 13

Moses and the burning bush; Moses confronts the Pharaoh; the ten plagues in Egypt (Exod 3:1—11:10)

1. And the Hebrews, who had been oppressed by the redoubling of the harshness of their slavery, directed their complaints to heaven and hoped for assistance from God. Then Moses, while tending sheep, saw a bush suddenly burn with flames that were nevertheless miraculously harmless to the plant. Dumbfounded by this novelty, he

went closer to the bush, and immediately God spoke to him in words that approximated these: he was the God of Abraham, Isaac, and Jacob, whose descendants were burdened by the domination of the Egyptians, and he wished to rescue them from these evils. Consequently, Moses was to go to the king of Egypt and present himself as the leader sent to restore the people to freedom. God strengthened the hesitating Moses with power and gave him the ability to perform miraculous works.

2. Therefore Moses traveled to Egypt, and after performing miracles among his own people, he came to the king with his brother, Aaron, as a companion. He revealed that he had been sent by God and that he spoke the words of God, so that the king might release the Hebrew people. The king denied that he knew the Lord, and he refused to obey the command. When Moses made a huge serpent from his staff, quickly converted all the waters into blood, and filled the entire land with frogs in order to validate the commands from God, similar deeds were performed by the Chaldeans.[27] Consequently, the king expressed the opinion that whatever miracles produced by Moses were accomplished through the magical arts, rather than the power of God. Finally, the land was filled with biting flies, and the Chaldeans were forced to admit that this was done through divine power.

3. Then the king, pressured by this hardship, called Moses and Aaron to him and gave the people permission to depart, provided that they removed the disaster that had overshadowed the Egyptians. But when the disaster was taken away, the king's heart, lacking self-control,[28] reversed itself, and he did not permit the Israelites to go as he had agreed. In the end, he was crushed by ten afflictions to his person and kingdom, and he was defeated.

CHAPTER 14

The institution of Passover, the exodus from Egypt;
the parting of the Red Sea and destruction of
the Egyptian army (Exod 12:1—14:30)

1. But the day before the people were to set out from Egypt, still ignorant of dates, they were instructed in a command from God that

they should regard the current month as the first of all the months. Consequently, a sacrifice was to be offered on that day in a solemn rite in the following years. On the fourteenth day of that month, a spotless lamb that was one year old, the sacrificial victim, was to be killed, and they were to smear the blood of this animal on their door posts. They were to eat its flesh completely, but break none of its bones. They were to abstain from yeast for seven days, consume unleavened bread, and pass this practice on to their descendants.[29] Therefore, the people burdened with wealth, both their own goods and the spoils of Egypt, set out. Their number had increased from the seventy-five Hebrews who had initially gone into Egypt, to six hundred thousand men. 430 years had passed since Abraham had first entered the land of the Canaanites, and this event took place 1,575 years after the flood.

2. And so a column of smoke during the day and a column of fire by night were held out in front of them as they quickly left Egypt. But when their route passed near the land of the Philistines[30] (because of the intervening coast of the Red Sea), in order to ensure that the Hebrews might not be presented with an opportunity to return by a familiar, overland route to Egypt should they reject the desert, the will of God turned the people aside and they were brought to the Red Sea where, lingering, they established their camp.

It was reported to the king that the Hebrews had lost their way and come to the blocking sea, and that they had no escape because of the opposing element. When he heard this, he went out of his mind, angered because so many thousands of men had abandoned his kingdom and power, and he quickly led out his army.

Then, in the distance, the soldiers, standards, and the extended battle lines, stretching widely across the plains, were spotted. The Hebrews were consumed with fear and gazed up into the sky, when Moses, following the command of God, struck the sea with his rod and divided it. A passage was made for the people, and with the water drawn back on either side, it was as if their journey was on dry land. The Egyptian king did not hesitate to follow those who were getting away, entering at the point where the sea stood open. Then he, along with his entire army, was destroyed when the waters came back together suddenly.

CHAPTER 15

Exultation after the escape from Egypt turns to rebellion;
quail and manna in the desert (Exod 15:1—16:36)

1. Then Moses, rejoicing because through the power of God, his people were safe and his enemies destroyed, sang a song to God, and the entire crowd of men and women[31] did the same thing. But after they entered the wilderness, when their journey was three days along, they were oppressed by a need for water, and the water they discovered could not be used because it was bitter. At that time, the defiance of the impatient people made its first appearance,[32] and from then on their defiance was directed against Moses. Instructed by God, Moses put a piece of wood into the waters, wood that had the power to restore the sweet taste of the stream.

2. Next, he settled the advancing flock at Elim, having discovered twelve springs of water and seventy palm trees. Once again the people, complaining bitterly about their hunger, protested against Moses; they were longing for their slavery in Egypt where they had enjoyed full bellies. Then a flock of quail, sent from above, filled the camp. Moreover, on the next day, those who had gone outside the camp noticed that the ground had been covered with small pods. These pods were an icy white, similar to that of the coriander seed,[33] as we see repeatedly in the winter months, when the land is covered with spreading frost. Then Moses warned the people that God had sent this bread to them as a gift, and that everyone ought to gather in prepared vessels only as much in one day as was required to satisfy each person. Nevertheless, on the sixth day of the week, because they were not permitted to collect food on the Sabbath, they could take a double portion. 3. But the people, as is typical of human nature, paid little attention to what had been commanded; they did not restrain their greed, but were making provision for a second day by hoarding. But the food that had been set aside kept bubbling up into maggots with an awful stench, although the food collected on the sixth day for use on the Sabbath remained untouched. This food was used by the Hebrews for forty years, and its taste was close to honey. Its name, we are told, was manna. Moses is said to have reserved a full gomor of it in a golden vase, to serve as a testimony to divine beneficence.

CHAPTER 16

Shortage of water at Rephidim; the battle with the Amalekites;
the arrival of Jethro; Mount Sinai and the Ten Commandments
(Exod 17:1—20:26)

1. After they had moved on from there, the people, when tested again by a shortage of water, were restrained with difficulty from destroying their leader. Then Moses, following the command of the Lord, made a supply of water in large quantities by striking a rock with his staff at the place named Horeb. When they reached Rephidim, they were ravaged by attacks of the Amalekites. Moses, when his own forces were drawn out into battle, placed Joshua in charge of the fighters. Taking Aaron and Ur, he planned to observe the battle, while at the same time, he climbed a mountain in order to pray for God's favor. Although the outcome of the clash between the armies seemed uncertain, the victor, Joshua, supported by Moses' prayers, slaughtered the enemy until night came.

2. At the same time, Jethro, Moses' father-in-law, along with his daughter, Zipporah (who had married Moses and then stayed at home while he had traveled to Egypt), and their children came to him. They had learned of what was being done through Moses. Following Jethro's counsel, Moses arranged the divisions of the people. Placing tribunes, centurions, and decurions[34] over the people, he established a necessary habit of discipline for future generations. Jethro then returned to his homeland.

3. Next, they came to Mount Sinai. There the Lord told Moses that the people would have to be purified because they would be hearing the words of God; this was carried out with great care. When God approached the mountain, the air shook with the violent blasts of trumpets, and the dark clouds writhed, split by numerous bolts of lightning. Moses and Aaron were at the summit of the mountain near the Lord while the people stood around the base. In this way, the law was given in God's words; it is complex, elaborate, and often repeats itself. If anyone has more curiosity about this law, let them go to the source itself, for we are only discussing it briefly here. "You will not," the Lord said, "take foreign gods for yourselves in preference to me; you will not fashion an idol for yourself; you will not take the name of your God in vain; you will do no work on the

Sabbath; honor your father and mother; you will not kill; you will not commit adultery; you will not steal; you will not speak false testimony against your neighbor; you will not long for any of your neighbor's possessions."

CHAPTER 17

The laws of Israel (Exod 21:1—23:12)

1. After God spoke these commandments, while the trumpets sounded, the lamps blazed, and smoke covered the mountain, the people, unable to bear the words of God, shuddered with fear. They demanded a promise from Moses that God would speak to him alone, and he would relate what he had heard to the people. Now these were God's edicts to Moses:

2. A Hebrew slave, purchased with money, will serve six years; after that, the slave will be freed. Nevertheless, if the slave should freely choose to remain in servitude, it will be pierced in the ear. He who kills a man will be subjected to capital punishment; he who does so unintentionally will be exiled in the customary manner. He who strikes father or mother or speaks to them abusively, will be punished with death. If anyone should kidnap and sell a Hebrew, he will be put to death. If anyone should strike his own male or female slave, and that slave dies from the blow, the case shall be handed over for judgment. If anyone should cause the abortion[35] of a woman's fetus that is not deformed, he shall be given to death. If anyone should gouge out the eye or tooth of a servant, that servant, touched by the staff of manumission,[36] shall be liberated.

3. If a bull kills a man, it will be stoned; if a master, knowing the viciousness of the beast, did not take action, he also will be stoned, or he will redeem his life with a price as great as his accuser demands. If the bull kills a servant, a fine of thirty didrachmas will be paid to the servant's master. If anyone should fail to cover a cistern that has been dug in the ground, and a farm animal falls into the cistern, he will give the price of the animal to its owner. If one bull should kill the bull of another man, the first bull shall be put up for sale and the owners will share the proceeds and divide the dead bull. But if the owner knew the vicious nature of the bull, yet failed to take appropriate measures, he

will surrender the bull. If anyone steals a calf, he shall repay it fivefold. If he steals a sheep, he will pay a fourfold penalty. If living cattle are found in the care of a rustler, he shall restore twice as many.

4. It is permissible to kill a thief at night, but not during the day. If a man's flocks graze on the crops of another, the owner of the flock will restore what has been damaged. If a deposit should be lost, the person who held the deposit will swear that he has not acted fraudulently. A thief who has been discovered will restore twice what he stole. A man shall not pay compensation for a farm animal in his care that is killed by a wild animal. If anyone should defile a girl who is not yet pledged in marriage, he shall provide a dowry for the girl and take her as his wife; if her father should reject the marriage, the ravisher will provide a dowry. If anyone has sexual relations with a farm animal, he shall be killed.

5. Anyone who sacrifices to idols must be killed. Widows and orphans must not be oppressed. A poor man who owes a debt should not be hounded, nor should interest be demanded. The clothing of a poor man should not be accepted as collateral for a loan. No one should protest against the leader of the people. Every firstborn thing must be offered to God. No one may eat meat that has been taken away from a wild animal. No one may conspire with others to offer false testimony in order to produce any evil whatsoever. You will not pass by a straying herd that belongs to your enemy, but rather you will return it. If you find an animal of your enemy that has fallen under its burden, you will be obliged to get it upright again. You will not kill the innocent and the just. You will not accept bribes to pardon a wicked man; bribes should not be accepted. A foreigner is to be received kindly. Six days are for work, the sabbath is for rest. You will not harvest your crops in the seventh year, but leave them for the poor and the needy.

CHAPTER 18

Moses on Mount Sinai; Aaron and the golden calf;
the tabernacle and pillar of cloud (Exod 24:3—40:38)

1. Moses carried the words of God, similar to these, back to the people, and he constructed an altar from twelve stones at the base of

the mountain. Then he ascended the mountain again upon which God was remaining. He took Aaron, Nadab, Abihu, and the seventy oldest men with him. These men were unable to gaze upon God; nevertheless, they saw the place in which God was standing. They reported God's amazing form and exceptional brightness. Moses, when God summoned him, entered the inner cloud that stood around God; it is said that he remained there forty days and the same number of nights. During this time, he was taught through God's words about building the temple and the ark and the rites connected with offering sacrifices. Because these commands seem very lengthy, I have decided that they should not be inserted in a work as short as this.

2. Now when Moses was delayed longer than expected, since he spent forty days with God, the people lost hope that he would return and compelled Aaron to construct idols. Then a calf's head was produced, made from melted metals. The people, unmindful of God, offered sacrifices to the calf, and they devoted themselves to wine and to their stomachs. God, seeing their actions and motivated by a well-founded anger, would have destroyed the rebellious people, except he was won over by Moses. When Moses returned, he carried two tablets of stone written by the hand of God. When he found that the people had given themselves over to extravagance and sacrilege, he smashed the tablets, believing that the tribe to whom the law of the Lord had been given was unworthy of it. Nevertheless, after rebuking the multitude, he gathered the Levites to himself and he ordered them to draw their swords and slaughter the people. In this attack, they say, twenty-three thousand[37] men were massacred.

3. Next Moses set up a tent outside the camp. Whenever he entered the tent, a column of cloud was seen to stand before the door, indicating that God was speaking to Moses face-to-face. When Moses begged that he be allowed to see the Lord in his own majesty, he was told that mortal eyes were unable to look upon the form of God; nevertheless, God permitted Moses to see his back. The tablets that Moses had shattered earlier were also restored. It is said that Moses spent forty days with God engaged in this discussion. When he descended from the mountain carrying the tablets, his face shone so brightly that the people were unable to look at him. When he was to present God's commands, he covered his face with a veil, and in this manner, spoke the words of God to the people. The construction of the tent

and its interior are reported in this place.[38] When this was completed, the cloud descended from above and covered the tent so that it excluded Moses himself from the entrance. These events are contained in two books, Genesis and Exodus.

CHAPTER 19

The numbering of the Israelites; the punishment of quail; the Hebrews reach the promised land (Num 1:1—14:45)

1. Next follows the book titled Leviticus, in which the laws for atonement are handed down. Commands are added to the law that had been laid down earlier, all replete with priestly customs. Anyone who wishes to learn about these laws will grasp them more perfectly there; for I, keeping to the plan for the work I have undertaken, am describing history only.[39] And so, after the tribe of Levi was set apart for the priesthood, the remaining tribes were counted and it was found that they numbered 603,500 men.

Well then, when the people were eating the bread of manna, as I related above,[40] with so many great blessings of God, as always, the ungrateful wretches desired the cheap foods that they had grown used to in Egypt. Then God brought an immense multitude of quail to the camp; the people tore these birds apart eagerly, but then began to die as the flesh was brought near their lips. There was a great disaster in the camp that day as at least twenty-three of the men[41] are said to have perished. In this way, the people were punished by that very food they desired.

2. After that, the crowd advanced and came to Paran. God informed Moses that the land that he had promised to give to the people was now near. Those who were sent to explore the land reported that it was a fruitful region abounding in all things, but the tribes were powerful and the towns were fortified with enormous walls. When the people learned this, a great fear spread through the minds of all. They were brought to such a point of wickedness that, rejecting the authority of Moses, they prepared to elect a new leader for themselves who would guide them back to Egypt.

3. Then Joshua and Caleb, who had been among the explorers of the land, wept and tore their garments, imploring the people not

to believe the scouts who had returned the alarming reports. They argued that although they had been together with them, they had discovered nothing worthy of fear in that land. Those who had been sent out should trust in God's promises, for their enemies would become spoils of war rather than the cause of their destruction. In spite of this, the unmanageable people, wrongly resisting sound council, were carried away to their ruin. God was provoked by these events, and he exposed part of the people to slaughter by their enemies. The spies were killed in order to frighten the people.

CHAPTER 20

The rebellion of Dathan and Abiram; rebellion at Kadesh;
Moses strikes the rock; wars with the Canaanites, Amorites,
and Midianites; the death of Moses (Num 16:1—Deut 34:12)

1. Then followed the insubordination of those who, with the leaders Dathan and Abiram, attempted to set themselves up against Moses and Aaron. But the earth opened its mouth and swallowed the men alive. Not long after these events, all the people rose in sedition against Moses and Aaron. They even rushed into the tabernacle, which no one except the priests was allowed to enter. Then death ran riot among them in great crowds. Everyone would have been killed in a moment, but the Lord, appeased by Moses' prayers, called off the massacre. Nevertheless, the number of the dead totaled 14,700.

Not long after, another rebellion of the people arose on account of a water shortage, as had already happened often. In response, God instructed Moses to strike a rock with his staff. It was a familiar experience, since, in fact, he had done this before. So he struck the rock once and then again, and water poured out. It is reported that God reproved Moses over this matter, because due to his lack of faith, he had been unable to draw water from the stone except through repeated blows. Because of this sin, he was not permitted to enter the promised land, as will be described below.

2. Next, Moses moved on from that place. When he was preparing to lead the people past Edom, he sent emissaries to the king and requested an opportunity to pass, thinking that the right of kinship required him to abstain from war. This was because these people were

the descendants of Esau. Unfortunately, the king, rejecting Moses' entreaties, denied safe passage and prepared to resist them with weapons. Then Moses turned the journey aside to Mount Hor, avoiding the prohibited path, so that he would not provide a pretext for war between relatives. While on this course, he destroyed the king of the Canaanites. He also overthrew Sihon, the king of the Amorites, and gained possession of all their towns. He also conquered the Kings Bashan and Balak. He built a camp on the Jordan River, not far from Jericho. Then he fought against the Midianites, defeated them, and they were suppressed.

3. Moses died after he had led the people for forty years in the desert. It is said that the Hebrew people stayed in the desert for such a long time for this reason: they stayed until everyone who had not believed the words of God died. Apart from Joshua and Caleb, no one who had been more than twenty years old when they came out of Egypt crossed the Jordan. The fact that Moses himself only saw the promised land but did not touch it is attributed to his sin. At the time when he had been ordered to strike the rock and produce water, he had doubted after so many trials of his own power. He was 120 years old when he died. The site of his tomb is unknown.

CHAPTER 21

The entry into the promised land; the conquest of Jericho and Ai (Joshua 1:1–8:29)

1. With the death of Moses, supreme power was in the hands of Joshua, son of Nun; for Moses had designated Joshua, a man who possessed very similar virtues to himself, as his successor. Now, shortly after taking command, he sent messengers throughout the camp to inform the people that they were to prepare a dependable grain supply. Three days later, he announced a journey into the neighboring country. Unfortunately, the very powerful Jordan River barred their crossing because there were not enough boats for their purpose, and they were unable to stand against the river, which was then filling the riverbed. And so Joshua ordered the ark to be brought forward by the priests so that they might position themselves upstream with it. It is reported that this act caused the Jordan to split, and the multitude

crossed over on dry land. 2. Now there was a town in these lands named Jericho, defended by the strongest walls, which would not easily yield to assault or siege. Joshua, confident in God, approached the town with neither arms nor strength. He ordered the ark of God to be carried around the walls, and the priests to advance before the ark and to sound their trumpets. When the ark had circled the town seven times, the walls and towers collapsed, and the town was sacked and burned. Then Joshua is said to have [...] God [...].[42] From there he led the army against Ai,[43] and when ambushes had been placed behind the city, Joshua pretended to be afraid and retreated before the enemy. When the men who were in the city saw this, they opened the gates and pursued the retreating Israelites. Those who had waited in ambush captured the empty city and slaughtered all of the inhabitants, leaving none to escape. The king was captured and executed.

CHAPTER 22

The covenant with the Gibeonites; the war with neighboring kings; excursus on bishops; the land divided; the death of Joshua (Josh 9:1—24:33)

1. When the kings of the neighboring tribes learned of this, they united in battle to drive out the Hebrews by force. But the Gibeonites, a strong people from a wealthy city, had surrendered to the Hebrews without being asked. They promised to carry out all orders and were received under the protection of the Hebrews. They were ordered to gather wood and water.[44] But their surrender had stirred up anger among the kings of the nearby towns. And so after these kings brought up their forces, they surrounded one of their towns, named Gibeon, with a blockade. The townspeople, motivated by their dire straits, sent messengers to Joshua so that he might come to the assistance of the besieged. Making a rapid journey, Joshua came upon the unsuspecting armies unexpectedly and slaughtered several thousand enemy soldiers in a massacre. When daylight began to fail as they slaughtered them, and night seemed as if it would protect the vanquished enemy, the leader of the Hebrews held back the night by the strength of his faith, lengthening the day so that there was no escape for their enemies. Five

kings were captured and killed. The neighboring towns were also added to Israel's rule in the same assault, and their kings were killed.

2. Because of my decision not to explain all these events in detail, as I aim for brevity, I will take care to note only this: twenty-nine kingdoms were subjected to Hebrew rule. Their land was distributed, man by man, throughout the eleven tribes. The Levites, having been taken into the priesthood, were given no portion of the land in order that they might serve God more freely. For my part, I must not pass over this example in silence, and would like to make this compulsory reading for the ministers of the churches.[45] For they seem to me not only negligent with respect to this precept, but they even go so far as to be completely ignorant of it. A great greed, like gangrene, is occupying their spirits in this age. They are eager for possessions, they cultivate farms, they brood over gold, they buy and sell, they desire a profit in all things. But even those with a better intention, neither owning things nor engaging in business, are doing something much more disgraceful: they expect money for being idle, and they have corrupted all that is honorable in life by their mercenary behavior while they profess a sanctity that is virtually for sale. But I have digressed further than I wanted as our times pain and irk me; let me return to what I had begun.

3. And so, as I said above, after the captured land was divided among the tribes, the Hebrews enjoyed great peace. The neighboring lands were too terrified by war to test in battle those who were distinguished by so many victories. During this period, Joshua died, in his 110th year. I will not offer a definite opinion about the length of his rule; it is a common view that he governed the Hebrews for twenty-seven years. If this is the case, then he died in the 3,884th year after the creation of the world.

CHAPTER 23

The conquests of Judah; the Israelites conquered and enslaved by Mesopotamia; Israelites enslaved by Moabites; Deborah; the Midianites conquer Israel (Judg 1:1—6:6)

1. After Joshua's death, the people were living without a leader. But when a war was to be fought against the Canaanites, Judah was

employed as the general for the war. Under his leadership, everything went well; at home and in the field there was perfect peace. The people governed the nations that had been conquered or received in surrender.

Then, as always seemed to happen in prosperous times, they forgot their customs and teachings and began to marry people from the conquered nations. Gradually they adopted foreign customs and, shortly thereafter, sacrificed to idols in profane rituals. This shows that all fellowship with foreign nations is extremely ruinous.[46] God, having foreseen this long before, had instructed the Hebrews in a beneficial oracle[47] to completely destroy conquered nations. But the common people, in their lust for power, preferred to rule the conquered to their own ruin.

2. Consequently, when they abandoned God and worshiped idols, they were stripped of divine assistance, conquered by the king of Mesopotamia, and the subjugated people suffered eight years in captivity.[48] Then they were restored to freedom by the leader Othniel and became masters of their own affairs for fifty years. Corrupted a second time by the evil of a long peace, they sacrificed to idols. Punishment quickly appeared for their sin: they were defeated by Eglon, king of the Moabites, and enslaved for eighteen years. Then Ehud, at God's instigation, killed the king of Israel's enemies by a trick and, gathering a hastily drafted army, won Israel's freedom in battle. Ehud presided over the Hebrews for eighty years in peace. Shamgar came after Ehud, and fighting against the Philistines, he waged a battle that had a successful outcome.

3. Once again, the king of the Canaanites, whose name was Jabin, subjugated the Hebrews, who were carving idols, and he exercised the most severe domination of the people for twenty years, until Deborah, a woman, restored their former state. The people were so devoid of faith in their leaders that they were defended by the aid of a woman. Nevertheless, she was sent ahead as a type of the church whose aid has driven away captivity.[49] The Hebrews were under this female leader, or judge, for forty years. Then once again, on account of their sins, they were handed over to the Midianites and held under harsh rule. Afflicted by the evil of slavery, they called out for divine assistance.

4. Thus it always went: in prosperous times, ignoring heavenly benefits, they worshiped idols, but in adverse times, they called out to

God. When I think back over this history, it seems that even though the people were so obligated to the benefits from God, so coerced by disasters when they sinned, and although they experienced both the mercy and severity of God, they were never made better at all.[50] Although they always received a pardon for their errors, they always sinned again after that pardon, and so it does not seem surprising that they did not receive Christ, when already they had been caught so many times rebelling against the Lord; what is even a greater wonder is that whenever these people—who were always sinning and never following God—asked him, they never failed to receive clemency.

CHAPTER 24

Gideon defeats Midianites; Gideon refuses to rule Israelites (Judg 6:7—8:23)

1. And so when, as we related above, they were dominated by the Midianites, they turned back to the Lord, demanding the customary mercy, and obtained it. There was among the Hebrews a certain man, Gideon by name, a just man, dear and pleasing to God. An angel came to this man when he was returning home from harvesting his field and said, "The Lord is with you, mighty man of valor." But Gideon, with a humble voice, was groaning that God was not with him, because in fact he had burdened the people with captivity, and weeping, he recalled the strength of the Lord, which had led the people from the land of Egypt.

Then the angel said, "Go in this spirit by which you have spoken, and deliver the people from their captivity." But Gideon denied that he could endure so great a burden, as the strength of his people had been broken, and he was the least of them. The angel insisted that he should not doubt that he would be able to do what God was telling him to do.

2. Gideon offered a sacrifice and then destroyed an altar that the Midianites had consecrated to an idol of Ba'al. Next, after going to his own people, he established a camp near the camp of the enemy. The people of Amalek had allied themselves with the Midianites, but Gideon had prepared an army of no more than thirty-two thousand soldiers. Before Gideon could fight, God told him that this great

number was larger than he wanted led into battle; the Hebrews, on account of their customary faithlessness, would not ascribe the outcome of the battle to God, but rather to their own valor. Therefore he should offer those who would leave an opportunity to depart. When this was proposed to the people, twenty-two thousand soldiers withdrew from the camp. But from the ten thousand who had remained, Gideon, warned by God, kept no more than three hundred; the rest he sent away from the army.

3. Gideon entered the enemy camp in the middle of the night, and ordering all of his soldiers to play their trumpets, he unleashed a great terror that none of the enemy had the courage to resist. They succumbed to disgraceful flight, running anywhere they could. The Hebrews ran in from every side, and the enemies fell as they fled in disorder. Gideon chased the kings across the Jordan and killed those he captured. In this battle, 120,000 of the enemy were killed and 15,000 were taken into captivity. Then, with the support of all, the Israelites proposed that Gideon should be the leader of the people. Gideon rejected this plan, as he preferred to live by a common law with the people rather than to rule them. And so the people, having been freed from the captivity that had lasted seven years, enjoyed peace for forty years.

CHAPTER 25

Abimelech seizes power; the rule of Tola and Jair;
Israel conquered by the Philistines; Jephthah;
the sacrifice of Jephthah's daughter (Judg 8:33—12:15)

1. But after Gideon died, Abimelech, his son, who had been born from a concubine, killed his brothers with the consent of the worst men and especially the princes of Shechem who were lending assistance, and he took the kingship. During the civil strife, in the course of military action against his own people, he tried to attack a certain tower into which those fleeing a fallen city had withdrawn. When he approached the tower carelessly, he was struck by a stone thrown by a woman, and he died.

2. He had held power for three years. Tola succeeded him, and he held the kingship for twenty-two years.[51] Jair came after Tola. When

he had held power for a similar length of time, twenty-two years, the people abandoned God and sold themselves to idols. On account of this, the Israelites were conquered by the Philistines and Ammonites, and they were under their power for twenty years.[52] At that time, those who were calling upon God were given a divine response: they should call upon their statues instead, because he would no longer show mercy to the ungrateful. Weeping, the people confessed their error and prayed for forgiveness. After throwing away their idols, they appealed to God and received the mercy that had been withheld.

3. And so with Jephthah as their leader, they came together in a great number to win their liberty on the battlefield. Emissaries were first sent to the king of the Ammonites, telling him to be content with his own lands and abstain from war. But the king, rather than shrinking from combat, deployed a battle line. Then Jephthah, before hostilities commenced, is said to have pledged that if he should fight successfully, the person he met first when coming back from the field would be offered as a sacrifice to God.

His enemies were defeated, and when Jephthah returned home, his daughter rushed out to meet him. She wanted to welcome her victorious father and had gone out joyfully with drums and singers. Jephthah was shocked and, tearing his robes in his grief, revealed to his daughter the binding nature of his vow. With unfeminine steadfastness, she did not offer objections to her death; nevertheless, she did request two more months of life to see her own friends before dying. When the two months had finally passed, she returned to her father of her own accord and fulfilled the vow made to God.[53] Jephthah held power for six years. He was followed by Ibzan, whose power was exercised in tranquil times. Ibzan died in his seventh year. After Ibzan, Elon the Zebulunite held power for ten years, and likewise, Abdon for eight years. In a time of peace, they did nothing that is recorded by history.

CHAPTER 26

Israel conquered by the Philistines; Samson (Judg 13:1—15:19)

1. Once again, the Israelites returned to their idols. Stripped of divine protection and conquered by the Philistines, they paid the penalty for their faithlessness through forty years of captivity. At this

time, it is said, Samson was born. His mother, who had been barren for a long time, saw an angel, and the angel told her that she must abstain from wine, intoxicating drinks, and unclean things; thus it would happen that she would bear a son who would win freedom for his people and punish their enemies. Subsequently, the mother gave birth to a son and gave him the name Samson.

2. He, with uncut hair, is said to have possessed astonishing strength, to the extent that he tore apart a lion he met on the road with his hands. He had a Philistine wife.[54] When he was away, she entered into marriage with another man. Resenting the fact that his wife had been snatched away, he undertook the destruction of her people. Relying upon God and his own powers, he was openly afflicting Israel's conquerors with disaster. In fact, after capturing three hundred foxes, he tied flaming torches to their tails and sent them into the fields of his enemies. By chance, the harvest was ripe at that time and it caught fire easily; the vines and olive orchards were burned down. He seemed to have achieved vengeance for the abduction of his wife through the great damage done to the Philistines.

3. The Philistines, stirred to anger by this attack, burned the woman who was the cause of so great an evil, along with her house and father. Sampson, judging that he had not achieved enough revenge, did not stop harassing the profane people with every annoyance. Then the Jews, under compulsion, bound him and handed him over to the Philistines. But after he was handed over, Samson broke his chains. Seizing the jawbone of an ass, which chance had offered as a weapon, he struck down one thousand of his enemies. When the sun's heat bore down and he was afflicted by thirst, he called upon God and water flowed from the bone[55] that he held in his hand.

CHAPTER 27

Samson trapped by the Philistines; the death of Samson;
the punishment of the tribe of Benjamin (Judg 16:1—21:25)

1. During the time Samson governed the Hebrews, the Philistines were vanquished by the strength of this one individual. They plotted to kill him, but not daring to attack him openly, they bribed the wife he had taken later with money, so that she might reveal the source of her

husband's strength. She approached him with the seductive charms of women, but he deceived her for a long time; although he hesitated many times, she finally compelled him to reveal that his power lay in his long hair. Soon after, ambushing him in his sleep, the woman cut his hair and handed him over to the Philistines. Although he had often been betrayed before, they had been unable to capture him. They cut out his eyes, shackled him with chains, and threw him into prison. But, as time passed, his shorn hair began to grow, and with it his strength returned. Samson, aware of his returning strength, was just waiting for the right time to exact his righteous vengeance.

2. There was a Philistine custom, when they celebrated their festival days, of bringing Samson out, as if for a public parade, so that they might mock the captive. It happened that on a certain day, when they had given a public feast in honor of their idol, they ordered Samson to be exhibited. The temple in which all the people and the leaders of the Philistines were banqueting was supported by two columns of an astonishing size. Samson was led out and placed between the columns. Then, seizing the opportunity, having already called upon the Lord, he tore down the columns. The whole crowd of Philistines was buried under the ruins of the temple, and he, avenged, lay with his enemies after he had led the Hebrews for twenty years.

3. Symmachar succeeded him, but the Scripture has told us nothing more about him. I could not discover the end date of his rule, and I find that the people appear to have been without a leader.[56] Thus, when there was a civil war against the tribe of Benjamin, Judah temporarily was taken on as the leader for the war. But a good number of authors who wrote about those times record that his command was only for a year. Nevertheless, several writers pass over him, and they place the priest Eli after Samson.[57] We shall leave this matter unresolved, as it is poorly authenticated.

CHAPTER 28

The offense of the Benjaminites and their defeat
by the eleven tribes (Judg 19:10—20:48)

1. During these times, as we said, a civil war had flared up, and the cause of the disturbance was the following: a certain Levite was

making a journey with his concubine. Compelled by the approach of
night, he had taken shelter in the town of Gibeah, which was held by
the Benjaminites. Although a certain old man received him with
benign hospitality, some young men from the town surrounded the
guest and prepared to rape him.[58] Strongly rebuked by the old man
and persuaded with difficulty to desist, at last they accepted the sub-
stitution of the concubine's body as their plaything. They spared the
stranger and returned the concubine the next day after abusing her
all night long. But she—whether because of the injury of the rape or
her shame, I cannot determine—breathed out her spirit when she saw
the Levite.

Then the Levite, in testimony against this cruel wickedness, cut
her body into twelve parts and sent the parts to each of the twelve
tribes in order to more easily stir up all the Israelites by the evil that
had been committed. 2. When they learned of this, the remaining
eleven tribes allied together in war against Benjamin. In the war,
Judah, as I have said, was the leader, but the first two battles were
fought poorly. Finally, in the third battle, the tribe of Benjamin was
defeated, and its men were put to the sword to the point of extinction.
Thus, for the wickedness of a few, the entire tribe was punished with
ruin.

3. These events are also contained in the Book of Judges. It is followed by the Books of the Kings. But in my opinion, as I pursue this
project of laying out a methodical arrangement of the years and a
sequence of times, the history seems to fit together poorly. For
although Semigar was a judge after Samson, and a little later, the history records that the people were without judges, Eli also was said to
have been a priest in the Books of the Kings,[59] but the Scriptures
reveal little about how many years there were between Eli and
Samson. I see that there was a certain intermediate span of time that
has produced ambiguity. Nevertheless, there were 418 years from the
date of Joshua's death until that time when Samson died, and from
the beginning of the world, 4,303 years. Although I know that others
disagree with my computation, I do not think that I have been careless in my exposition of the hidden order of the years, until I come to
these times, and I acknowledge that I have doubt about them. Now let
me pursue the remaining events.

CHAPTER 29

Hannah gives birth to Samuel; Eli's corrupt sons;
the death of Eli (1 Sam 1:1—4:18)

1. And so, as I related above, the Hebrews were living under their own authority, without a judge or leader. Eli was the high priest. During his tenure, Samuel was born. Samuel's father was Elkanah, his mother, Hannah. She had been infertile for a long time, and she is said to have made a vow when she asked God to allow her to conceive: if she bore a son, the boy would be dedicated to God. For this reason she gave the boy she had produced to Eli, the priest. Later, when he had entered adolescence, God spoke to the boy. God announced his anger toward Eli because of the lifestyle of his sons. They had turned the priesthood of their father into a source of profit, demanding payments from those who came to offer sacrifices. Although Eli was said to have rebuked them many times, his too-lenient scoldings had not sufficed as a form of discipline.

2. The Hebrews were rushing out to meet the Philistines who were pouring into Judea. Having been defeated, the Hebrews were preparing to reestablish their battle line, and they carried the ark of the covenant with them into battle. The sons of the priest walked with the ark because Eli, weighted with years and fading eyesight, had been unable to perform his duty. When the ark was brought into the enemies' sight, they were terrified, as if by the majesty of the presence of God, and they prepared to flee. But after the Philistines regained their self-control (and this change of heart came through God), they attacked with all of their strength. The Hebrews were defeated, the ark was captured, and the sons of the priest were killed. Eli was shocked and breathed his last when the news of the disaster was brought to him. He had held the priesthood for twenty years.[60]

CHAPTER 30

The ark of the covenant in Philistine hands;
the ark returned to Israel (1 Sam 5:1—6:21)

1. Victorious in this second battle, the Philistines carried the ark of God, which had fallen into their power, to the town of Ashdod and

placed it in the temple of Dagon. But the idol, dedicated to the demon, fell over when the ark was introduced into the temple. After they had restored the idol to its place, it was mutilated during the following night. Then mice,[61] having appeared throughout all the land, brought death to several thousand people through their harmful bites. This evil forced the people of Ashdod to transfer the ark of God to Gath in order to avoid any more calamities. The people of Gath, when they were afflicted with a similar disaster, transported the ark to the city of Ashkelon. Then after the leaders of that city were summoned, they decided to return the ark of the Lord to the Hebrews. So, by the judgment of the kings, augurs, and priests, the ark was placed upon a cart with many gifts and sent back. A great marvel then occurred: they yoked cows to the burden, and although they kept their calves at home, the beasts made the journey into Judea with no leader, forgetting the maternal feeling they had for the calves that had been left behind. Because of the miraculous nature of this event, the kings of the Philistines who were escorting the ark to the Hebrew lines carried out a religious ritual.

2. Now the Jews, when they saw that the ark had been returned, eagerly rushed out from the town of Beth-shemesh with great joy to meet it, hurrying, exulting, and offering thanks to God. Quickly the Levites, who had this duty, offered a sacrifice to God, and they burned the cows that had drawn the ark. But it was not possible to keep the ark in the town of Beth-shemesh, which I mentioned above. After there had been indiscriminate violence in the entire town,[62] in accordance with the will of God, the ark was moved to the town of Kiriath-jearim, where it stayed for twenty years.

CHAPTER 31

Samuel as high priest; Israel demands a king
(1 Sam 7:1—8:22)

1. At this time, Samuel the priest presided over the Hebrews. The years were free from war, and the people spent their time at leisure. Then the peace was broken by an invasion of the Philistines, and all the people grew nervous because they were aware of their sin. Samuel, after slaughtering the sacrificial animals, placed his trust in

God and led his people into battle. The enemy was scattered with the first rush, and victory belonged to the Hebrews. 2. But when fear of the enemy abated in the subsequent tranquil period, their decisions were corrupted, and following the way of the mob, in whom distaste for the present always provokes a desire for something they do not have, the people were demanding the authority of a king, which is hateful to nearly all free people.[63] Clearly they thought it preferable, as attested by this notable example of folly, to exchange liberty for slavery.

Crowds besieged Samuel so that he might choose a king for them, because he was elderly by that time. Samuel, calmly, with a salutary oration, directed the people away from their insane desire. He expounded on kingly domination and the arrogance of power; he praised liberty, and condemned servitude. Finally, he warned of the divine wrath that might strike them if in fact the men became corrupted in their thinking and, after having God as a king, demanded a king for themselves from among men. These words and others in a similar vein were spoken in vain; when the people persevered in their purpose, Samuel consulted God. God had been stirred up by the senseless madness of the people, and he responded that nothing was to be refused to those who were seeking something that would harm them.

CHAPTER 32

Saul becomes king; Saul's illicit sacrifice; Jonathan and the honeycomb; Saul spares the Amalekites and their goods (1 Sam 9:1—15:9)

1. Consequently, Saul, after first being anointed with oil by the high priest Samuel, was made king. Saul was from the tribe of Benjamin, the son of Kish. His character was modest; he had a sound physique, so that the dignity of his body rightly harmonized with the dignity of the kingship. At the beginning of his reign, a considerable part of the people had revolted against him, as they had not wanted to be ruled by a king, and they had joined themselves to the Ammonites. Saul punished them vigorously. His enemies were conquered, the Hebrews were forgiven, and it is said that Samuel then anointed Saul a second time.

2. Then, with another incursion of the Philistines, a bloody war
arose. Saul had fixed a place for his army to assemble in Gilgal. He
waited there seven days for Samuel, so that a sacrifice could be offered
to God. But Samuel was delayed, and when the people began to slip
away, King Saul, with unlawful presumption, offered the sacrifice in
place of the priest. Samuel scolded him vigorously, and Saul acknowledged his sin with a late repentance. Because of the king's sin, fear
pervaded the entire army. The enemy's camp, placed nearby, was presenting an immediate threat, and none of the Israelites had the heart
to march out to battle; in fact, many slipped away into the marshes.
Apart from the lack of courage of those who were thinking that they
had been estranged from God because of the king's offense, the army
desperately needed iron weapons, so much so that it is said that no
one had an iron sword or spear apart from Saul and his son Jonathan.
For the Philistines, victorious in an earlier war, had forbidden the use
of grindstones among the Hebrews, and none of the Hebrews had
retained the ability to manufacture military spears or farming tools.

3. And so Jonathan made an audacious decision and entered the
enemy camp with only his armor bearer as a companion. There he
killed nearly twenty enemy soldiers and filled the rest of the Philistine
army with terror. Then, in fact, by the will of God, the Philistines took
flight, obeying no commands, observing no order, and their only idea
of protection was to run away. When Saul noticed this, he summoned
his forces without hesitation, pursued them as they fled, and won a
victory. It is said that on that day, the king ordered that no one was to
take any food unless the enemies had been destroyed. But Jonathan,
unaware of the king's order, had found a honeycomb, stabbed it with
his spear point, and had eaten the honey. When the king learned of
this, because of God's anger that the vow had been broken, he commanded that his son be put to death. But the people's support preserved Jonathan from destruction.

At the same time, Samuel was warned by God and he went to the
king, bearing the words of God, namely, that he should make war upon
the Amalekites, who once had prevented the Hebrews from crossing
their land while they were fleeing from Egypt; and he added a further
command: Saul was not to desire any of the spoils from the conquered. Then the army was led against the enemy country, their king
was captured, and the people were conquered. Saul, overwhelmed by

the magnitude of the spoils, forgot the divine command and ordered the captured goods to be spared and carried back to Israel.

CHAPTER 33

God turns against Saul; Samuel anoints David; David and Goliath; David marries Michal (1 Sam 15:10—18:27)

1. God, offended by what had happened, told Samuel that he deeply regretted that he had appointed Saul king. The priest reported what had been spoken to the king. Shortly thereafter, Samuel, following God's command, anointed David with the royal perfume. David was still a small boy, living under his father, herding sheep, and often accustomed to play the lyre. Because of his musical talent, he was later taken by Saul and enrolled among the king's servants.

2. At this time, war had flared up between the Philistines and Hebrews, and when they had established battle lines opposite one another, a certain Philistine named Goliath, a man of amazing size and strength, walked out in front of their lines and, flinging abuse with ferocious words against his enemies, called for single combat. Then the king promised rewards and the hand of his daughter to anyone who brought in the spoils of the challenger's equipment, but no one from the large Hebrew army dared to attack Goliath. Then David, although still a boy, offered himself for battle. Rejecting the weapons that were too burdensome for his young body, he went into battle with only a staff and five stones that he had picked up. With his first cast, he launched the stone from the sling and struck the Philistine. Then he cut off his head, carried away the man's equipment, and later placed the sword in the temple. All of the Philistines took flight, conceding victory.

3. After returning from the battle, the considerable support for David inflamed the jealousy of the king. Nevertheless, the king was afraid to kill a man so dear to all while under the influence of envy and a curse.[64] Consequently, employing the pretext of honor, he decided to expose David to many dangers. First, he appointed David tribune, so that he would take charge of the war; then, although he had pledged his daughter to him, he broke his promise and gave her to another. Soon a younger daughter who had been born to the king,

Michal by name, began to burn with love for David. Saul suggested a
condition for David's marriage to Michal: if David brought back one
hundred foreskins from the enemy, the royal daughter would be given
to him in marriage. Saul was hoping that the young man, risking so
many dangers, would easily be killed. But it turned out far differently
from what he had expected, for David promptly secured one hundred
foreskins from the Philistines, as Saul had proposed, and thus he
received the king's daughter in marriage.

CHAPTER 34

*Saul tries to kill David; David flees from Saul; David and Saul
at the cave of Adullam; David flees to the Philistines
(1 Sam 19:1—25:44)*

1. The king's hatred against David grew in those days, stimulated
by jealousy, because evil people always pursue the good. The king
ordered his servants and his son, Jonathan, to prepare snares against
David's life. But David was dear to Jonathan and had been kindly
received by him from the beginning. Consequently, Jonathan scolded
the king, and Saul revoked the bloodthirsty order. But the evil do not
remain good for very long. For once when Saul was being battered by
the spirit of error and David was standing near him, playing his lyre to
calm the king, Saul tried to spear him with a lance. He would have succeeded, except David quickly dodged the lethal blow.

2. From that time onward, Saul no longer hid his intentions, but
openly attempted to kill him. David no longer entrusted himself to
the king. He fled, going first to Samuel, then to Ahimelech, and at last
to the king of Moab. A little later, having been warned by the prophet
Gad, he returned to the land of Judea where his life was in danger. At
this time, Saul killed the priest Ahimelech, who had sheltered David.
Because none of the king's servants dared to lay a hand upon the
priest, Doeg, the Edomite, carried out the bloody service. After this,
David sought the desert. Saul followed him there as well, but his
attempts to destroy the one whom God was protecting proved to be in
vain.

3. There was a cave in the desert[65] that opened into a vast chamber. David had dashed into its interior. Saul, unaware of this fact, had

entered the first chamber of the cave for a rest, and there he fell fast asleep. When David became aware of the king's presence, all of his men began to encourage him to take advantage of this opportunity. Nevertheless, he refused to kill the king, although he did carry off his cloak. He then left the chamber and spoke to Saul from a safe distance behind him. He reminded Saul of his services, that he had often exposed his life to dangers for the king, and of how, finally, at the present time, he had refused to kill the man who had been handed over to him by God. Saul acknowledged his fault in these matters, prayed for forgiveness, wept tears, praised the piety of David, blamed his own malice, and called him king and son.

4. The king was so greatly changed from that earlier ferocious spirit that you might believe he would dare nothing more against his son-in-law. But David, who had carefully watched and understood the malice of the king's mind, resolved to believe nothing the king said and continued to stay in the desert. Saul was driven mad because he lacked the power to apprehend his son-in-law. He gave his daughter Michal, who, as related above, had married David, to a certain Palti in marriage. David fled to the Philistines.

CHAPTER 35

Saul and the Witch of Endor; the death of Saul; the chronological problems associated with Saul's rule (1 Sam 25:1—31:13)

1. During this time, Samuel had died. When the Philistines launched a war, Saul consulted God, but he received no response. Then, through a woman whose heart was filled with a spirit of error,[66] he consulted Samuel, who had been summoned from the dead. Samuel told him that on the next day, he and his sons would be defeated by the Philistines, and they would fall in battle. The Philistines placed their camp in enemy territory and drew up a battle line on the next day. Nevertheless, David had been sent away from their camp because they did not believe that he would stand faithfully with them against his own people. The battle was joined, the Hebrews were dispersed, and the king's sons were killed. Saul, having fallen from his horse, did not want to be captured alive by his enemies, and so he fell upon his own sword.

2. I have discovered little with certainty about the length of his rule, except that in the Acts of the Apostles, he is said to have reigned for forty years.[67] But I think that Samuel's years must have been added to the length of this king's reign by Paul,[68] whose preaching is related in Acts. Nevertheless, there are many who have written[69] about these times and have stated that he ruled for thirty years, an opinion that we definitely cannot endorse. For at the time when the ark was moved from the town of Kiriath-jearim, Saul had not yet begun to rule, and it is said that the ark was removed from that town by King David after it had stayed there for twenty years.[70] And so, since Saul reigned and died within that time period, he held power for a very short span of time indeed.

The same obscurity clouds our calculation concerning the times of Samuel, who is said to have been born during the priesthood of Eli and was still serving as a priest when an old man. Nevertheless, some who have written about these times, because the sacred histories expressed almost nothing about his years [...] by many[71] it is related that he led the people for seventy years. Nevertheless, I have been unable to discover the source of this opinion. In the face of such an abundance of errors, I have followed the notation of the Chronicles,[72] because I deem its dating, as I mentioned above, to have been drawn from the Acts of the Apostles, and I report that Samuel and Saul held power for forty years.

CHAPTER 36

David learns of Saul's death; the opposition and death of Abner; David conquers many nations; the insulting behavior of Hanun of the Ammonites (2 Sam 1:1—11:1)

1. After Saul had been destroyed, David was in the land of the Philistines. He received a message about Saul's death, and he is said to have wept in an amazing example of piety. Then he set out for the town of Hebron in Judea. There, for the second time, he was anointed with the royal oil and named king. But Abner, who had been the commander of the army for King Saul, rejected David and made Ishbosheth,[73] the son of Saul, the new king. This was followed by numerous clashes between the generals of the kings. Abner was frequently

defeated; nevertheless, while fleeing, Abner killed the brother of Joab, who was the army commander on David's side. Later, because of his grief, Joab ordered Abner's throat to be cut after Abner had surrendered himself to King David. David was deeply grieved because Joab had stained his honor with blood.

2. During the same time, almost all of the older Hebrew men, with universal agreement, conferred kingship of all the tribes upon David. During his first seven years, he had ruled only in Hebron. He was anointed king for a third time when he was around thirty years old. He repulsed the Philistines who were invading his kingdom in a series of battles. At this time, he transferred the ark of God, which was in the town of Kiriath-jearim, as I said above,[74] to Zion. And when he had it in his mind to build a temple to God, a divine reply was given that told him to reserve that project for his child. Next, he mastered the Philistines in battle, subjugated the Moabites, and conquered Syria and imposed a tribute upon them. He carried away an immense quantity of gold and bronze from the spoils of war. Then he made war against the Ammonites because of an injury given by their king Hanun.[75] The Syrians also rebelled again and joined with the Ammonites in the war. David relinquished command of the operations to Joab, the army's leader, while he himself, far from the scene of battle, stayed in Jerusalem.

Chapter 37

David and Bathsheba; the rebellion and death of Absalom;
Sheba's rebellion; David takes a census; the death of David and
the ascension of Solomon (2 Sam 11:2—1 Kgs 2:12)

1. At this time, David committed adultery with a certain Bathsheba, a woman of marvelous beauty. She is said to have been the wife of a certain Uriah, who was in the army camp. David saw to it that this man would be defending a dangerous place on the battlefield so that he would be killed by the enemy. Thus he added the widowed woman to the number of his wives, as she was already pregnant from the adultery. Then he was harshly scolded by the prophet Nathan, and although he openly acknowledged his error, he did not escape God's correction. For after a few days, he lost the son produced by that

secret intercourse, and many evil curses fell upon his household and
family. Ultimately, his son Absalom impiously took up arms against his
father, hoping to dislodge David from the kingship. Joab clashed in
battle against Absalom, although the king had ordered him to spare
the boy when he was defeated. But Joab ignored the command and
took revenge with his sword for the attempted parricide. This victory
is said to have brought tears to the king; his piety was so great that he
even wanted to forgive his parricidal son.

2. This war barely seems to have ended when another rose to
take its place, led by a certain general named Sheba, who stirred all
the wickedest people to arms. This uprising of all the people was
quickly suppressed with the death of their leader. Next, David had
numerous battles against the Philistines with favorable results. He subdued the neighboring countries in battle, and with both external and
internal disturbances quelled, he maintained his flourishing kingdom
in peace.

3. Then a sudden desire struck him to take a census of the people in order to estimate the strength of his empire. Joab, the commander of the soldiers, counted 1,300,000 citizens. What had been
done soon pained him, and he repented and sought forgiveness from
God, asking why the idea had arisen in his heart that he should judge
the power of his kingdom based more upon the strength of the multitude than upon divine favor. An angel[76] was sent to him. It announced
three possible punishments and gave him the opportunity to choose
one. Three years of starvation, three months of exile, or three days of
death[77] were proposed; detesting exile and starvation, the king chose
death, and, in a moment of time, seventy thousand of his men were
killed. David, who could see the angel whose right hand was destroying his people, prayed for forgiveness and presented himself as the
one person who should be punished on behalf of all his people; he
deserved destruction because he had sinned. Because of this, the punishment of the people was suspended. David then established a temple to God in the place where he had seen the angel.

4. Soon, bowed down by his years and sickness, he appointed
Solomon, the son he had conceived with Bathsheba, the wife of
Uriah, to be his successor in the kingdom. Solomon was anointed with
the royal oil by Zadok the priest and, with his father still alive, was
named king. David died after he had reigned forty years.

Chapter 38

The wisdom and discernment of Solomon (1 Kgs 3:1–28)

1. Solomon, at the beginning of his reign, encircled the city with a wall. He had a dream in which God seemed to stand near him, offering the option of claiming what he wanted. But Solomon asked God to grant him nothing more than wisdom, believing everything else to be of less value. Thus, inspired by this dream, when he stood before the shrine of God, he gave an example of the wisdom that God had imparted to him.

2. As it happened, two women lived together in one house. They had given birth to sons at the same time, and on the night of the third day, one of the two children had died. The mother of the dead child waited for the other mother to fall asleep, and then put the dead child beside her and took the living baby. This led to an altercation between the two over the identity of the boy, and in the end, the matter was brought to the king. Lacking witnesses, it was difficult to decide between the women; both were denying the other's version. Then Solomon, employing his gift of divine wisdom, ordered the remaining child to be killed and his corpse to be divided between the fighting women. When one of the women consented to the decision, but the other preferred to surrender the child rather than have him destroyed, Solomon awarded the boy to the second woman, inferring from her feminine affection that she was the true mother of the child.

This judgment sparked the admiration of those who were standing around, since, in fact, his foresight had unveiled a hidden truth. Thus, in admiration of his intellect and foresight, the kings of all the neighboring peoples sought friendship and a treaty with him and prepared themselves to carry out his orders.

Chapter 39

Solomon builds the temple; Solomon's wives (1 Kgs 5:1—11:13)

1. Solomon trusted in his wealth and set out to construct a temple to God of immense size. He raised funds for three years, and then he laid the first foundation in about the fourth year of his reign.

Measured from the Hebrews' departure from Egypt, this was approximately the 588th year, although it is clearly stated in the Third Book of Kings as 440 years.[78] It is impossible to reconcile this difference, for in fact, in the sequence outlined above, it would have been easier if perhaps I had recorded fewer years rather than more. But I do not doubt that the truth has been corrupted, especially in such a long intervening age, by the negligence of the copyists rather than by any error on the part of the prophet. We believe that the same thing will happen in this little book of ours, as careless copyists will spoil what we have so carefully arranged.

2. He arranged to begin building the temple in his twentieth year. Then—after Solomon celebrated with a sacrifice in the same place and offered a prayer with which he blessed the people and the temple—God spoke to him and announced what would happen if ever they sinned and abandoned God: the temple would be razed to the ground. We see that long ago this prophecy was carried out, and shortly I will explain the inevitable sequence of events. Meanwhile, Solomon grew very wealthy, the wealthiest of all the kings who had ever lived and, as is always the order of things, was dragged down by his wealth into luxury and vice. Against the command of God, he took wives from foreign peoples; he had seven hundred wives and three hundred concubines. He also set up idols, in accordance with the rites of their countries, for his women to worship. God was repelled by these deeds and, after a severe scolding, announced a penalty: the greater part of the kingdom would be taken from his oldest son and given to his servant. And this is what happened.

CHAPTER 40

Solomon's death; Rehoboam and Jeroboam; Jeroboam establishes idolatry in the North; the death of Rehoboam
(1 Kgs 11:41—14:31)

1. Solomon died in his fortieth year of power, and Rehoboam began to rule his father's kingdom at age sixteen. At this time, he offended a portion of the people and they broke away. For when they demanded that the tax that Solomon had imposed so heavily be mitigated, Rehoboam refused the entreaties of the supplicants and lost

the support of all the people. With everyone's agreement, dominion was granted to Jeroboam. He had risen from a middle-class family and for some time had served Solomon. But when Solomon had discovered, through the oracle of the prophet Ahijah, that the Hebrew kingdom had been promised to Jeroboam, Solomon had resolved to kill him secretly. Fearing this, Jeroboam fled into Egypt, and there he took a wife from the royal line.[79] Finally, when he learned that Solomon had died, he returned to the land of his fathers and, with the support of the people, as I noted above, assumed power.

2. Nevertheless, two tribes, Benjamin and Judah, remained under the control of Rehoboam. He gathered an army of three hundred thousand men from them.[80] When the battle lines advanced, the people were warned by the words of God to refrain from battle, for Jeroboam had received the kingdom by God's will. Consequently, the people rejected Rehoboam's rule, the army fell apart, and Jeroboam's rule was strengthened.

Since Rehoboam held Jerusalem, where the people were accustomed to offer sacrifice to God in the temple built by Solomon, Jeroboam resolved to occupy their minds with a superstition; he was afraid that religion would turn the people away from him. He set up a golden cow in Bethel and a second near Dan for the people to worship. He also established priests from the people, passing over the tribe of Levi. But a protest followed this scandalous behavior that was so hated by God. Next, there were numerous wars with mixed outcomes between the kings, as each held onto their kingdom. Rehoboam, after finishing his seventeenth year of power, came to the end of his life.

Chapter 41

Kings Abijam, Asa, Nadab, Baaha, Elah, Zimri, Omri, Jehoshaphat (1 Kgs 15:1—22:41)

1. In Rehoboam's place, Abijam,[81] his son, held the kingship in Jerusalem for six years, although in the Chronicles he is said to have reigned for three years.[82] His son, Asa, succeeded him, about the fifth from David, his great-great-grandson. He was a most religious worshiper of God, for he destroyed the altars and sacred groves of the

idols and thus removed the remnants of his father's faithlessness. He established a treaty with the king of Syria; with his help, he attacked the kingdom of Jeroboam, which was then held by Jeroboam's son, and brought great destruction; defeating his enemies frequently, he carried back plunder from his victories. After his forty-first year, he died from a sickness of the feet. A threefold sin is ascribed to this man: one, that he had relied too greatly on his alliance with the king of Syria; two, that he had thrown one of God's prophets, who had been scolding him for his alliance with Syria, into prison; and three, that he had placed his hope, not in God, but in doctors, to heal the illness of his feet.[83]

2. At the beginning of Asa's rule, Jeroboam, king of the ten tribes, died. He passed the kingdom to his son, Nadab. He, with evil works as hateful to God as his father's offenses, was unable to hold the kingship beyond his second year, and his unworthy children were stripped of power. His successor was Baasha, son of Ahijah, a man who was also very hostile toward God. Baasha died in his twenty-sixth year of power.[84] Kingship then devolved to his son, Elah, who was unable to retain it beyond his second year. Zimri, the leader of his cavalry, killed him while he was at a banquet. Zimri assumed the kingship, a man impious in the same way toward God and men. Part of the people seceded from this man; the title of king was conferred on a certain Thamni.[85] But Zimri, before this, ruled seven years, and with Thamni, he ruled twelve more. And in the part held by the tribe of Judah, Asa died, and his son, Jehoshaphat, began to rule. Jehoshaphat was a man who was distinguished by the merit of his religious virtues. He had peace with Zimri and died after he had ruled twenty-five years.

CHAPTER 42

King Ahab and Elijah (1 Kgs 16:29—19:18)

1. During the reign of Jehoshaphat, Ahab, son of Ambri,[86] was the king of the ten tribes and impious beyond all the others toward God. For after taking Jezebel—a daughter of Ethbaal, king of Sidon—in marriage, he established an altar and sacred groves to Ba'al, and killed the prophets of God. 2. At this time, the prophet Elijah closed heaven with his prayer so that it would not give any rain to the land,

and he announced his action to the king, so that the king would know that his own impiety was the cause of the drought. The waters were retained in the sky and the entire land was scorched by the burning sun, so that it no longer provided food for men or fodder for livestock.

The prophet also experienced the danger of the famine. At this time, he went out into the desert, and he lived on food from ministering ravens. A nearby stream provided water until it ran dry. Then, prompted by God, he traveled to the town of Zarephath and stayed with a widowed woman. When he became hungry and sought bread from her, she gave him the excuse that she had nothing more than a handful of grain and a trifling amount of oil; when that food was gone, she expected to die with her son. When Elijah promised, through the words of God, that neither the urn of grain nor the vase of oil would have to be diminished, the woman did not hesitate to believe the prophet who was demanding faith, on the condition that the amount taken out each day was replaced daily. During this time, the widow's son died and Elijah restored him to life.

3. Then, by the command of God, Elijah went to the king. After reproaching him for his sacrilege, Elijah demanded that he gather all the people together. When the people convened hastily, the priests who served the idols and sacred groves, nearly 450 of them, were summoned, and at that place an altercation broke out between them: while Elijah was praying to God, they were defending their own superstitions. Finally, it was agreed that a trial of danger should be attempted. A sacrificial offering would be slaughtered, and if fire fell from heaven to consume the offering, the people would adopt the religion that had demonstrated such power. The priests slaughtered a young calf and began to call upon their idol of Ba'al. After they had used up all their invocations without effect, they quietly professed the helplessness of their god.

Then Elijah ridiculed them: "Is it not possible that he sleeps? Scream louder, so that he might wake from the dream that holds him." Of course those miserable men were beginning to mutter and to watch to see what Elijah would do. Elijah laid down a slaughtered calf after he had soaked the altar with water. He called upon the Lord, and with everyone watching, fire fell from heaven and consumed both the water and the sacrifice. Then, in fact, the people fell to the ground, worshiped God, and rejected their idols.

Afterward, on Elijah's command, the profane priests were seized, led to the river, and killed. The prophet followed the king who was returning from the river. But because Jezebel, the king's wife, was preparing a fatal trap for him, he withdrew to a remoter place. God spoke to Elijah there, announcing that there were still seven thousand men who had not given themselves to idols. This amazed Elijah, who believed that he was the only one free from sacrilege.

CHAPTER 43

Ahab and Naboth, the death of Ahab *(1 Kgs 20:1—22:40)*

1. At this time, King Ahab of Samaria desperately wanted the vineyard of Naboth, which adjoined his own land. When Naboth refused to sell his vineyard to the king, he was killed by the cunning of Jezebel. Ahab acquired the vineyard, although it is reported that he mourned Naboth's death. Soon he was scolded by the words of God that Elijah delivered. Acknowledging his crime, he put on sackcloth and is said to have become repentant. Through this act, he averted the punishment that threatened him.[87] For in fact, the king of Syria with his great army and thirty-two kings associated in a war alliance had penetrated the borders of Samaria, and had begun to besiege the city with its king.[88]

When the condition of the besieged became too difficult to bear, the Syrian king gave his terms of war: if they handed over gold, silver, and their women, he would spare their lives. His terms were so unjust it seemed preferable to endure extreme hardships. Then, when everyone had already despaired of rescue, God sent his prophet to the king. He encouraged him to go out in battle, and he strengthened the hesitant king in many ways. Thus a breakout was engineered, the enemy was dispersed, and a great amount of loot was seized.

2. A year later, after rebuilding his forces, the Syrian returned to Samaria, wanting to exact revenge for the disaster that had occurred. He was defeated again. In this battle, 120,000 Syrians were killed. Ahab forgave the Syrian king and granted him both his kingdom and his former status. Then Ahab was scolded by the word of

God delivered through the prophet, who asked why he had misused divine beneficence and spared the enemy who had been handed over to him. Three years later, the Syrian king attacked the Hebrews. Ahab, spurred on by false prophets, went down to fight a battle against the king. Ahab had rejected the prophet Micaiah and thrown him into prison after the prophet had announced that the war was going to be fatal for the king. Ahab was killed in battle, leaving his power to his son, Ahaziah.

CHAPTER 44

Kings Ahaziah and Jehoram;
the prophetic ministry of Elisha;
the rebellion of Jehu (2 Kgs 1:1—9:28)

1. Ahaziah's body was sick, and when he had sent some of his servants to consult an idol about his health, Elijah, having been informed of their mission by God, met them on the way and scolded them. He then ordered the men to announce to the king that he was about to die. The king then ordered his men to apprehend Elijah and bring the prophet to him, but they were consumed by fire that fell from heaven.[89] The king, as the prophet had predicted, died. His brother, Joram, was his successor. He held power for twelve years. And in the part of Israel made up of two tribes, King Jehoshaphat died and his son, Joram,[90] held the kingship eighteen years. He took one of Ahab's daughters as his wife, and he resembled his father-in-law more than his father.

2. After Joram, his son, Ahaziah, inherited power. While he was ruling, it is said that Elijah was carried away.[91] At that time, Elisha, one of his disciples, displayed his power with many signs. All of these are too well-known to need a platform. He brought the son of a widow back to life; he cleansed a Syrian leper; during a time of famine, he brought a great quantity of food of all types, which had been taken from fleeing enemies, into the city; he produced water for the use of three armies; from a woman's small amount of oil, he was able to pay her debt in large increments, and he provided her with enough oil to support herself.[92] In their times, as I said, Ahaziah was king of the two tribes, and Joram, as I related above, ruled the other ten. They made

a treaty between themselves, joining their forces to fight both against the Syrians and against Jehu, whom the prophet had anointed as king of the ten tribes. Side by side they went into combat, and they both perished in the same fight.

CHAPTER 45

Kings Jehu and Ahaziah; Athaliah takes the throne; Jehoash, Amaziah, Jehoahaz, Jehoash (2 Kgs 9:30—14:22)

1. Jehu held the kingdom of Joram. After Ahaziah, a king of Judea who had reigned one year, his mother, Athalia, seized power, usurping the rule of her grandson, who at that time was a small boy; his name was Jehoash. But eight years later, the priests and people restored the power that his grandmother had snatched away, and she was driven out. From the beginning of his reign, he paid very close attention to divine worship, and he supplied the temple with many expensive decorations. Later, he was twisted by the adulation of the leading men,[93] and he deserved wrath after they began to worship him. Hazael, the king of Syria, attacked him, and with the battles going against him, he took gold from the temple to purchase peace. Nevertheless, he did not gain peace; this action made him very unpopular, and his own people killed him in the fortieth year of his reign.

2. Amaziah, his son, succeeded him. In the land of the ten tribes, Jehu had died and his son, Jehoahaz, reigned. God hated him because of his wicked deeds, and because of this, his kingdom was looted by the Syrians until the enemies were driven out by the mercy of God, and they returned to their former condition. When Jehoahaz died, his kingdom was handed on to his son, Jehoash. He brought civil war to Amaziah, king of the two tribes. After winning a victory, he carried a great quantity of loot back to his own kingdom. It is said that this happened to Amaziah because of his transgression, for in fact, when he, victorious, had entered the borders of Idumea, he had adopted the idols of its people. It is written that he ruled for nine years;[94] this much I have discovered in the Books of Kings. But in Chronicles and in the *Chronicles* (of Eusebius), it is noted that he held power for twenty-nine years. What is easily ascertained from those books naturally persuades

me of this calculation. For Jeroboam, king of the ten tribes, is said to have begun his rule in the eighth year of Amaziah's reign, and to have held power for forty-one years; then four years into the rule of Uzziah, son of Amaziah, Jeroboam died. By this calculation, it is shown that there were twenty-nine years in the reign of Amaziah. Consequently, I am following this chronology, because it seems right to adopt this calculation of the dates, and I align myself with the authority of the Chronicles.

CHAPTER 46

Kings Uzziah, Jeroboam, Zechariah, Jotham (2 Kgs 15:1–38)

1. And so, Uzziah,[95] son of Amaziah, came to power. Among the ten tribes, Jehoash had died, but he had made a place for his son, Jeroboam, and after Jeroboam, his son, Zechariah, ruled. I do not think that the times of these kings, and of all those who ruled the ten tribes of Samaria, need to be recorded, because, aiming for brevity, I have omitted superfluous events. I have thought that to secure an understanding of the most important part, I must focus on the years of the part that held their kingdom for a longer time than the part that was led away into captivity first.[96]

2. And so Uzziah, after he attained the kingdom of Judah, had a particular eagerness to know the Lord, and he relied heavily upon Zechariah the prophet. Isaiah is also said to have begun to prophesy under Uzziah. Because of this merit, Uzziah fought and won wars against the neighboring countries. He even defeated the Arabs. He also shook Egypt by the terror of his name, and having been made proud by his later deeds, he dared illicit things and offered incense to God, which, according to custom, only the priests were allowed to do. He was scolded by the priest Azariah and forced to withdraw from that place. When he flared up in anger, his body was completely covered with leprosy, and then he withdrew. He ended his life afflicted with this disease after he had reigned fifty-two years. Next, the kingdom was given to his son, Jotham. He is said to have been very holy, and he administered his realm successfully. He compelled the Ammonites,

who had been conquered in battle, to offer a tribute. He ruled for sixteen years and then his son, Ahaz, took his place.

CHAPTER 47

The story of Jonah (Jonah 1:1—4:11)

1. The well-known anecdote about the faith of the Ninevites is said to have happened in these times. That town, originally founded by Asshur,[97] a son of Shem,[98] was the capital of the Assyrian kingdom. At that time, it was crowded with a multitude of inhabitants, supporting 120,000 men, and as is often the case in a large population, it abounded in vice. God, having been aroused by these vices, instructed the prophet Jonah to travel from Judea and announce the destruction of the city, just as Sodom and Gomorrah had once been destroyed by divine fire. But the prophet rejected this prophetic ministry, not out of insubordination but from foreknowledge, through which he saw that God would be placated by the repentance of the people. Jonah boarded a ship heading for Tarshish, which was in a very different direction from Assyria. In the middle of the crossing, the savagery of the seas compelled the sailors to draw lots in order to discover who was the cause of the evil that had fallen upon them. When the lots had settled upon Jonah, he was cast into the deep sea as propitiation to the storm. He was caught and swallowed by a whale (a marine monster). After the third day, he was ejected on the shores near Nineveh, and he preached the message that had been imposed on him, that the city would be destroyed in three days[99] because of the sins of the people.

2. The voice of the prophet was heard, without any pretense that it had not been, as had happened before in Sodom.[100] And immediately, by the order and example of the king, all the people—even newborns—abstained from food and drink. In the same way, the beasts of burden and animals of all kinds were made to go hungry and thirsty, demonstrating a form of lamentation alongside the humans. In this way, the impending evil was averted. When Jonah complained bitterly in God's presence that what had been promised had not come to pass, God said in response that it was impossible to deny forgiveness to the penitent.

CHAPTER 48

Kings Shallum, Menahem, Pekahiah, Hoshea;
the Assyrians deport the ten tribes;
King Ahaz of Judah
(1 Kgs 15:10—17:41)

1. In Samaria, a certain Shallum killed the very impious King Zechariah, who, as I said above, was ruling, and Shallum seized the throne. Shallum was killed through the snares of Menahem, who simply followed Shallum's example. Menahem held the power he had snatched from Shallum, and he passed it on to his son, Pekahiah. But this king was killed by a certain Pekahiah, a man who had the same name,[101] and the second Pekahiah seized the throne. Shortly thereafter, he lost power, killed by Hoshea through the same wickedness he had used to assume power. This man, impious beyond all the earlier kings,[102] deserved both the punishment God sent upon him and the perpetual captivity of his people. For Shalmaneser, king of the Assyrians, attacked him, and Shalmaneser made the conquered king pay tribute. Forming secret conspiracies, Hoshea prepared to rebel, and he summoned the king of Ethiopia, who at that time was occupying Egypt, to assist him. When Shalmaneser discovered this plot, he bound Hoshea forever in chains and threw him into prison. Then he destroyed the city and abducted the entire population of his kingdom.[103] Assyrians were placed in the hostile country to guard it. From then on, that part of the country was called Samaria, because in the language of the Assyrians, guards are called Samaritans.[104] Many of the Assyrians adopted the divine ceremonies while the rest continued to persevere in the error of the Gentiles.

2. During this war, Tobias was led into captivity. In the part of the country held by the two tribes, King Ahaz, whom God hated on account of his impiety, was frequently oppressed by wars with the surrounding countries. Ahaz decreed that the gods of the Gentiles were to be worshiped, undoubtedly because the victors had stood firm with their help during the frequent wars. Thus he died in this criminally wicked state of mind after he had ruled for sixteen years.

CHAPTER 49

King Hezekiah; Judah besieged by Sennacherib (2 Kgs 18:1—19:8)

1. Hezekiah, Ahaz's son, succeeded him. Hezekiah was very different in character from his father. At the beginning of his reign, he encouraged the people and priests to worship God, and he spoke at length about how those who had frequently been punished by the Lord often attained mercy, and how ultimately the ten tribes had recently been led away into captivity and disbanded as a punishment for their sacrilege; they must make sure that they would not deserve to suffer the same fate.

So, with the minds of all turning back to religion, Hezekiah arranged for the Levites and all the priests to offer sacrifices according to the law, and he commanded that Passover be celebrated, because that festival had been omitted for a long time. When the holiday was at hand, he sent messengers throughout all the land and proclaimed the day of gathering, so that, if any had settled in Samaria after the abduction of the ten tribes, they might come for the holy rite. Thus, in a very crowded gathering, the holy day was spent with public rejoicing, and the religious observation found in the law was reestablished, after a very long interval, by Hezekiah.

2. Next, he took charge of the military with an industriousness equal to his care for divine things, and he crushed the Philistines in numerous battles. Then Sennacherib, king of the Assyrians, attacked him; he penetrated his borders with a great army, laid waste to the undefended fields in every direction, and then established a blockade of the city. Hezekiah, with a smaller force, did not dare fight hand to hand, but he was defending himself within the city walls. The Assyrian king assaulted the gates, threatened destruction, and demanded surrender. He claimed that Hezekiah trusted in God in vain and that it was actually the will of God that had led him to take up arms; the people would be unable to escape the conqueror of all nations and the destroyer of Samaria unless they looked after themselves with an opportune surrender. In this state of affairs, Hezekiah, relying upon God, consulted the prophet Isaiah. The prophet's response taught him that there was no danger from the enemy;

divine aid would not be absent. Not long after these events, Tarraca, king of Ethiopia, invaded the kingdom of the Assyrians.

CHAPTER 50

An angel slaughters the Assyrians;
the death of Hezekiah; Kings Manasseh and Amon
(2 Kgs 19:9—21:26)

1. Upon receipt of this message, Sennacherib turned his attention to defending his own country. Grumbling and claiming that victory had been snatched from the victor, he abandoned the war. He sent a letter to Hezekiah, denouncing him with abusive words, claiming that soon, after he had settled matters in his own country, he would return at an opportune time and destroy Judea.

Hezekiah, unmoved by these threats, is said to have prayed to God that he not permit the great insolence of the king to remain unavenged. Consequently, on that very night, an angel entered the Assyrian camp and killed many thousands of men. The frightened king fled back to the city of Nineveh. There he was killed by his sons, a destruction that he deserved. At the same time, Hezekiah, sick with a physical ailment, took to his bed. And when Isaiah conveyed the words of the Lord to him, that he had come to the end of his life, it is reported that the king wept. As a result, he deserved to have fifteen years added to the span of his life. When these were completed, in his twenty-ninth year of power, he died. He relinquished the kingdom to his son, Manasseh.

2. Manasseh fell well short of his father, and having abandoned God, he cultivated impious forms of worship. On account of this, he was handed over into the power of the Assyrians, and driven by this punishment, he acknowledged his error and exhorted the people to abandon their idols and worship God.[105] He did nothing else worth remembering, although he ruled for fifty-five years. Next, his son, Amon, gained the kingdom, although he held power for no more than two years. An heir of his father's impiety, he neglected God and perished, the victim of a surprise attack by his own people.

CHAPTER 51

King Josiah (2 Kgs 22:1—23:30)

1. Power devolved to Amon's son, Josiah. He is said to have been very religious and to have looked after religious matters with great care, employing Hilkiah the priest well. When he had read a book discovered in the temple by a priest, in which the words of God had been written, and which contained a prophecy that the Hebrew people would be destroyed on account of their repeated impieties and sacrileges, he turned aside the impending disaster with pious prayers to God and constant weeping. When he learned, through the prophetess Huldah, of the favor shown him, he felt obligated, as one might expect, to the divine favors, and he supervised God's cult with even greater care. He burned all the vases that had been consecrated to superstitious idols by earlier kings.

2. The profane rituals had grown stronger, to the point that the people granted divine honors to the sun and moon and also erected shrines made of metals to the same. Josiah reduced these to dust and also killed the priests of the profane temples. But he did not even spare the tombs of the impious, as he carried out a punishment once foreseen by the prophets. Passover was celebrated in the eighteenth year of his reign. Nearly three years later, he went out to battle against Neco, the king of Egypt, who was waging war against the Assyrians. Before the battle lines drew together to fight among themselves, he was struck by an arrow.[106] He was carried into the city but died from that wound. He had ruled for twenty-one years.

CHAPTER 52

Kings Jehoahaz, Jehoiakim, Jehoiachin; the beginning of the Babylonian Exile; King Zedekiah; Jehoiachin released from prison (2 Kgs 23:31—25:30)

1. Next, his son, Jehoahaz, acquired the throne and held it for three months, but he was destined for captivity on account of his impiety. For King Neco of Egypt took Jehoahaz away as a captive in chains. He died not long after, still in chains. The Jews were ordered to pay

an annual tribute, and the victorious Egyptians decided to make Eliakim their king. Later, Eliakim changed his name and was called Jehoiakim. He was the brother of Jehoahaz, the son of Josiah, and since he was more like his brother than his father, God hated him for his sacrilege.

2. When he proved subservient to the king of Egypt, since he paid tribute to him, Nebuchadnezzar, the king of Babylon, occupied the land of Judea with arms, and the victor held the land for three years by the right of conquest. After the Egyptian king withdrew and the imperial borders were drawn between them, it was agreed that the Jews would belong to the Babylonian empire. Jehoiakim completed his eleventh year in power and then made way for his son, who had the same name.[107] The younger Jehoiakim roused the anger of the Babylonian king against himself, an act that was surely prompted by God,[108] who had decided that the Judean people were to be handed over to captivity and extermination. Nebuchadnezzar entered Jerusalem[109] with an army and razed the walls and temple to the ground. He hauled away a vast quantity of gold and the sacred ornaments, both public and private, and all the adults of both the male and female gender. Those whose age or infirmity made them repugnant to the victors were left behind. This group, deemed useless for slavery, was given the job of working and cultivating the fields, so that the land would not lie fallow.

3. King Zedekiah[110] was put in charge of the people, and with all of his powers stripped away, he was granted the empty title of king. Jehoiakim held power for three months. He was carried away to Babylon with the people and was thrown in prison. Thirty years[111] later, he was released and received by the king in friendship, sharing his table and councils. He died with the consolation of having had his calamity set aside.

CHAPTER 53

King Zedekiah and Jeremiah; the second deportation; Gedaliah placed over Judea (Jer 37:1—40:12)

1. Meanwhile, Zedekiah was king over a useless crowd, although he lacked power. Untrustworthy of mind and neglectful of God, he

did not understand that the captivity was produced by the people's offenses, and finally, having been destined for the ultimate misfortunes, he offended the mind of the king. Consequently, after nine years of rule, Nebuchadnezzar attacked him, and for three years, he besieged Zedekiah, who had been forced to flee inside the walls.

2. At this time, the king consulted the prophet Jeremiah,[112] who had foretold that the capture of the city was imminent; he asked the prophet if, by chance, any hope remained. But Jeremiah was aware of heaven's anger. Having been asked the same question often, he responded by announcing that a special punishment had been prepared for the king. Then Zedekiah, stirred to anger, ordered the prophet to be thrown into prison. Soon the cruelty of what he had done bothered him, but opposed by the leaders of Judea, whose custom, even from the beginning, had been to oppress the good, he did not dare release the innocent prophet. Driven by these same men, the prophet was cast into a horrible cistern[113] of great depth, into the mud and filth from which a deadly stench arose, so that he might not even come to his end in a simple death. But the king, although clearly impious, was nevertheless somewhat milder than the priests, and he ordered the prophet to be taken out of the cistern and returned to the custody of prison.

3. Meanwhile, the besieged were being pressured by hunger and enemy force. Everything that could be eaten had been consumed and hunger was growing. Consequently, when the defenders grew exhausted from starvation, the city was captured and burned. The king, as the prophet had said, had his eyes gouged out[114] and was carried away to Babylon. Jeremiah was released from prison by the mercy of the enemies. When Nebuzaradan, one of the king's generals, led him away as a captive with the others, he offered Jeremiah a choice of whether to remain in the deserted and desolate land of his fathers or to go with Nebuzaradan and receive the highest honors in Babylon. Jeremiah preferred to live in his fatherland.[115] Nebuchadnezzar, after abducting the people, established Gedaliah, a man of Judea, over those who remained behind, those who had been abandoned under terms of war or because the victors had rejected them as loot. Gedaliah held neither royal rank nor imperial title because there was no honor in governing so few in such a blighted place.

BOOK II

CHAPTER 1

Daniel in King Nebuchadnezzar's court; Daniel and Susanna (Dan 1:1–21; 13:1–64)

1. The times of captivity were made glorious by the prophecies and acts of the prophets, especially in Daniel's exceptional perseverance in keeping the law, in the acquittal of Susannah by divine counsel, and Daniel's other deeds, which I will now explain in sequence.

Daniel was captured during the reign of King Jehoiakim and led away to Babylon while a very small boy. Later, because of his elegant appearance, he was enrolled among the king's attendants, together with Hananiah, Mishael, and Azariah. When the king had ordered them to be provided with more luxurious foods, and he had given that duty to the eunuch Ashpenaz, Daniel, mindful of the tradition of his fathers, did not want to partake of the food of Gentiles that was brought from the king's table. He asked the eunuch to permit them to eat only vegetables. Ashpenaz protested that their ensuing thinness would reveal that the king's order was being ignored. Daniel, confident in God, promised that their appearance would be of greater beauty from vegetables than from the king's food. His words carried conviction, and their appearance was thought not at all comparable to those who were maintained by imperial expense. And so the king accepted them into honor and favor, and after a short time, they were preferred over all the men around the king because of their prudence and discipline.

2. At the same time, there was Susanna,[1] the wife of a certain Joachim, a woman of conspicuous beauty, who was desired by two priests. When she did not acquiesce to the lustful men, she was falsely accused of a crime: the two priests charged that they had surprised a young man who was together with her in a remote place, but that young man had energetically eluded the grasp of the older men. The testimony of the priests was deemed trustworthy, and Susanna was condemned by the judgment of the people.

When she was being led away to a punishment that was in accordance with the law, Daniel, then only twelve years old, began scolding the Jews, asking why they had handed an innocent person over to death. He demanded she be returned to court and her case be heard again.

The crowd of Jews who were present at that time believed that a boy of such contemptible youth would not have burst out so firmly in this matter apart from God, and with their support, the case was returned to council. The trial resumed once more. It was placed in Daniel's hands so that he sat among the elders. He ordered that the accusers be separated, and he asked each man individually the type of tree under which the adulterous woman had been caught. The difference between their answers proved the false nature of the charge. Susanna was absolved, and the priests, who had manufactured danger for the innocent woman, were executed.

Chapter 2

Nebuchadnezzar's dream (Dan 2:1—3:35)

1. At the same time, Nebuchadnezzar had a dream that was remarkable in that it disclosed the mystery of coming events. When he was unable to interpret the dream on his own, the Chaldeans were brought in to explain it. These are men who are said to know hidden things and to predict future events through their magical arts and the examination of the organs of sacrificed animals. The king was afraid they would offer an interpretation in accord with the customs of men and not the truth—that is, a pleasing interpretation of the king's dream. Consequently, he kept what he had seen secret and demanded that they, if there was truth in their divination, tell him the content of his dream. He would only believe their interpretation if they first made a test of their art by revealing his dream. 2. But they, refusing so great a task, admitted that this was not within human power. The king, stirred up, asked why they should be allowed to lead men into error through their false declaration of the ability to divine, when the present matter forced them to admit that they knew nothing. Thus, by a royal edict, they were punished, and everyone who practiced their arts was executed publicly.

When Daniel learned this, he sent for a relative of the king and promised that he could reveal the dream and interpret it. The message was handed on to the king and he summoned Daniel. God had already disclosed the mystery to Daniel, and he recounted and explained the visions of the king.

This work demands that I explain the king's dream, the interpretation of the prophet, and the confirmation revealed in the subsequent events. 3. The king had seen a figure in his dream with a head made of gold, a chest and arms of silver, a stomach and thighs of bronze, and legs of iron; the iron part ended in the feet, and a part of the feet was made of clay. But the iron and earth, although mixed together, were unable to stick together. Finally, a stone, torn off with no hands touching it, ground down the figure. After all the parts of the figure had been reduced to rubble, it was blown away by the wind.

CHAPTER 3

The interpretation of Nebuchadnezzar's dream (Dan 2:36–45)

1. And so, according to the interpretation of the prophet, the figure that had been seen represented the world. The golden head symbolized the Chaldean Empire,[2] since in fact we understand that the Chaldean Empire was the first and the wealthiest. The silver chest and arms proclaim the second kingdom, for Cyrus conquered the Chaldeans and Medes and brought power to the Persians. In the bronze belly, the third kingdom was announced as a prediction, and we see that this has come to pass, since Alexander claimed the empire, snatched from the Persians, for the Macedonians. The iron thighs stand for the fourth empire, and this is understood to be that of the Romans, for it is more powerful than all the kingdoms that went before. But the feet, part iron, part clay, show that the Roman kingdom is to be divided as it will never be able to form a whole among itself.

That has already happened, since in fact the Roman state is ruled not by one emperor, but rather by many, and they are always disagreeing among themselves with armies or party factions.[3] 2. Finally, the clay and iron, mingled but never combining into a material that will hold together, signify the future of the human race, disagreeing with one another in turn, since in fact it is common knowledge that Roman land has been occupied by foreign or rebellious people or given to those who surrendered in the guise of peace.[4] We also see the barbarous peoples mixed into our armies, cities, and provinces, and especially the Jews,[5] who live among us even though they do not adopt our customs. The prophet announced that these would be the last things.

3. But in the stone, torn off with no hands touching it, which smashed the gold, silver, bronze, iron, and clay, we see the figure of Christ.[6] For he came forth, not from the human condition, since he was not born from the will of a man, but from God; he will reduce this world, in which the earthly kingdoms are to be nothing; he will establish another kingdom that will be incorruptible and perpetual; in other words, he will establish the future age that has been prepared for the saints. The faith of certain people still wavers about this one point: they do not believe prophecies about future events, although they have been proven wrong by what has happened in the past.

And so the king presented Daniel with great riches, set him over Babylon and the entire empire, and held him in the highest honor. By his decision, Hananiah, Azariah, and Mishael were promoted into positions of the highest dignity and power as well. At nearly the same time, the splendid prophecy of Ezekiel[7] appeared, as the mystery of coming events and the resurrection had been revealed to him. The book of this great work is extant and should be read with care.

CHAPTER 4

Ishmael kills Gedaliah; Ishmael driven out of Judea; the people
flee to Egypt (2 Kgs 25:25–26; Jer 41:1—43:7)

1. Meanwhile in Judea, which, after the destruction of Jerusalem, had been placed under Gedaliah, as I noted above,[8] the people were resenting a leader of Judea who was not from the royal line but, rather, a man who had been imposed by the victor's decision. Following the leadership of a certain Ishmael, the instigator of a wicked conspiracy, the people killed Gedaliah in an ambush set at a banquet.

Those who had not been part of this conspiracy, wanting to avenge the crime, quickly took up arms against Ishmael. But since he knew that he was about to be destroyed, he abandoned the army he had assembled and, with no more than eight companions, fled to the

Ammonites. Then fear spread throughout all the people that, owing to the wickedness of a few, the king of Babylon would come as an avenger and destroy all the people; for many Chaldeans had been killed along with Gedaliah.

2. It was decided that they should flee to Egypt, but first the crowds went to Jeremiah, asking for a divine response. That man encouraged all the people with the words of God, stating that they should remain in their homeland; if they did that, God's protection would guard them and there would be no danger from the Babylonians; if, on the other hand, they went to Egypt, they would all die: by the sword, by hunger, or by various other forms of death. But the common people, with their usual evil, unaccustomed to complying with wise counsels and the divine command, went into Egypt.[9] The sacred texts are silent about what happened to them afterward, and I have discovered nothing about their fate.

CHAPTER 5

Nebuchadnezzar builds a golden idol for the people to worship;
the Israelites in the furnace; Nebuchadnezzar punished
(Dan 3:1—4:37)

1. During this stretch of time, Nebuchadnezzar, made haughty by his prosperity, erected an immense golden statue of himself, and he ordered that it should be worshiped as a sacred image. Although this was done eagerly by all, since the spirits of all the people had been corrupted through fawning, Hananiah, Azariah, and Mishael abstained from this profane obligation, knowing that honor was owed to God alone. As a result of this, they were pronounced guilty by royal edict; they were shown a blazing furnace, the form their punishment was to take, so that fear of what they saw would compel them to worship the statue. They preferred immolation in the flames to offering a sacrifice.

2. Consequently, after being shackled with chains, they were thrown into the middle of the flames. The flames devoured the servants of this damnable work while they were too eagerly pushing the condemned men into the fire. The fire did not touch the Hebrews, an outcome that is amazing to relate and hard to believe for those who

did not witness it, although those who were watching saw them walking around in the furnace and speaking a psalm to God. They also saw a fourth figure, in the form of an angel, with the men among the flames. Nebuchadnezzar, seeing correctly, confessed that he had seen the son of God. Then the king, with no doubt that divine power was present in this matter, sent proclamations throughout his entire kingdom to make it publicly known that a miracle had occurred, and he confessed that honor should be offered to God alone.[10]

3. It is said that, not long after this, he was given a warning in a dream that came to him, and then also by a voice that came out of the sky; he set aside his royal power, and far away from all human interaction, maintaining his life by eating grass alone, he served a penance. His power was preserved for him by the will of God. After seven years, when the period of punishment had been completed and he finally acknowledged God, he was restored to his monarchy and his former condition.

After this, he defeated Zedekiah, as I said above,[11] who was taken as a captive to Babylon; Nebuchadnezzar is said to have reigned another twenty-six years, although I do not find this written in the Holy Scriptures. 4. But it happened, by chance, that while I was studying many things, I discovered this annotation in a book damaged by age, one that lacked the name of the author; in this book, I discovered a chronological record of the Babylonian kings. I did not believe that this information should be passed over, since in fact it both agrees with the Book of Chronicles and its account fills out these years for us. Thus it covers, through its arrangement of kings, whose times are contained there, a seventy-year period, down to the first year of King Cyrus.[12] This is the length of time reported in the sacred history from the captivity until Cyrus.

CHAPTER 6

King Belshazzar gives a banquet; Daniel interprets the writing on the wall; Darius seizes the kingdom and favors Daniel (Dan 5:1–30)

1. After Nebuchadnezzar, his son acquired the kingdom, who, in the Book of Chronicles,[13] I find was named Evil-merodach. He died in

the twelfth year of his reign, and his younger brother, named Belshazzar, took his place. When, in his fourteenth year, he gave a public banquet for his princes and prefects, he ordered the sacred vases to be brought out. Nebuchadnezzar had taken these vases from the Jerusalem temple; the king did not use them, but kept them stored in the treasury.

2. And when all of the men and women, his wives and concubines, were sharing them in the extravagant and licentious conduct of the royal banquet, suddenly the king caught sight of a hand writing on the wall, and the letters that were written appeared to form a verse. Unable to find anyone who could read the writing, the terrified king summoned the magicians and the Chaldean astrologers.

3. After they muttered over it but were unable to offer an interpretation, the queen reminded the king that there was a certain Hebrew named Daniel who once had revealed the hidden mystery of Nebuchadnezzar's dream and then had been granted the highest honors on account of his evident wisdom. Daniel was summoned and he read the text; then he offered an interpretation: because of the king's offense—defiling the vases that were sacred to God—his destruction was imminent and his kingdom would be handed over to the Medes and Persians.

4. Shortly thereafter, this happened. For on the same night, Belshazzar died, and Darius, a Mede by nationality,[14] seized his kingdom. Darius placed Daniel, who was known to have a noble reputation, over the entire kingdom, following the judgment of the earlier kings. For Nebuchadnezzar had put him in charge of the kingdom, and Belshazzar had established him as the third leader of the kingdom, giving him a purple garment and a golden collar.

CHAPTER 7

Daniel in the lion's den (Dan 6:1–28)

1. And so those men who were sharing power along with him were stirred to envy because a foreigner of a captive nation had been made their equal. They convinced the king, who had been corrupted by their fawning, that for the next thirty days, the people should offer him divine honors, and no one would be permitted to pray to any God

except the king. Darius was easily persuaded to do this because of the foolishness found in all kings who claim divine honors for themselves.

2. And so it was that Daniel, neither unaware nor ignorant of the fact that prayers should be offered to God rather than to men, was found guilty of failing to obey the edict of the king. For a long time, Darius refused this request; Daniel was dear to him and the king had always welcomed him, but ultimately the other leaders convinced him that Daniel should be dropped into a pit. But even when exposed to wild animals, he was in no danger. When the king had seen this, he ordered Daniel's accusers be given to the lions. These men did not enjoy a similar fate; they were immediately gulped down and sated the hunger of the beasts. Daniel was even more famous than he had been before. The king rejected his own edict and proposed a new one: errors and superstitions should be abandoned and worship must be offered to Daniel's God.

3. Daniel's visions, in which he revealed the order of the coming ages, still exist; he announced—having also grasped the number of years—when Christ would descend to earth, just as it happened; he also clearly revealed that the antichrist will come. If anyone wants to be more diligent, let him investigate this more thoroughly by looking in that place; I propose simply to join together an arrangement of events. Darius is said to have reigned eighteen years; during this time, Astyages was ruling the Medes.[15]

CHAPTER 8

Cyrus conquers Babylon and issues edicts that allow
the Jews to return to Judea; Daniel and Bel
(Ezra 1:1–7; Dan 14:1–40)

1. Cyrus, a grandson of Astyages through his daughter, used the Persian armies to drive this man from his kingdom. Because of this rebellion, the greatest power was transferred to the Persians. The Babylonians also came under Cyrus's power and jurisdiction.[16] And so, from the beginning of his reign, in edicts that were publicly distributed, he gave the Jews the right to return to the land of their fathers, and he even returned the sacred vases that Nebuchadnezzar had taken from the temple in Jerusalem. At that time, a few men returned to

Judea. As for the others, I have discovered little about whether they lacked the courage or the opportunity to return.

2. There was at this time, among the Babylonians, a statue made from bronze of Bel,[17] the most ancient of the kings, whom even Virgil mentions.[18] This statue had been consecrated by the superstition of men, and Cyrus also customarily worshiped it, having been led astray by a trick of its high priests. The priests claimed that the statue ate and drank when they themselves secretly consumed the daily ration of food that was brought for the idol. And so, when Cyrus was treating Daniel as a close friend, he asked him why he did not worship the statue, when there was clear evidence that the god was alive, since it consumed the food brought to it. Daniel, laughing at the error of the man, said that it was not possible for a bronze statue—that is, one made of insensate materials—to consume food or drink.

3. The king ordered the priests to be summoned (for there were about seventy), and having employed terror against them, he demanded to know who was consuming the expensive foods, since Daniel, a man distinguished for his good sense, contended that it was impossible for an inanimate statue to do this. Then they, confident in the trick that had been prepared, demanded that the usual food should be brought in and the king should then seal the temple. Then, unless everything had been consumed by the next day, they should be arrested and would pay their penalty by death, while the same condition should also await Daniel. The temple was sealed with the king's seal, although earlier, unknown to the priests, Daniel had sprinkled the pavement with ashes, so that the footsteps of those going in might reveal hidden doorways.

The next day, when the king entered the temple, he noticed that the food he had ordered to be placed before the idol had been consumed. Then Daniel disclosed the hidden fraud that was revealed by the footprints: the priests, together with their wives and children, had entered through a hole dug under the temple, and they had consumed the food that had been served to the idol. Thus all the priests were executed by the order of the king; the temple and its statue were handed over to the power of Daniel and destroyed by his decision.

CHAPTER 9

Opposition to the rebuilding of the temple;
a list of Persian kings (Ezra 4:7–23)

1. Meanwhile the Jews, who, with the permission of Cyrus, had returned to their homeland, as we noted above,[19] undertook to rebuild the city and temple. The few, poor people were making little progress, until in approximately the one-hundredth year,[20] with King Artaxerxes[21] ruling Persia, they were deterred from rebuilding by those who were preeminent in the land. For even then, Syria and all of Judea were under the power of Persia, and they were still being ruled through magistrates and military commanders. These leaders decided to write to King Artaxerxes that the Jews should not be given an opportunity to rebuild their city; they had a natural inclination to insubordination, and with their power restored and accustomed to rule over other nations, they would not tolerate living under a foreign power. This decision of the military commanders was approved by the king, and the rebuilding of the city was hindered, until in the second year of King Darius,[22] the decree was set aside.

2. In this examination of the times, I will insert a list of those kings who ruled the Persians, through which a sequence of the years, arranged in order, may be more easily recorded. After Darius the Mede, who I indicated had reigned eighteen years,[23] Cyrus was the master of affairs for thirty-one years.[24] While fighting the Scythians, he fell in combat, during the second year after Tarquinius Superbus had begun to rule in Rome.[25] Cambyses, Cyrus's son, succeeded him. Cambyses ruled for nine years.[26] After he had suppressed and subjugated both Egypt and Ethiopia in battle and was returning to Persia as a victor, he wounded himself in an accident and perished from the blow.

3. After his death, two brothers who were magicians from the country of the Medes held the kingdom of the Persians for seven months. Seven of the most noble men of Persia bound themselves together in a plot to kill them. Darius,[27] the son of Hystapes, was the leader of the conspirators. He was the son of Cyrus's brother on his father's side. With the consent of all, the kingship was conferred upon him. He reigned for thirty-six years. This man, four years before he died, fought at Marathon in the most celebrated battle of Greek and

Roman history. That took place in about the 260th year after the foundation of Rome, with Macerinus and Augurinus as consuls. That is 888 years ago, if my investigation of the Roman consulships has not gone astray. For I have put every period in order up to the consulship of Stilicho.[28]

4. Xerxes came after Darius; he is said to have ruled for twenty-one years, although in many sources I discovered that the length of his reign was twenty-five years.[29] Artaxerxes, whom we mentioned above, succeeded him.[30] When this man ordered the rebuilding of the Jewish city and temple to be held back, the suspended work was put on hold until the second year of king Darius.[31] But in order that the arrangement of the periods may be joined up to him: Artaxerxes reigned forty-one years, Xerxes for two months, and after him, Sogdianus ruled for seven months.[32]

CHAPTER 10

The reconstruction of the temple and Jerusalem
(1 Esd 3:1—4:48; Ezra 7:1–10)

1. Then Darius, under whom the temple was restored, obtained the kingdom; his name then was Ochus.[33] This king had three Hebrew youths[34] of proven trustworthiness as bodyguards, and one of their number had displayed such good sense that he had attracted the admiration of the king. When he was offered the chance to request something for himself if there was anything his heart desired, groaning over the ruin of his homeland, he asked for the opportunity to restore his city. Furthermore, if he deserved a favor from the king, he also asked to be placed in charge of the local rulers and military leaders and that he might speed up the reconstruction of the sacred temple by paying for the costs. As a result, the temple was finished in four years, in the sixth year after Darius began to reign,[35] and the Jews thought that was enough. Because this diffident people thought it was too much trouble to restore the city and they did not have enough trust in their own strength to begin so difficult a work, restoration was confined to the temple.

2. Ezra, a scribe of the law, lived during this same period, approximately twenty years after the temple had been completed.[36]

Darius, who had ruled for nineteen years, had died by then, and with the permission of Artaxerxes II (not the man who had ruled between the two Xerxes, but the one who had succeeded Darius Ochus), Ezra set out from Babylon with many following him.[37] He brought vessels of various kinds to Jerusalem, gifts that the king had sent to the temple of God, and twelve Levites.

It is reported that this number could hardly be found from that tribe. When Ezra discovered that the Jews were frequently intermarrying with Gentiles, he scolded the people and commanded them to renounce this form of marriage and expel from among them the children produced by these unions. They all obeyed his word. The people were purified and were living by the rite of the old law. Otherwise, I find that Ezra did nothing about rebuilding the city,[38] and I believe that he considered that reforming the corrupted customs of his people was a greater concern.

CHAPTER 11

Nehemiah rebuilds the city
(Neh 1:1—8:30)

1. Nehemiah, a Jewish man, was a minister of the king at this time in Babylon. Artaxerxes regarded him most favorably because of the value of his services.[39] He had questioned the Jews to determine the state of the city, and when he discovered that his homeland still lay in ruins, he was greatly disturbed. It is said that he prayed to God with groaning and many tears, thinking back over the offenses of his people and begging for divine mercy.

2. When the king noticed his unusual sorrow during the banquets, he demanded that Nehemiah should explain the reason for his grief. Then Nehemiah bitterly lamented the hardships of his own people and the ruin of the city, which, having stood devastated to its foundations for nearly 250 years,[40] now served as evidence of its woes and a spectacle for the wicked; he begged that the king should grant him the power to go and rebuild the city. The king complied with these pious requests and at once sent Nehemiah with a bodyguard of cavalry, who would ensure that the trip was made safely. He was also

given letters to the praetors,[41] so that they would supply whatever was necessary.

When Nehemiah reached Jerusalem, he distributed work on the city to individual people, and everyone carried out his commands zealously. Soon the scaffolds had advanced to half the height of the original walls.[42]

3. This stirred up the envy of the neighboring peoples, and the cities conspired to interrupt the works and prevent the Jews from rebuilding the city. But Nehemiah arranged guards against those who would attack the city and, unafraid, completed what had been begun. With the wall finished and the folding doors of the gates perfected, he measured the space within the city so that families could build their homes.

He calculated that the number of people was insufficient for the size of the city, for he discovered no more than fifty thousand people of intermingled sex and class. Many from the formerly large number of people had been destroyed in the frequent wars or detained in captivity. In the past, after they had separated from the ten tribes, the two tribes of which these people were the remainder had armed 320,000 soldiers. Because of their sin, God had given them over to death and captivity until they had been reduced to this small number.

4. But these people, as I said, were the commoners of the two tribes; the ten tribes had been dispersed earlier among the Parthians, Medes, Indians, and Ethiopians;[43] they never returned to the land of their fathers and, to this day, are still dwelling in the empires of the barbarian peoples. It is reported that the reconstruction of the city was completed in the thirty-second year of Artaxerxes's reign.

5. There were 398 years from this time until the crucifixion of Christ, which happened during the consulship of Fufius Geminus and Rebellius.[44] Otherwise, from the restoration of the temple until its destruction, which was carried out by the Caesar Titus during the consulship of Vespasian Augustus,[45] there were 483 years. This had been predicted earlier by Daniel, who had prophesied that from the renewal of the temple to its overthrow, there would be sixty-nine weeks.[46] From the date of the captivity of the Jews until the time when the city was rebuilt, there were 260 years.

CHAPTER 12

Queen Vashti set aside; Esther marries the Persian king
(Esth 1:1—2:18)

1. I have decided that Esther and Judith[47] belong to this period; however, I am not able to ascertain easily to which kings their exploits should most easily be linked. For although it is reported that Esther lived under King Artaxerxes, I find that there were two Persian kings[48] by that name, and I feel great hesitation about linking her to the times of either man. Still it seems apparent to me that the story of Esther should be connected with Artaxerxes II, under whom the temple was restored, because it is implausible that, if she had lived under the earlier Artaxerxes, a period that embraced the times of Ezra, there would have been not so much as a reference to this illustrious woman, especially since it is known, as I reported above, that the reconstruction of the temple was delayed by that Artaxerxes.[49] Esther would not have suffered this if she had been married to him at that time.

2. Now I will discuss her acts. There was, at that time, a certain wife of the king named Vashti, a woman of exceptional beauty. The king praised her appearance to all, and on a certain day when he was offering a public banquet, he ordered the queen to make an appearance to display the charm of her beauty. But she, more prudent than the stupid king, was ashamed to offer the spectacle of her body to the eyes of the men, and she refused his commands. At this disobedience, the king's barbarous heart was stirred up, and he expelled his wife from both the marriage and the palace.

And so, when a girl was sought to be a wife for the king in her place, Esther was reported to surpass all others of her gender. She was from Judea, of the tribe of Benjamin, and having been orphaned by the death of both parents, she was raised by her cousin Mordecai. When she was led to the royal wedding, she followed the command of her guardian and concealed her race and homeland, although she was warned not to forget the tradition of her fathers, and even if she was entering into marriage with a foreigner as a captive, she should not eat Gentile foods.

Consequently, after being joined with the king, in a short amount of time, as it sometimes happens, she easily captured his entire heart through the power of her beauty, to such a degree that he gave her an equal symbol of imperial power, a purple robe.

CHAPTER 13

Haman plots against Mordecai;
Haman executed (Esth 3:1—7:10)

1. At this time, Mordecai was among those nearest to the king, and he served as the overseer of domestic affairs to the best of his ability. He revealed a plot to the king that had been formulated by two eunuchs. Because of that, he was regarded with greater favor and given the highest honors.

2. There was also at this time a certain Haman who was very close to the king; he was made equal to the king, and in accordance with the custom of the Persian kings, the king ordered that Haman should be worshiped. Mordecai was the only one among all the people who disdained to do this, and the Persian began to hate him. And so Haman, aiming his mind at the ruin of the Hebrew, went to the king and asserted that there was in his kingdom a class of men hated by both God and men for their wicked superstitions, men who were living by foreign laws and deserved destruction.[50] It would be right to hand all of these men over to death, and Haman promised that great wealth could be extracted from their holdings. He had no difficulty persuading the barbarous king; an edict was issued to kill the Jews and copies of the order were sent immediately throughout the entire kingdom, from India to Ethiopia.

When Mordecai learned of the edict, he tore his clothes, covered himself with sackcloth, sprinkled himself with ash, and then went straight to the palace where he filled the entire place with great lamenting and complaints: it was wicked and unworthy, he said, to destroy an innocent people who had never offered any justification for their destruction.

3. Esther learned what was happening from the loud sound of lamenting, but she could not decide what to do because she lacked the power of approaching the king (for in accordance with the custom of the Persians, the queen was not permitted to go to the king unless summoned, and in fact she was not admitted whenever the king pleased, but only at an appointed time). Then, as it so happened, Esther was held, separated from the presence of the king, for the next thirty days. Consequently, thinking that something should be attempted on behalf of her people even if she courted certain death,

prepared to die in this beautiful cause, she first called upon God, then slipped into the king's inner court.

The barbarian king was struck by this unusual conduct, but he was gradually calmed by his wife's flattery and finally was led to the queen's banquet, together with that Haman who was the favorite of the king and the enemy of the Jewish people.

After the courses, when the king had begun to grow flushed with the many drinks served at the banquet, Esther fell prostrate before his knees and interceded against the evil being done to her people. Then the king promised that nothing that she was seeking would be denied if there was anything more she wanted.

4. Then Esther, seizing the moment, demanded Haman's death to avenge the people he had wanted to destroy. The king, mindful of his friend, hesitated for a moment and then withdrew in order to consider the matter. When he returned, he saw Haman clutching the knees of the queen. His anger boiled over. Decrying the assault on the queen, he ordered Haman to be put to death. Then, when the king discovered that Haman had prepared the penalty of crucifixion for Mordecai, Haman was nailed to the same crucifix. All of his possessions were given to Mordecai, and the Jews were set free. Artaxerxes reigned sixty-two years and Ochus followed him.

Chapter 14

The identity of Nebuchadnezzar

1. I will rightly connect the activity of Judith to this period in the order of events. For it has been handed down that she lived after the captivity, but the divine history does not reveal who ruled the Persians at that time. It calls Nebuchadnezzar king when these deeds were performed, but this is definitely not the same man who captured Jerusalem.[51] I do not find another man with that name, after the captivity, who ruled the Persians, unless it is because of the violence and his attempt to be equal with that man that this king was called Nebuchadnezzar by the Jews. Nevertheless, there are many who believe[52] that this was Cambyses, the son of King Cyrus, because he, as a conqueror, invaded Egypt and Ethiopia. But the same sacred history rejects this view, for Judith is said to have lived in the twelfth

year of this king,[53] but Cambyses did not hold power beyond his eighth year.

If it is permitted to make a conjecture on the course of this history, I believe that these events transpired under King Ochus,[54] who followed Artaxerxes II. I make this conjecture based on the fact that this same Ochus, as it has been written in the secular accounts, is said to have had a merciless nature and a hunger for war. For he brought armies against his neighbors and recaptured Egypt, which had revolted several years earlier.

2. At this time, he is said to have mocked their holy sites and Apis, who had been accepted as a god.[55] Later, Baguas, his Egyptian eunuch, was outraged, and he avenged the king's affront to the people by killing him. The divine histories mention this Baguas: when Holofernes, by the king's order, led an army against the Jews, Baguas is said to have been in the same camp.[56] This information supports my conjecture, and so I suggest that the king called Nebuchadnezzar was Ochus, and Baguas, according to the secular historians, lived under his reign.

3. But it should not amaze anyone that the writers of secular volumes have not discussed any of those things that were written in the sacred books. Influenced by the Spirit of God, unsullied by corrupt speech or the interweaving of truth and lies, the history is bounded by its own great mysteries, which, separated from the concerns of the world and brought forward in so many sacred words, should not be mixed with other historical works as if they were equal. It would be most inappropriate to mix the sacred histories with secular histories that are seeking or doing different things. But I must continue on to other topics and, as I am able, explain a few things about what was done through Judith.

Chapter 15

Nebuchadnezzar attacks Israel; Holofernes and Achior;
Achior converts to Judaism; the Israelites besieged by Holofernes
(Jdt 1:1—7:32)

1. As I stated above, the Jews had returned to the land of their fathers, but the disposition of the state of the city and its affairs had not yet been arranged. The Persian king attacked the Medes and

fought in formation against their king, Arphaxad,[57] with a favorable outcome. Upon the death of Arphaxad, the Persian king added the Medes to his empire. He did the same thing to the remaining nations, sending out Holofernes, whom he had chosen to be the leader of the army, along with 120,000 foot soldiers and 12,000 cavalrymen. Holofernes devastated Cilicia and Arabia in battle, and he either captured many cities through force or compelled them to surrender out of fear.

The army, advancing to Damascus, struck great fear among the Jews. They were not up to the challenge of resisting, nor did their minds find any solace in the idea of surrender, because they had experienced the evils of captivity in the past. Consequently, crowds of people flocked to the temple. There, the people prayed for divine assistance, groaning and wailing in unison that they had fully paid the penalties to God for their sins and crimes; he should at least spare the remainder, who had only recently returned from slavery.[58]

2. Meanwhile, Holofernes had received the Moabites in surrender, and they had been added as allies in the war against the Jews. When he asked the Moabite leaders about the powers that the Hebrews relied upon, those that did not allow them to give up their minds to surrender, a certain man named Achior explained what had been discovered, namely, that the Jews were worshipers of God, well established in that pious ritual by their forefathers, and once they had been enslaved in Egypt. They had been led out by divine kindness and had crossed a dried sea on foot. Finally, having conquered all the other nations, they had received the lands inhabited by their ancestors.

From that time onward, depending on the state of their affairs, they had either flourished, declined, or been overrun with evils; they experienced the alternating anger or pleasure of God, based on their merits. When they were sinning, they were coerced by enemy invasions and captivity; when the deity was favorably disposed, they could never be conquered. If, at the present moment, they were free of sin, there was no way they could be conquered; if, on the other hand, there was sin among them, they would be defeated easily.

3. In response to these words, Holofernes, made defiant by his many victories, thought there was no country he could not conquer. His anger boiled over at the notion that people might believe that his victory hinged on how much the people of Judea had sinned. He ordered

that Achior be thrown into the camp of the Hebrews so that he might perish with those whom he had claimed could not be conquered.

At that time, the Jews had moved to the mountains. Thus, those who had been charged with the task approached the foot of the mountain and left Achior there in chains. When the Jews noticed this, they released the man from his chains and led him up the hill. He explained the reasons for what had happened to those who were questioning him, and then he was received in peace and waited to see the conclusion of the conflict. Later, after the victory, he was circumcised and thus made a Jew.

When Holofernes discovered the impregnability of the Jewish defensive positions, he surrounded the mountains with his soldiers because he was unable to attack the high places, and he took pains to deny the Hebrews access to water. On account of this, the siege was felt more acutely. Overcome by the lack of water and inclined to surrender, the people all went together to Ozias, the leader. But he responded that they must hold on a little longer and await divine assistance. The date for surrender was set for five days later.

Chapter 16

Judith seduces and beheads Holofernes; the Jewish army defeats the invaders (Jdt 8:1—15:11)

1. Judith was the widow of a man. She was extremely wealthy, distinguished in appearance, but even more illustrious for her morals than for her face. She was in the camp at that time and discovered the plan to surrender. She reasoned that in the difficult circumstances her people faced, something—even an action certain to cause her destruction—ought to be dared and attempted. She braided her hair, washed her face, and in the company of a maid, entered the enemy camp. Having been led immediately to Holofernes, she stated that the ruined condition of her people had led her to save her life by crossing over to the enemy. Then she asked the leader for freedom to go outside the camp at night for the purpose of prayer. Holofernes issued an order for that to the guards and the gatekeepers.

2. When, through her custom of going in and out over the course of three days, she had gained the trust of the barbarians,

Holofernes was incited by lust to use his prisoner's body, for the Persian was easily aroused by her excellent figure. The eunuch, Baguas, led her to the leader's tent, and having begun a feast, the barbarian swamped himself with too much wine. Then, after his servants had withdrawn, he fell asleep before he could rape the woman. Judith, snatching the opportunity, cut off the head of her enemy and took it away with her. And when, following her normal practice, it was believed that she was simply going out of the camp, she returned to the Jews unharmed.

3. The next day, the Hebrews displayed the head of Holofernes from the heights, and then, breaking out, they continued toward the enemy camp. At that time, the barbarians were demanding an order to fight, and crowds collected around the general's tent. When the headless body was reported, a dreadful fear gripped the soldiers, and they turned to flight, showing their backs to their enemies.

The Jews followed them as they ran away. They slaughtered several thousand soldiers and took over the camp and its loot. Judith was honored with the highest praise, and it is said that she lived for 105 years.

4. If these events, as I believe, took place in the twelfth year of King Ochus's reign, then twenty-two years elapsed between the time Jerusalem was rebuilt and this war. However, Ochus ruled for twenty-three years.[59] Nevertheless, he was the cruelest of all and more than a barbarian in spirit. The eunuch Baguas offered poisons to him when he was ill.[60] After him, Arses, his son, held power for three years,[61] and then Darius was in power for four years.[62]

CHAPTER 17

The conquests and death of Alexander the Great;
his empire divided among his generals;
the Jews begin to compete for the office of high priest

1. Alexander of Macedonia[63] fought against this king in battle. When Darius was conquered, Alexander took the empire away from the Persians. It had stood for 250 years from its beginning with Cyrus.[64] Alexander conquered nearly all the nations, and he is said to have gone up to the temple in Jerusalem and to have brought gifts.[65]

He proclaimed throughout the entire empire he had brought under his rule that the Jews living in his empire were to be allowed to return freely to their fatherland. When he had finished his twelfth year in power, in the seventh year after he conquered Darius, he died near Babylon.

2. His friends, who earlier had carried out those very great wars alongside him, divided his kingdom.[66] For a certain amount of time, they administered the parts they had received without making use of the royal title, and it seems that power was given to a certain Philip Arrhidaeus, the brother of Alexander, who was ruling as a very weak leader, in name only. Real power was in the hands of those who had distributed the army and provinces among themselves. This state of affairs did not last very long, for all the generals wanted to call themselves kings. The first king in Syria after Alexander was Seleucus,[67] who also subjugated Persia and Babylon.

3. At this time, the Jews were paying an annual tribute of three hundred silver talents to the king. They were not, however, ruled by foreign magistrates, but by their own priests. They were living by the rites of their fathers until many of them, again corrupted by the long peace, began to confuse and stir up everyone in seditions, aspiring to the high priesthood out of lust, avarice, and the desire to dominate others.[68]

CHAPTER 18

The high priests Onias, Jason, Menelaus, and Lysimachus;
King Antiochus bans Jewish worship (2 Macc 3:1—5:21)

1. Onias,[69] a man of holiness and integrity, was the first priest under King Seleucus,[70] the son of Antiochus the Great.[71] A certain Simon had been unable to dislodge Onias by making false charges against him before the king.[72] Then, after time had passed, Jason, the brother of Onias, went to King Antiochus,[73] who had succeeded his brother Seleucus. He promised a larger tribute if he was given the job of high priest.[74] Although it was uncommon and had never been permitted before to hold the priesthood perpetually, the king's heart was stirred up, depraved with avarice, and he was easily convinced.[75]

2. Onias was expelled and Jason was given the position of high priest. He relentlessly attacked the people and the fatherland in the

foulest manner. Then, since he had sent the money promised to the king through a certain Menelaus, the brother of that Simon, the way of ambition opened again, and through the same arts that Jason had employed earlier, Menelaus obtained the priesthood.[76] Not long after, when the full amount of promised silver failed to arrive, Menelaus was expelled from his position, and Lysimachus was put in his place.[77] From this action, foul battles arose between Jason and Menelaus until Jason withdrew, an exile from his fatherland.[78]

From these beginnings, moral decay developed to such an extent that many of the people asked Antiochus to permit them to live by Gentile customs.[79] When the king granted what they were seeking, all the worst people began, as if in a competition, to construct shrines, to worship idols, and to profane the law.

3. Meanwhile Antiochus, returning from Alexandria (for at that time, he had fought against the king of Egypt, a war that he ended on an order from the senate and people of Rome, during the consulship of Paulus and Crassus),[80] approached Jerusalem. When he discovered that the people were in an uproar over the superstitions that had been imported, he demolished the law and favored those who were engaged in impiety.[81] He withdrew all the ornaments from the temple, and he laid waste to it with great bloodshed.[82] This was done in the 151st year after the death of Alexander, with, as I said, Paulus and Crassus serving as consuls, around the fifth year after Antiochus had begun to rule.[83]

Chapter 19

A discussion of the chronology of the Seleucid rulers; Antiochus IV Epiphanes orders all the Jews to follow pagan religious practices (1 Macc 1:41–59)

1. But, so that an arrangement of the times might be set in order and it be made even clearer who this Antiochus was, I shall detail the kings who came after Alexander in Syria, recording both their names and their dates.[84] After King Alexander died, as I related above,[85] his entire kingdom was divided among his friends, and for some time, each region bore the name of the man who administered it. Seleucus was named king after nine years in Syria, and he reigned for thirty-two years. His son, Antiochus, reigned nineteen years after him. Next was

his son, Antiochus, who also had the cognomen Theus; he ruled fifteen years. After him was his son, Seleucus, with the cognomen Callinicus; he reigned twenty-one years. He was followed by another Seleucus, son of Callinicus, who reigned for three years. When he died, Antiochus, the brother of Callinicus, held Asia and Syria for thirty-seven years. Lucius Scipio Asiaticus fought against this Antiochus.[86] Antiochus was defeated in battle and fined part of his empire. He had two sons, Seleucus and Antiochus, whom he gave as a hostage to the Romans.[87]

2. Thus, with the death of Antiochus the Great, Seleucus, the older of his two sons, obtained the kingdom. Under this man, as we said, Onias the priest was charged by Simon.[88] Then the Romans released Antiochus. Demetrius, the son of King Seleucus, who was ruling at that time, was given as a hostage in his place. Upon the death of Seleucus,[89] in the twelfth year of his reign, his brother, Antiochus, who had been a hostage in Rome, took the kingdom.[90] He, five years after he had begun to rule, as I explained above, had pillaged Jerusalem. He was paying a heavy tribute to the Romans, and he was driven, almost as a necessity, by these great expenses to search for wealth that could be confiscated and to overlook no occasion for looting.

3. After the second year, with the Jews again being afflicted with a similar disaster, he placed a garrison in the citadel[91] so that the Jews, compelled by such frequent evils, might not begin a war. Then, undertaking to overturn the sacred law, he sent out an edict that all the people must abandon the traditions of their fathers and live in the Gentile manner.[92] There was no shortage of those who were willing to comply with the profane order. The order was followed by a horrible spectacle: throughout all the cities, sacrifices were offered openly in the streets and the sacred volumes of the law and prophets were burned in fires.

CHAPTER 20

Mattathias Maccabee rebels; the seven martyred brothers and their mother (1 Macc 2:1; 2 Macc 7:1–41)

1. At this time, Mattathias, son of John, was a priest. When he was pressured by the king's men to comply with the edict, he despised

the profane orders with commendable constancy and, in front of all the people, cut the throat of a Hebrew who had profaned himself. Now that a leader had finally been discovered, a rebellion broke out. Mattathias went out from the city and, gathering many people to him, formed a kind of righteous army. All of these people shared a set purpose: to take up arms against the profane empire, and even to meet death in battle rather than submit to impious ceremonies.

2. Meanwhile, Antiochus was compelling reported Jews to sacrifice throughout the Greek cities that were in his empire, and he was afflicting those who were reluctant with unheard of tortures. At that time, the most illustrious of these cases was the seven brothers and their mother. Coerced by tortures to violate the law of God that had been established by their ancestors, the seven brothers chose death. In the end, their mother had also accompanied them, sharing their punishments and eventual deaths.

CHAPTER 21

Mattathias dies and is replaced by his son, Judas; the Maccabees win many battles (1 Macc 3:1—4:35)

1. Meanwhile, Mattathias died; he put his son, Judas, in his place as leader of the army that he had prepared. Led by this man, the army successfully fought against the king's forces in numerous battles. First, he destroyed Apollonius,[93] the leader of the enemies, together with all his army, who had arrived at the battle in great numbers. Then, when a certain Seron, who at that time was ruling Syria, learned of this, he increased his forces and attacked Judas. Seron was aggressive because he had the superior numbers, but when he descended to the plain, his forces were routed. Forced to flee, he returned to Syria, having lost nearly eight hundred men. Antiochus's anger and grief were kindled when he learned of this, and he suffered because his generals, along with their great armies, had been defeated. He assembled reinforcements from his entire kingdom, and a donative was paid to the soldiers that completely depleted the treasury.

2. As a matter of fact, he was seriously hampered by a shortage of funds at that time. For the Jews, who had provided more than three hundred talents each year in taxes, broke free from his control. They

were joined by the Greek cities and many regions that, having been disturbed by the evil of this persecution, also stopped paying their taxes. He had not even spared the Gentiles, whom he had tempted to abandon long-standing superstitions and to follow a single rite. Naturally, those people, who hold nothing sacred, easily relinquished their practices, but nevertheless, all the people were affected by fear and defeat.

Antiochus was seething over these problems, for he himself, once richer than all of the other kings, was feeling his own poverty, the consequence of his wickedness. He divided his forces with Lysias and entrusted Syria and the war against the Jews to him. Antiochus advanced into Persia to collect taxes. Lysias selected Ptolemy, Gorgias, Doron, and Nicanor[94] to be the generals for the war. Forty thousand foot soldiers and seven thousand cavalrymen were assigned to them.

3. In the first attack, they brought great terror to the Jews. Then Judas exhorted all the despairing people: they should descend with a brave spirit to battle; relying upon God, they could not be defeated; and often in the past, battles against a superior force had turned out well for the smaller army. A fast was proclaimed, a sacrifice was celebrated, and they went down arrayed for battle. The enemy forces were driven off, and Judas acquired their camp where a large amount of gold and Phoenician dyed garments were discovered. Syrian merchants, with no doubt about the victory, had followed the king's army in the hope of purchasing captives, but they had become booty themselves. When Lysias learned of these things from messengers, he prepared his forces with greater care and, in the next year, attacked the Jews with a larger army. When he was defeated, he returned to Antioch.

CHAPTER 22

The victorious Judas cleanses the temple; Lysias defeated again;
Antiochus in Persia; the death of Antiochus
(1 Macc 4:36—6:17)

1. After Judas drove off the enemy forces, he returned to Jerusalem and focused his mind on cleansing and restoring the temple, which, having been ruined by Antiochus and profaned by the Gentiles, was presenting a foul sight. Unfortunately, the Syrians held

the fortress, which was connected to the temple and, by the nature of the place, was higher and impregnable. The adjacent part was inaccessible, blocked by frequent sorties from above. Judas set up a very powerful battle line of his own men to oppose this interference. Thus he was able to begin the work of restoring the sacred temple and surrounding it with a wall, and he posted soldiers to maintain a perpetual armed guard around the temple.

2. Lysias, after rebuilding his forces, returned to Judea but was defeated again. It was great disaster for his army and the reinforcements who had been sent to him from various cities and had fought on his side in the battle.

Meanwhile, Antiochus, who, as I said above, had gone into Persia,[95] had attempted to loot the town of Elymus. Elymus was the wealthiest town of that region, and the temple placed there was crammed with gold. But a multitude of men, pouring in from all sides to defend that place, forced him to flee. In addition, he received a message from either Lysias or Lysias's friends that events had not turned out well.

3. Consequently, from the distress of his spirit, he fell physically ill. Troubled by internal sorrows, he recalled the evil acts by which he had tormented the people of God, and he acknowledged that his own afflictions had fallen upon him justly. He died a few days later after he had ruled for eleven years. The kingdom was handed over to his son, whose name was Eupator.[96]

CHAPTER 23

Judas Maccabee besieges and overcomes the Syrians; Antiochus V Eupator dies and Demetrius I Soter becomes the new king; the Jews make an alliance with Rome; the death of Judas Maccabeus; Bacchides sues for peace (1 Macc 6:16—10:73)

1. At this time, Judas was besieging the Syrians who were stationed in the fortress. When they began to feel the pangs of hunger and shortages, they sent messages to the king, appealing for assistance. Thus Eupator came with one hundred thousand soldiers and twenty thousand cavalrymen to support them. Elephants led the battle line, spreading great terror. Then Judas relaxed the blockade

and marched out to meet the king. He defeated the Syrians in the first battle. The king began to negotiate for peace, but because of his treacherous nature, he used this peace badly, and vengeance pursued his treachery. When Demetrius, the son of Seleucus, who, as I said above, had been given to the Romans as a hostage,[97] heard that Antiochus had died, he asked to be returned to rule the kingdom. When this request was denied,[98] he secretly fled from Rome and arrived in Syria and took over the kingdom. The son of Antiochus, who had ruled one year and six months, was killed.[99]

2. Once this man began to rule, the Jews sought friendship and an alliance with the Romans; their delegation was received in a friendly manner and, by a senatorial decree, the Jews were named allies and friends.[100]

Meanwhile, Demetrius was waging war against Judas through his generals. At first the army was led by a certain Bacchides and Alcimus of Judea.[101] After Nicanor had been given command of the war, he fell in battle. Then Bacchides and Alcimus, their strength reinstated and with expanded forces, fought against Judas. The victorious, blood-stained Syrians exploited their victory to the limit in this battle. In place of Judas, the Hebrews selected Jonathan, his brother.[102] 3. Meanwhile, Alcimus died after he had laid waste to Jerusalem in the foulest manner.[103] Bacchides, deprived of his ally, returned to the king. Two years later, Bacchides again brought war to the Jews and, after he was defeated, made peace. This was given under certain conditions, namely, that the refugees, captives, and everything that had been seized in the war should be returned.

CHAPTER 24

The usurpations of Alexander and Demetrius II
(1 Macc 10:1—11:17)

1. While these things were taking place in Judea, a certain young man named Alexander,[104] who had been educated in Rhodes, asserted that he was the son of Antiochus (which was false) and, supported by the wealth of King Ptolemy of Alexandria, entered Syria with an army. He overcame Demetrius and killed him in battle; Demetrius had ruled for twelve years. This Alexander, before he defeated Demetrius,

had made a treaty with Jonathan and had given him a purple robe and
the insignia of a king. Because of this, Jonathan had lent him assistance, and when Demetrius was defeated, Jonathan was the first of all
to hurry to him with congratulations. Alexander did not later break
faith with his treaty.

2. Thus, during the five years of his reign, the Jews enjoyed
peace. Then Demetrius,[105] son of Demetrius, who had fled to Crete
after the death of his father, was goaded into action by Lasthenes, the
leader of Crete, and he tried to reclaim his father's kingdom through
battle. Inferior in strength, he begged Ptolemy Philometor, king of
Egypt and father-in-law of Alexander, who was even at that time hostile toward his son-in-law, to provide support for him. Ptolemy, not so
much because of the begging entreaties but rather out of the seductive prospect of occupying Syria, joined his forces with Demetrius and
gave the daughter who had been married to Alexander to Demetrius.
Alexander fought against them in battle. In this battle, Ptolemy fell,
but Alexander was defeated. Shortly thereafter, he was killed;[106] he had
ruled five years or, as I have found in several other authors, nine
years.[107]

CHAPTER 25

Tryphon kills Jonathan; Simon becomes high priest
(1 Macc 12:46)

1. Demetrius, after winning the kingdom, treated Jonathan in a
kindly manner and made a treaty with him. He allowed the Jews to
govern themselves by their own laws. Meanwhile, the king put
Tryphon, who had been a supporter of Alexander,[108] in charge of Syria
to keep him from going to war. Jonathan came down against him with
a frightful army of forty thousand soldiers. Tryphon, when he discerned that his forces were unequal to Jonathan's, pretended peace,
received him in friendship, and then killed the man he had invited to
Ptolemais.

After Jonathan, the supreme control of the state was passed to
his brother, Simon. Simon carried out his brother's funeral with magnificence and constructed those seven pyramids of the most noble
craftsmanship, in which he placed the bones of his brothers and father.

2. Then Demetrius renewed the treaty with the Jews, and in considera-
tion of the disaster that had been brought upon them by Tryphon—for
after the death of Jonathan, Tryphon had devastated their cities and
fields in a war—he suspended their annual taxes forever. Up to that
time, they had paid a stipend to the Syrian kings unless they were at war
with them. 3. This was done by King Demetrius in his second year,
which I have singled out here, because until this year, I have hurried
through the times of the Asian kings, so that the calculation of the dates
that has been offered might be clear.[109] Nevertheless, now I will offer an
account of the events from the time of those Jews who were either kings
or priests, until the birth of Christ.

CHAPTER 26

The high priests from Jonathan to the arrival of Pompey and the Romans

1. After Jonathan, his brother Simon, as I said above,[110] led the
Hebrews by the right of the high priesthood. He was granted that
position of honor by his own people and the Romans. He began to
lead the people in the second year of King Demetrius, but he was
killed after eight years, caught up in the snares of King Ptolemy.[111]
John, his son, followed Simon. After he had fought exceptionally well
against the Hyrcanians, a very powerful nation, he received the cognomen Hyrcanus.[112] John died after holding power for twenty-six
years.

2. Aristobulus was installed as high priest, the first of all the leaders after the captivity to assume the title of king, and he placed a
crown upon his head. He died after exactly one year.[113] Then
Alexander, his son, was both king and high priest at the same time. He
ruled for twenty-seven years. I have found nothing worth mentioning
in his acts, apart from his cruelty. When he died, he left behind two
young sons, Aristobulus and Hyrcanus. His wife, Salome Alexandra,
held power for nine years.[114] After her death, a disgraceful struggle
broke out between the brothers over the kingdom.

3. Hyrcanus obtained power first; soon, however, he was
attacked by his brother, Aristobulus,[115] and he fled to Pompey, who, at
that time, had finished the war against Mithridates. Having pacified

Armenia and Pontus, Pompey, the conqueror of every nation he had attacked, was hoping to continue inward and join all the neighboring countries to the Roman Empire; consequently he was looking for justifications for war and an opportunity for further conquest. He welcomed Hyrcanus with open arms and, under his leadership, attacked the Jews.[116] The city was taken and destroyed but he spared the temple. Pompey sent Aristobulus to Rome in chains, and he restored the right of being high priest to Hyrcanus. He imposed a tribute on the Jews and selected a man named Antipater, from Ashkelon,[117] to be their procurator. Hyrcanus, after holding power for thirty-four years, was captured while fighting against the Parthians.

CHAPTER 27

King Herod; the advent of Christ; the sons of Herod; Christ is crucified

1. Then Herod,[118] a foreigner who was the son of Antipater of Ashkelon, requested and received the kingdom of Judea from the senate and people of Rome. This man was the first foreign king of the Jews.[119] For with Christ about to arrive, it was necessary, according to the predictions of the prophets, for them to be deprived of their own leaders so that they would not expect anyone beyond Christ.[120] Christ was born under the reign of this Herod, in the thirty-third year of his rule, during the consulship of Sabinus and Rufinus, on the eighth day before the calends of January.[121]

2. But I do not dare address these events, which are contained in the Gospels and then in the Acts of the Apostles, out of fear that the abbreviated nature of this work might detract from the dignity of those events. I shall pursue what is left over. Herod ruled for four more years after the nativity; the total length of his reign was thirty-seven years. The tetrarch Archelaus, who ruled for nine years,[122] came after him, and Herod, who ruled twenty-four years.[123] In the eighteenth year of Herod's reign, the Lord was fixed to a cross during the consulship of Fufius Geminus and Rubellus Geminus.[124] There are 372 years from this date until the consulship of Stilicho.

Chapter 28

The scandalous behavior of Nero; Peter and Paul in Rome

1. Luke covered the acts of the apostles up to the time when Paul was escorted to Rome,[125] during the rule of Nero. I will not call Nero a king,[126] but he was quite rightly deemed the foulest of all men and even monstrous beasts; he was the first to start a persecution.[127] I do not know whether he will also be the last, coming as the antichrist,[128] as is thought by many. The nature of his crimes would have demanded that I cover these matters thoroughly, but it is not possible to enter into such a lengthy undertaking in a work of this kind. I am content to have only noted that this man, in all of his deeds, showed himself to have gone so far in the most foul and cruel deeds as to kill his own mother,[129] and later to make a mock marriage to a certain Pythagoras in the manner of a solemn wedding. The emperor wore a bridal veil; a dowry, conjugal bed, wedding torches, and everything else that accompanies a wedding were displayed; even among women, these items are not displayed without modesty.[130] I am not certain whether it is more painful or more shameful to discuss the rest of his actions. He was the first to attempt to abolish the name *Christian*. Clearly, vices are always the enemies of virtues, and all the best people are perceived as hypercritical by the wicked.

2. The divine religion had grown stronger in the city at that time; Peter held the bishopric there,[131] and Paul, after he had appealed to Caesar from the unjust judgment of the governor, was taken to Rome.[132] Many people assembled in order to hear him; these people had understood the truth and were motivated to join in the worship of God by the virtues that the apostles had then strongly displayed.

Peter and Paul held their famous meeting against Simon at this time. Simon, using his magical arts in an attempt to prove that he was a god, had flown into the air, supported up by two demons. When, by the prayers of the apostles, the demons were put to flight, Simon fell to the earth and was shattered, with the people looking on.[133]

CHAPTER 29

The fire in Rome; Nero persecutes the Christians;
the beginning of the Jewish revolt; Nero kills himself

1. Meanwhile, with the number of Christians already expanding, it happened that Rome was burned up in a fire.[134] At this time, Nero was at Antium.[135] The universal opinion of the people laid the blame for the fire on the emperor, as it was believed that the emperor wanted the glory of renovating the city. Nero was unable to devise any strategy to convince people that he had not ordered the fire.

Consequently, he turned prejudice against the Christians, and the cruelest tortures were carried out against the innocent. As a matter of fact, new forms of death were devised; some were covered with skins of animals and died after being ripped apart by dogs; many were nailed to crosses or burned in the flames; a few were held back so that on the appointed day, they might be burned to serve as a source of light at night.[136]

2. The desire to practice brutality against the Christians sprang from this beginning. For afterward, the religion was forbidden by published laws, and edicts were openly displayed that stated that it was not permitted to be a Christian.[137] Then Paul and Peter were condemned to death; Paul had his neck cut by a sword, while Peter suffered crucifixion.[138] While these events were unfolding in Rome, the Jews, chafing under the injustices of their governor, Festus Florus,[139] began to rebel. Nero sent Vespasian[140] against them with the power of a proconsul, and after many hard-fought battles, he compelled the defeated people to seek refuge within the walls of Jerusalem.

3. Meanwhile, Nero, who now had grown hateful even to himself because of his awareness of his wicked acts, was removed from human affairs. It is not certain if he killed himself, for his body was never found.[141] From this it is believed that, even if he had run himself through with a sword, he was preserved by the healing of his wound, according to what was written about him.[142] The death blow was healed, and he was sent away until the end of the age, so that he might carry out the mystery of iniquity.[143]

CHAPTER 30

The year of the four emperors (AD 69); Vespasian takes control of the empire; Titus besieges Jerusalem; the hardships of the Jews; the destruction of the Jews had been predicted by the prophets

1. After the destruction of Nero, Galba seized power; soon Galba was killed and Otho held the office. Then Vitellius, relying on the soldiers from Gaul that he was commanding, entered the city. Otho was killed and Vitellius usurped the highest power. Next, that power was granted to Vespasian in what was clearly a bad precedent; nevertheless it had the good effect of saving the republic from wicked men.[144] While Vespasian was blockading Jerusalem, he assumed power and, as is the custom, the diadem was placed on his head[145] and he was saluted by his army. He made his son, Titus, Caesar. Titus was given command of some of the troops and the duty of besieging Jerusalem. Vespasian returned to Rome, where he was received with great favor by the senate and people. After Vitellius killed himself,[146] Vespasian strengthened his power.

2. The Jews, meanwhile, were blockaded by the siege. Because they were not offered an opportunity for peace or surrender, they were, in the end, perishing from hunger. Everywhere corpses began to fill their streets, as they could no longer carry out the duty of burying the dead. This led all of them to try every unspeakable dish, and they did not refrain from eating even human corpses, except those that decay had made unsuitable for use as food. Then, when the defenders had weakened, the Romans broke into the city. At this time, it was nearly the day of Passover, and a great multitude from the farms and other towns of Judea had come together. No doubt this pleased God, for in the same season this impious people had nailed the Lord to the cross, they were handed over to extermination.[147]

3. The Pharisees bitterly resisted for a while in front of the temple; then, with their spirits set on death, they hurled themselves freely into the fires that had been set. 1,100,000 were reported killed, with one hundred thousand captured and sold.[148] Titus, in a council that had been summoned prior to this, is reported to have deliberated as to whether he should destroy a temple of such impressive work. For it seemed to some that a famous, sacred shrine, beyond all mortal creations, should not be destroyed. If preserved, it would serve as a testi-

mony to the restraint of the Romans, but if destroyed, a perpetual sign of their cruelty.

4. Against this view, other men and Titus himself advised that the temple should be destroyed at once;[149] in this way, the religion of the Jews and Christians would be more thoroughly destroyed. Clearly, these religions, although opposed to one another, had nevertheless evolved from the same founders. Christianity had sprung from the Jews; with the root destroyed, the branch would more easily wither. Thus, by the will of God, the hearts of all were stirred up and the temple was torn down, 331 years ago.[150]

These events—the final destruction of the temple and the last captivity of the Jews, in which the exiles from the fatherland are seen to have been dispersed throughout the entire world—are a daily testimony to the world. They are being punished for no other reason than they laid impious hands upon Christ. For although there were other instances when they were handed over into captivity on account of their sins, they never served a sentence of enslavement that lasted more than seventy years.

Chapter 31

The persecutions of Domitian and Trajan; the Bar Kochba revolt under Hadrian

1. Then, after some time had passed, Domitian, the son of Vespasian, persecuted Christians.[151] At this time, he banished the Apostle and Evangelist John to the island of Patmos.[152] John, after arcane mysteries were revealed to him, wrote the book that recorded the holy apocalypse. This book, though, is not accepted by many, whether out of impiety or stupidity.

After a short interval, there was a third persecution under Trajan.[153] He discovered, through tortures and investigations, that the Christians did nothing that deserved punishment or death, and so he opposed brutalizing them any further.[154] Under Hadrian, the Jews wanted to rebel, and they attempted to seize Syria and Palestine.[155] An army was sent and they were subdued. At this time, Hadrian, believing that the Christian faith could be destroyed by an insult to that place, set up images of demons in the temple and on the site of the Lord's passion.[156]

2. Because people believed that Christians came from the Jews—for at that time in Jerusalem the church would not admit a priest unless he was circumcised—Hadrian ordered a cohort of soldiers to stand as guards forever to keep all the Jews from approaching Jerusalem.[157] This action actually advanced the Christian faith, because at that time nearly all the people who believed that Christ was God were observers of the law. Hadrian's action was undoubtedly arranged by the Lord,[158] so that the slavery of law would be abolished by the liberty of faith and church. As a result, Mark, the first convert from the Gentiles, became the bishop in Jerusalem.[159] The persecution under Hadrian was counted as the fourth, although later he prevented its implementation, announcing that it was unjust that anyone concerned should be judged without a crime.[160]

CHAPTER 32

The persecutions from Hadrian to Diocletian

1. After Hadrian, when Antoninus was ruling, the churches had peace. Then, under [Marcus] Aurelius,[161] the son of Antoninus, a fifth persecution was set in motion. This was the first time that martyrdoms were seen in the Gallic provinces,[162] since the religion of God had been received later across the Alps. Next, when [Septimus] Severus was ruling, the sixth trial of Christians occurred. At this time, Leonidas, the father of Origen, poured out his holy blood in martyrdom.[163] This was followed by thirty-seven years of peace for the Christians, except when, in the middle of this span, Maximinus [Thrax] troubled the priests of certain churches.[164]

2. Then, when Decius was already ruling, the seventh persecution raged among the Christians.[165] Next was Valerian, the eighth enemy of the saints.[166] Nearly fifty years of peace followed Valerian.[167] Then, with Diocletian and Maximianus ruling, the harshest persecution began, which ravaged the people of God for ten consecutive years.[168] During this storm, nearly the entire world was stained by the holy blood of the martyrs. Obviously, those who were eager for glory

were dashing into the contest. Back then they sought martyrdoms through glorious deaths; now they are more accustomed to compete for bishoprics because of their depraved ambitions.

3. The world was never exhausted by greater wars, nor did we ever prevail with a greater triumph than when we were not conquered by ten years of devastation. The outstanding sufferings of the martyrs of this time exist in writings that I do not believe should be appended here, lest I exceed the bounds of this work.

CHAPTER 33

Constantine becomes emperor, ending the persecutions; Helena in Jerusalem

1. That persecution ended eighty-nine years ago when Christians began to become emperors. For then Constantine,[169] who was the first Christian among all the Roman emperors, became master of the state. Next, of course, Licinius, who fought against Constantine for power, ordered his own soldiers to make the sacrifices.[170] He expelled those who refused from the army. This action is not counted among the persecutions. In fact it was too unimportant a matter to be classed as having done the churches any harm.

2. Since then, we have been enjoying peace in these quiet times. We do not believe that another persecution is about to happen, except for the one that the antichrist will carry out right at the end of the age. For the sacred prophecies proclaimed that the world would be struck by ten blows.[171] Consequently, since nine persecutions have occurred, the one that remains will be the last.[172]

During this protracted period, it is amazing how much the Christian religion has grown, inasmuch as Jerusalem, once lying in ruins, has been adorned with numerous, magnificent churches. For Helena, the mother of the Emperor Constantine, who as empress shared power with her son, when she conceived a desire to know Jerusalem,[173] crushed the idols and temples she discovered there. Later, drawing upon the powers of the monarchy, she established basilicas in the places that marked the passion, resurrection, and ascension of the Lord.[174]

3. Here is something amazing:[175] that place that the divine foot-steps last touched before the Lord was carried in a cloud up to heaven could not be joined with a pavement to the remaining part of the street. Indeed, the earth, no longer accustomed to bearing human steps, rejects any stones that are laid and the marble is often tossed back into the teeth of those laying it. As a matter of fact, it is such an everlasting piece of evidence that God trampled the dust, that the footsteps pressed into the earth may still be seen. Faith compels those who come here every day to take a little sand from those places in which the Lord walked; nevertheless, the sand does not experience damage, and the earth continues to retain the same appearance as if it had been sealed with the impression of his feet.

Chapter 34

Helena discovers the One True Cross

1. The cross of the Lord was then discovered through the help of the same empress.[176] It was not possible to consecrate this cross at the beginning of the Christian movement because the Jews opposed it, and afterward, the city was demolished and buried under crushed stone. It did not deserve to be revealed except to someone hunting so faithfully. And so, Helena first was informed about the site of the passion. Approaching with a band of soldiers and a crowd from all the provinces who were competing with the queen in their enthusiasm, she ordered them to dig up the ground and clear away each adjoining area and the most extensive of the ruins. Soon, as a prize for their faith and labor, three crosses were discovered, side by side, just like those that had been set up for the Lord and the two thieves.

2. Everyone's hearts and minds were disturbed by the great difficulty of discerning which of the crosses the Lord had hung upon; they worried that, perhaps through mortal error, they might consecrate the cross of a thief in place of the Lord's cross. Then they seized upon a plan: they would bring someone who had recently died to the crosses. Without delay, as if by the will of God, the funeral of a man who had died was passing with solemn rites. The corpse was taken from its litter by those gathered at the site. The body was first brought to two crosses without result; when it touched Christ's cross—this is

amazing—the body was thrown off, startling everyone, and in the sight of the onlookers, stood up. The true cross was identified and the throng consecrated it with honor.

CHAPTER 35

The beginning of the Arian heresy; the Council of Nicaea; the treachery of the Arians

1. These deeds were accomplished through Helena; meanwhile the world had received, from the Christian emperor, liberty and an example of faith. Unfortunately, this peace produced a far greater danger for all of the churches.[177] For next, the Arian heresy erupted and it shook the entire world, which had been infected by this error. As a matter of fact, even the emperor was corrupted by the two Arians, the most energetic proponents of this treachery;[178] the emperor thought that he was carrying out the duty of religion, and he employed the power of persecution.[179] Bishops were driven into exile, brutality was employed against priests, and punishment inflicted on the laypeople who had separated themselves from communion with the Arians.

2. The ideas that the Arians proclaimed[180] were as follows: God, the Father, for the purpose of creating the world, produced a Son and, through his own power, from nothing, made a new and second God, of a new and second substance; consequently, there had been a time when the Son had not existed.[181] To address the cause of this evil, a synod was convened near Nicaea,[182] drawn from the bishops of the entire world, since indeed 318 came together. The bishops composed a complete creed, the Arian heresy was condemned, and the emperor adopted the episcopal decree.

3. The Arians, who did not dare suggest anything against this sound faith, mixed themselves among the churches, just as if they were acquiescing and not thinking something else. Nevertheless, there remained planted in their hearts a hatred against the Catholic men. Unable to master them in debates about the faith, they attacked them through suborned accusers and fictitious charges.

CHAPTER 36

The attacks on Athanasius, Marcellus, and Photinus;
the synod of Serdica (343); Ursacius and Valens appeal to
Pope Julius for resumption of communion

1. And so they first attacked and condemned the absent Athanasius, the bishop of Alexandria,[183] a holy man who had been a deacon at the synod of Nicaea. For they were joining to the charges, which false witnesses brought against him, that he had received, with improper eagerness, the heretical priests Marcellus and Photinus,[184] who had been condemned by the judgment of the synod. Now, in the case of Photinus, there is no doubt that he deserved condemnation; with respect to Marcellus, it appears that nothing at that time was found in his views that justified condemnation. Moreover, his innocence was strengthened by the enthusiasm of that faction, as there was no doubt that the same judges who had condemned him were heretics.

2. Still, the Arians did not want to remove them more than they wanted to depose Athanasius. They petitioned the emperor so frequently that Athanasius was sent as an exile to Gaul.[185] Shortly thereafter, eighty bishops who had assembled in Egypt pronounced that Athanasius had been condemned unjustly. The matter was then referred to Constantine.[186] He ordered the bishops from the entire world to assemble in Serdica;[187] they were to review the entire trial in which Athanasius had been condemned. While this was happening, Constantine died.[188] The synod that gathered under the Emperor Constantius[189] absolved Athanasius. Marcellus was also returned to his bishopric. But in the case of Photinus, the sentence was not reversed; for in our contemporaries' judgment, too, he is shown to be a heretic.

3. Nevertheless, the charge itself was weighing heavily upon Marcellus, because Photinus was known to have been one of his students in his youth. Still, an action of Ursacius and Valens, the leaders of the Arian party, added to the absolution extended to Athanasius and Marcellus. When they appeared to be separated from communion after the synod of Serdica, they publicly begged forgiveness from Julius, the bishop of Rome, when brought before him, for having condemned an innocent man; moreover, they professed that the sentence of absolution, given to Athanasius at the Council of Serdica, was justified.

Chapter 37

Athanasius disavows Marcellus,
creating an opportunity for the Arians

1. Next, after time had passed, Athanasius suspended Marcellus from communion when he discovered that he had drifted too far away from sound faith. Marcellus retained a sense of modesty, so that, having been reproached by the judgment of such a great man, he yielded of his own accord. Although he was innocent before this, afterward he was corrupted. It can be demonstrated that, by the time he received judgment from Athanasius, he had already become harmful.

The Arians, seizing the opportunity offered in this condemnation, conspired to overturn the decrees of the synod of Serdica. 2. For a pretext now seemed to be available to them, as it could be argued that the judgment made in Athanasius's favor had been as unjust as Marcellus's acquittal, since now even Athanasius condemned Marcellus as a heretic. For Marcellus had stood out as a defender of the Sabellian heresy; but Photinus had already advanced a new heresy by this time, differing only in a single point from Sabellius by proclaiming that Christ had his beginning from Mary.[190]

3. Consequently, the Arians, through clever counsel, mixed the innocent with the criminals and secured a condemnation of Photinus, Marcellus, and Athanasius under the same sentence.[191] They were deceiving inexperienced minds in such a way that those who had perceived the truth about Marcellus and Photinus would not be believed to have judged wrongly about Athanasius.

4. Nevertheless, at this time, the Arians were concealing their treachery; they did not dare to openly assert their own dogma of errors, but instead they were passing themselves off as Catholics. They decided that the first thing they needed to do was expel Athanasius from the church, the man who had always blocked them like a wall. Once he was driven off, they hoped that the rest would yield to their will.

Some of the bishops, who were following the Arians, accepted the long-desired condemnation of Athanasius; another group, driven by fear and factionalism, joined in the enthusiasm of the first group; a few bishops, to whom the precious faith and truth was more important, did not accept this unjust judgment. Paulinus was among them, the bishop of Trier. It is said that when a letter was delivered to him, he signed his consent to permit the condemnation of Photinus and Marcellus, but he refused to approve the condemnation of Athanasius.

CHAPTER 38

Arian bishops gain influence over Emperor Constantius II;
Bishop Valens tricks Constantius at Mursa

1. Then the Arians, after they had made little progress through cunning, decided to use force. For whatever they dared or attempted happened easily, as they were supported by the friendship of the king, whom they had attached to themselves through sycophantic fawning. In fact, their position was strengthened because they were supported by the agreement of many; for nearly all the bishops of the two Pannonias, and most of the East, and all of Asia, had joined in their treachery. 2. Their evil leaders were Ursacius from Singidunum,[192] Valens from Mursa, Theodore from Heraclia, Stephen from Antioch, Acacius from Caesarea, Menofantus from Ephesus, George from Laodicea, and Narcissus from Neronopolis. These men occupied the palace, so that the emperor did nothing apart from their will. Although subservient to all the bishops, the emperor was especially devoted to Valens.

3. For at that time, when he had fought against Magnentius[193] near Mursa, Constantius had not dared to march down to battle in plain sight, so he had waited in the basilica of a martyr situated out-side the town. Valens, the bishop of that place, was retained to keep him company. However, Valens had arranged things cunningly with his own people, so that he would be the first to learn the outcome of the battle, and thus either win the gratitude of the king if he was the first to bring good news, or looking after his own life, he would have time to flee before he could be captured if the battle went poorly. Consequently, he was the first to announce to the few men who were gathered around the king, made jumpy with fear and the emperor's anxiety, that the enemies had fled. When the emperor demanded that he be introduced to the messenger, Valens, in order to build up the emperor's reverence for him, replied that an angel had brought him the news. The emperor easily believed this, and later

was accustomed to say that the credit for his victory belonged to the
merits of Valens rather than the valor of his army.

CHAPTER 39

The treachery of Valens and the Arians;
the Synod of Milan (345); some western bishops refuse
to sign the creed and are exiled

1. From this beginning, the Arians, who had misled the
emperor, gained fresh hope that they would be able to profit by royal
authority where they had not prevailed by their own authority. When
we did not accept the decision that they had issued concerning
Athanasius, the emperor published an edict that stated that those who
did not endorse the condemnation of Athanasius were to be driven
into exile. Some of us, when councils of bishops were held near Arles
and Bitteras, a town of Gaul, requested that before they were compelled to indict Athanasius, they should have more debate about the
faith, and they would only decide the matter once an agreement had
been reached about who would constitute the jury. 2. But Valens and
his allies wanted to extract a condemnation of Athanasius first, and
they did not dare debate the faith. Due to this conflict between the
parties, Paulinus was sent into exile.

Meanwhile a council met in Milan,[194] where the emperor was at
that time; that same controversy, in its turn, did not reach any resolution. Then the Bishops Eusebius of Vercelli and Lucifer from Cagliari
in Sardinia were removed. But Dionysius, a priest of Milan, agreed to
join in the condemnation of Athanasius, provided that the question
about the faith was raised among the bishops. But Valens, Ursacius,
and the others, out of their fear of the people, who with outstanding
diligence were preserving the Catholic faith, did not dare acknowledge their crimes publicly, but gathered in the palace.

3. They sent a letter from Milan that was infected with every kind
of perverse idea. It was issued under the name of the emperor, and
undoubtedly the Arians believed that if the people accepted this letter with open ears, they would advance their ideas under the authority of the state. If, however, these ideas were rejected, the ill will of all
the people would be directed against the king, and he would be for-

given for these views because, at that time, he was a catechumen and would rightly appear unable to understand the mystery of faith.[195]

The people rejected this epistle when it was read in church. Dionysius, because he did not support it, was expelled from the city, and immediately, Bishop Auxentius was proposed to fill his place. 4. Liberius, the bishop of the city of Rome, and Hilary of Poitiers[196] were also sent into exile. The same situation also ensnared Rhodianus, the chief priest of Toulouse; he was more relaxed by nature and had not complied with the Arians, more through his association with Hilary than his own inclinations. Nevertheless, all these men had been prepared to suspend Athanasius from communion, provided that an investigation into the faith took place among the bishops. 5. But it appeared best to the Arians to eliminate the most prominent men from the struggle.

Thus, those men whom I mentioned above were driven into exile forty-five years ago, during the consulship of Arbitis and Lollianus. Liberius, a short time later, was restored to the city because the Roman people rioted. Nevertheless, it is agreed that the exiles were honored by the support of the entire world, plenty of money was collected for their expenses, and they were frequently visited by emissaries of the Catholic people of nearly all the provinces.

CHAPTER 40

The introduction of the words homoiousion and anomoiousian; Ossius of Spain defeated

1. Meanwhile, the Arians—not secretly as before, but openly and publicly—were preaching their sacrilegious heresy. In fact, they had already interpreted the Nicene Council in their favor; they had corrupted it with the insertion of one letter and had thrown a certain cloak of darkness over the truth. For in the place where *homoousion* had been written, that is, "of one substance," they had claimed that it should be written *homoiousion*, which means "of a similar substance." They were conceding a similarity, although they took away the unity, because a similarity is quite different from unity. For instance, a picture of a human body would be similar to a man, but nevertheless, the picture does not possess the true nature of a human. But some of

them went further, advocating the term *anomoiousian*,[197] which means "of a dissimilar substance."

2. The effect of these conflicts was that this kind of sacrilege ensnared the entire world. For Valens, Ursacius, and others (whose names I have reported) had corrupted Italy, Illyricum, and the East. Saturninus, the bishop of Arles, an unstable and factious man, oppressed our Gallic provinces. There was a rumor that Ossius of Spain[198] had also joined in the same perfidy; this seemed amazing and incredible because for nearly the entire period, he had been the most steadfast member of our party, and people believed that the Nicene Council had been assembled under his authority. It could be that he had fallen apart and gone crazy in his old age, for he was more than a hundred years old, as Saint Hilary reports in his letters. 3. With these matters stirring up the entire world and a sickness weakening the churches, a concern, less acute perhaps but no less serious, was bothering the emperor: clearly the Arians, whom he was favoring, seemed superior, but still there was no agreement among the bishops concerning their faith.

CHAPTER 41

The Council of Rimini (359); the praiseworthy example set by the British bishops

1. Therefore, the emperor ordered a synod to be convened at Rimini,[199] an Italian city. He instructed Taurus, the prefect, to assemble the bishops in one place and to hold them until they had consented to one faith. Taurus was promised a consulship if he settled the matter. Imperial officials were sent throughout Illyricum, Italy, Africa, Spain, and Gaul. They summoned or compelled considerably more than four hundred bishops to assemble at Rimini. The emperor ordered that all these bishops should be given stipends and food. 2. This seemed inappropriate to our bishops, those of Aquitaine, Gaul, and Britain; correctly rejecting the imperial funding, they chose to live at their own expense. Only three bishops from Britain, having nothing of their own, used the public fund, since they had rejected the collection offered by others, believing it more holy to burden the imperial treasury than individuals. I have heard Gavidus, our bishop, often refer to

this action in a disparaging way, but to the contrary, I think otherwise: I praise the bishops who were so poor that they had nothing of their own nor did they take more from other people than from the treasury; through this action, they were a burden to no one. In both of these decisions, they offer an outstanding example. Concerning the rest of the bishops, nothing worth remembering is handed down, so I will return to my exposition.

3. After all the bishops, as I wrote above, had been gathered together as one, the factions separated. Our bishops were occupying the church, but the Arians had taken a shrine for their place of prayer, which was then deliberately left vacant. They did not have more than eighty partisans, while the remainder of the bishops were members of our party.

Despite frequent meetings, nothing was accomplished; our supporters were remaining in the faith, while the Arians refused to give up their perfidy. At last it seemed right to send ten emissaries to the emperor so that he could learn about the belief or opinions of the two parties, and he would discover that it was impossible for there to be peace with the heretics.

4. The Arians did the same, sending an equal number of representatives who were to argue against us in the emperor's presence. Young men were chosen from our party, men who were insufficiently learned and even less cautious. The Arians sent old men who were shrewd and intellectually able, men blackened with the old dirt of their treachery, men who easily appeared superior before the king. Our representatives were ordered not to enter into communion, in any form, with the Arians, and to reserve all discussion for a synod.

CHAPTER 42

The Council of Seleucia (359); Hilary of Poitiers defends the western beliefs

1. Meanwhile in the East, the emperor followed the example of the West and ordered nearly all the bishops to assemble at Seleucia, a town of Isauria.[200] At that time, Hilary[201] was then in the fourth year of his exile in Phrygia. The deputy and governor gave him permission to travel with the other bishops by the public post, and he was compelled

to go. Although the emperor had given no particular orders about him, the judges had followed the general directive to the letter; it had ordered all the bishops to assemble for the council. Thus they were willing to allow Hilary also to travel with the other bishops. I contend that it was by the will of God that they willingly let him go as well; this ensured that this man, who was the most learned in divine matters, would be on hand when there was a discussion about the faith.

2. When he reached Seleucia, he was received with great favor, and he converted the minds and inclinations of all to his position. First, he was asked to explain the faith held by the Gauls. The Arians had circulated lies about us, and at that time, it had been received among the Easterners that we believed in a threefold manifestation of a solitary god, following the view of Sabellius.[202] But he offered testimony to the eastern bishops, setting out our faith in accordance with the tenets that had been prescribed by the Nicene fathers. Thus, to everyone's relief, he was not only received into the knowledge of the communion and their society, but also admitted into the council.

3. Then the council began the task of identifying the authors of the depraved heresies and expelling them from the body of the church. Among their number were George from Alexandra, Acatius, Eudoxius, Uranius, Leontius, Theodosius, Evagrius, and Theodulus. After the decrees were prepared by the synod, an embassy was sent to the emperor to make him aware of what had been done. The condemned also made their way to the king, trusting in their allies and the fellowship of the emperor.

CHAPTER 43

The emperor forces representatives from Rimini and Seleucia
to meet at the Council of Constantinople (360)
and sign a watered-down creed

1. Meanwhile, the emperor compelled the legates from the Council of Rimini,[203] those from our party, to be united in communion with the heretics.[204] He gave them the confession that had been written by these unscrupulous men, overlaid with misleading words, which spoke with hidden deception about the Catholic discipline. For under a type of false reasoning, it omitted the word *ousia* as one that

was ambiguous and used at random by the fathers rather than produced from the authority of the Scriptures. The word was left out to ensure that no one would believe that the Son was of one substance with the Father. This confession declared that the Son was of a similar nature to the Father, but there was a deliberate error underlying this, namely, that the Son should be considered similar but not equal.[205]

2. After the representatives had been sent away, the emperor issued a command to the prefect that the synod was not to be concluded[206] before all the bishops publicly proclaimed with their signatures that they agreed with the creed that had been drawn up. If any should stubbornly refuse, provided that the number was less than fifteen, they were to be driven into exile. But when our representatives returned,[207] pleading against royal power, they were denied communion. For indeed, when the bishops learned what had been decreed, there was greater confusion of both actions and counsel. 3. Then, gradually, many of our bishops, partly from feebleness of mind, partly because they were overcome with exhaustion from traveling, gave up and surrendered themselves to their adversaries, who after the return of their representatives were greater in number. Our bishops were being dislodged by those who were taking control of the church. Once minds began to change, they went over to the other side in droves, until the number of our party was reduced to around twenty.

CHAPTER 44

Bishops Foegaudius and Servatius stand firm among the weakening western bishops; Valens and Ursacius propose altering the creed to accommodate western positions; Valens tricks the bishops with a new formulation; the Council of Rimini closes

1. Nevertheless, the strength of these men was in inverse proportion to their numbers. Our Foegadius[208] was regarded as the most steadfast among them, as well as Servatius, the bishop of the Belgians. Because they had not submitted to threats and terrors, Taurus approached them with entreaties, and with tears in his eyes, he appealed to them to reflect upon these matters in a calmer spirit. Already, he said, the bishops had been enclosed in one city for seven months; the severity of winter and lack of provisions offered no hope

for their departure. What, ultimately, would become of them? They should follow the example of the majority, and at least take their authority for this action from their regard for the majority. Despite this appeal, Foegadius publicly proclaimed that he was prepared to set out for exile and every punishment that was required of him, but he would not accept the formula of faith proposed by the Arians.

2. Several days were expended on this conflict; when they found themselves making little progress toward a peaceful solution, little by little, Foegadius weakened, and he was overcome at last by the solution that had been proposed. For Valens and Ursacius affirmed that the present formulation of the faith, conceived by Catholic reason and proposed by the eastern bishops with the authority of the emperor, could only be rejected by a criminal action. How would the discord ever end if the confession that pleased the eastern bishops displeased the Westerners? Finally, if what was produced appeared less complete than the present statement of faith, they themselves should insert those things that they thought need to be added. "And we," said Valens and Ursacius, "will secure agreement for what has been added." The popular declaration was readily welcomed by all, and none of our side dared to reject the proposal, as by whatever means we wanted to bring an end to this matter.

3. Next, the confessions conceived by Foegadius and Servatius began to circulate. In these, they first condemned Arius and all the rest of his perfidy; they then pronounced the Son of God to be equal to the Father, without a beginning and eternal. Then Valens, just as if he was encouraging us, added the sentence in which there was a hidden trick, namely that the Son of God was not a creature as others were creatures. He deceived those who heard his fraudulent confession. For by those words in which the Son was denied to be like other creatures, it was affirmed nevertheless that he was a creature, although greater than the rest. Consequently, neither side felt that they had won completely, nor did they believe that they had been defeated. The statement of faith favored the Arians, but the professions added afterward favored our side, except for that clause that Valens had inserted, which, although understood later, went unnoticed at the time. This agreement allowed the council to be dismissed, one that had begun well but was concluded most disgracefully.

CHAPTER 45

The eastern bishops at Seleucia are forced to sign the western formulation; Hilary attempts to debate the matter before the emperor but is ordered to return to Gaul; under Hilary's leadership, the Gallic churches embrace Nicene Christianity

1. The Arians hurried back to Constantinople, to the emperor, with matters settled all too successfully and proceeding according to their wishes. There, drawing on royal power, they compelled the representatives of the Synod of Seleucia, whom they met in Constantinople, to accept the warped statement of faith, following the example of the western bishops. Many of those who refused were harassed with harsh custody and starvation, and they surrendered their captive conscience. Many, who struggled with more perseverance, had their bishoprics taken from them; they were sent into exile, and their places were given to others. With the best priests eliminated through intimidation or exile, the remainder succumbed to the treachery of the few.

2. At that time, Hilary had come to Constantinople following the delegates from Seleucia, and with no certain commands about his fate, he was waiting for the decision of the emperor as to whether perhaps he would be ordered to return to exile. When he noticed the extreme danger facing the faith, with the western bishops deceived and the eastern bishops conquered by wickedness, he wrote three public petitions and demanded an audience with the king, so that he might openly debate the faith with his adversaries.

Naturally, the Arians vigorously rejected that proposal. Finally, as if he were a breeding ground of discord, a disturber of the East, he was ordered to return to Gaul, but the emperor did not cancel his decree of exile.

When Hilary had traveled across nearly the entire world that was infected by this evil wickedness, he became doubtful in his spirit and was agitated by a great number of concerns. When it appeared that many believed they should not join in communion with those who had accepted the formulation of the Synod of Rimini, he judged it best to call all those men back to an emendation of life and penance.

3. In frequent councils among the Gauls, and with nearly all of the bishops admitting the error, he condemned the decisions of

Rimini and restored the faith of the church to its former state. Saturninus, the bishop of Arles, resisted these sensible decisions; he was a man who was clearly one of the worst, possessing an evil, wicked mind. But he, apart from the infamy of heresy, was convicted of many shocking crimes and was thrown out of the church.

In this way, the power of the Arian party was broken by the loss of this leader. There was also Paternus from Perigueux, who was equally insane, and when he refused to recant his perfidy, he was expelled from the priesthood. Forgiveness was extended to the rest. What is agreed by all is that through the service of one man, Hilary, our Gallic churches were freed from the crime of heresy.[209]

4. But Lucifer,[210] then in Antioch, was of a different opinion. For he had condemned those who had met at Rimini to such an extent that he continued to disassociate himself from communion with those who had been readmitted after satisfaction or penitence. I would not dare say whether his decision was right or wrong. Paulinus and Rhodianus died in Phrygia. Hilary, in the sixth year after his return, died in his homeland.

CHAPTER 46

The Priscillian controversy; the heresy had its origin
in Egyptian gnosticism and was spread to Spain by Marcus;
the character and career of Priscillian; the movement
begins to spread in Spain

1. The serious and dangerous times of our own age[211] followed in which there was more than the customary evil polluting the churches and stirring everything up. For this was the first time that the infamous heresy of the Gnostics was detected in Spain; this heresy was a deadly superstition, cloaked in arcane secrets. The origin of this evil was the East, especially Egypt. It is not easy to explain its beginnings there, but Marcus, coming from Egypt[212] (having been born in Memphis), introduced it first in the Spanish provinces. His first students were a certain Agape, a woman who was certainly no commoner, and the rhetor Helpidius.

2. They taught Priscillian. Priscillian came from a noble, extremely wealthy family;[213] he was sharp, restless, eloquent, educated

through his study of many books, and always eager to engage in discussions and debates. He would have certainly been successful, if his great talent had not been corrupted by his depraved aims; many good qualities, of both mind and body, could be discerned in him: he was able to stay awake for a long time, to bear hunger and thirst, he had very little greed, and he was extremely frugal in using what he did have. But Priscillian was incredibly vain, and his knowledge of profane matters had inflated his self-opinion more than it should have. As a matter of fact, it is believed that he had practiced the magical arts from his boyhood.

After he had adopted that deadly doctrine, he attracted many of the nobility and a large number of the common people into allying themselves with him through his persuasive authority and the art of flattery. To this number, women—with a lust for new things, wavering in their faith, and with minds drawn to every new curiosity—flocked to him in great crowds. Clearly, by offering an appearance of humility in his speech and dress, he instilled reverence and honor for himself among his followers.

3. Already the disease of that perfidy had begun to penetrate the greater part of Spain. As a matter of fact, some of the bishops were tainted: Instantius and Salvian[214] had supported Priscillian, not only with their agreement but almost as if they were bound by an oath. This situation persisted until Hyginus, the bishop of Cordoba, coming from the neighboring region, reported what had been discovered to Hydatius, the priest of Emerita. Hydatius, without restraint and going further than he should have, challenged Instantius and his allies. This added a torch, as it were, to the fire springing forth: he incited the evildoers more than he restrained them.

CHAPTER 47

The Council of Saragossa (380) meets to consider the Priscillian problem; Instantius and Salvian consecrate Priscillian as bishop of Avila; Hydatius obtains a rescript from Emperor Gratian against the heretics

1. After many conflicts between them that do not deserve mention, a synod gathered in Saragossa[215] at which even the bishops of

Aquitaine took part. The heretics did dare entrust themselves to judgment. Nevertheless, a sentence was passed on the absent men: the Bishops Instantius and Salvinianus were condemned, together with the laymen Helpidius and Priscillian. The council also decided that anyone who received the condemned in communion should expect that the same sentence would be extended to themselves. This business was turned over to Bishop Ithacius of Ossonoba,[216] who was given the duty of bringing the decree of the bishops to the attention of all and ensuring that the bonds of communion with Hyginus were severed. Hyginus, although he had been the first of all the bishops to openly pursue the heretics, had grown scandalously depraved after the synod, and he had received them in communion.

2. Meanwhile, Instantius and Salvian, condemned by the judgment of the priests, decided that, for the purpose of consolidating their strength, they would appoint Priscillian—a layman, but the leader of all the wicked men who together with them had been censured by the Synod of Saragossa—as bishop in the town of Avila.[217] They evidently believed that if they armed the wily and cunning man with priestly authority, they themselves would be better protected.

Hydatius and Ithacius attacked more vigorously, believing that the trouble could be suppressed in its earliest stages. Unfortunately, through poor judgment,[218] they petitioned secular judges to have the heretics driven from the cities by their decrees and punishments. After many disgusting conflicts, Hydatius procured a rescript from Gratian, who was then the emperor,[219] in which all the heretics were ordered to depart, not just from the church and cities, but they also were to be driven out of all the Roman lands.[220] When this was published, the Gnostics, having no confidence in their own positions, did not dare to fight the judgment; those who appeared to be bishops quit of their own accord. Fear dispersed the rest.

CHAPTER 48

Bishops Instantius, Salvian, and Priscillian travel to Rome, hoping to gain support from Bishop Damasus; their mission rejected by both Damasus and Ambrose of Milan; they obtain a rescript from Macedonius, which allows them to return to their sees

1. Then Instantius, Salvian, and Priscillian headed to Rome, so that they might refute before Damasus, the bishop of the city at that time, the charges against them. Their journey passed near the interior of Aquitaine, where, having been magnificently received by those who were unacquainted with them, they sowed the seeds of wickedness. They perverted the people of Eauze, who at that time had been good and devoted to religion, with their depraved ideas. They were driven out of Bordeaux by Delphinus;[221] nevertheless they tarried for a little while on Euchrotia's estate[222] and infected some with their errors. Then they continued their journey with their clearly obscene and disgraceful companions: wives and unmarried females (among whom were Euchrotia and her daughter Procula). The rumor among the people was that Procula had been raped by Priscillian, and then the resulting pregnancy had been aborted with herbs.[223]

2. Upon reaching Rome, these men wanted to be exonerated by Damasus, but they were not even admitted into his presence. Then, returning to Milan, they discovered that Ambrose was equally set against them. Since they had not deceived these two bishops who, at that time, had the greatest authority, they altered their strategy. They decided that they would extract the support they wanted from the emperor by bribery and soliciting favor. They corrupted Macedonius, a master of the offices, and subsequently procured a rescript, which, overturning what had been decreed earlier, commanded that they be restored to their churches. Instantius and Priscillian, relying upon this order, returned to Spain, for Salvian had died in the city. And then, without any struggle, they received the churches that they had held before.

CHAPTER 49

Ithacius forced to flee; the usurpation of Magnus Maximus; the Synod of Bordeaux (384); Instantius deposed; Priscillian requests a trial before the emperor

1. Ithacius did not lack the spirit to fight them, but there was no opportunity, because the heretics, after corrupting the proconsul Volentius,[224] had established their powers. In fact, they even arraigned

Ithacius as a disturber of the churches. When it was ordered that he should be given a horrible execution, he fled to Gaul. There he appealed to the prefect Gregory.[225] When Gregory discovered what was happening, he ordered the instigators of the disturbances to be brought to him. He referred all of these matters to the emperor to deny the heretics a way of gaining influence. But that plan was useless, because owing to the caprice and power of the few, everything was for sale in the palace.[226]

2. And so the heretics, through their arts (and by giving a great deal of money to Macedonius), obtained a judgment that meant imperial authority was taken away from the prefect, and the trial was handed over to the *vicarius* of Spain,[227] for by this time, those provinces no longer had a proconsul. The magistrate sent officers to drag Ithacius, who had gone to Trier, back to Spain. The clever Ithacius frustrated their purpose, and later, having been supported by Bishop Britannius, he escaped.

Already at this time, a quiet rumor was beginning to spread that Maximus[228] had assumed power in Britain, and shortly he would be invading Gaul. Consequently, Ithacius decided to await the arrival of the new emperor, even though the situation was uncertain. Meanwhile, no actions were taken against him. When Maximus entered the city of Trier as a victor, Ithacius lodged many petitions against Priscillian and his wicked, criminal associates. The emperor was galvanized by these entreaties, and in letters sent to the prefect of Gaul and the *vicarius* of Spain, he ordered absolutely everybody who had been involved in these disgraceful acts to be brought to a synod in Bordeaux.[229]

3. When Instantius and Priscillian were brought, Instantius was ordered to state his case first. Afterward, having failed to justify himself, he was pronounced unworthy to hold the office of bishop. Priscillian, to avoid a hearing before the bishops, appealed to the emperor.[230] Our bishops surrendered the point with their usual inconstancy. They should have either rendered a sentence, even against a resistant man or, if they themselves were regarded with suspicion, should have reserved the case for other bishops. They should not have allowed the investigation of such blatant crimes to be referred to the emperor.

Chapter 50

The inappropriate zeal of Ithacius; Martin attempts
to intervene on behalf of the accused; Priscillian tried
and then sentenced to death by Maximus

1. Consequently, all those who were involved in this matter were led to the king. Bishops Hydatius, Ithacius, and their accusers followed. I would not censure their enthusiasm for overcoming heretics, if they had not fought with more of a desire for conquest than they ought to have exhibited. In my opinion, this affair is as displeasing as the conduct of the accusers, for I do not think Ithacius possessed any scruples or holiness. He was reckless, talkative, shameless, lavish, and treated his stomach and throat to every kind of food. This foolish man went so far as to include in his accusation—as if they were companions or disciples of Priscillian—all the holy men whose enthusiasm had been directed toward reading or to struggling with the flesh through fasting. That miserable man also dared at that time to openly charge Bishop Martin, a man clearly comparable to the apostles, with the disgrace of heresy.

2. When Martin came to Trier, he continued to scold Ithacius, enjoining him to desist from his accusation, and he implored Maximus to abstain from the blood of these unfortunate men.[231] He said that it was enough to have these condemned heretics expelled from the churches by the sentence of the bishops, and that it would be a brutal and unprecedented wickedness if a secular judge rendered judgment in a church affair.[232] The trial was delayed as long as Martin was in Trier. Shortly before leaving, through his extraordinary authority, he elicited a promise from Maximus that he would do nothing cruel in resolving these matters. But afterward, the emperor, having been led astray by Magnus and Rufus, turned away from milder advice and handed the matter over to the prefect Euodius, a man both harsh and severe.

3. This man pronounced Priscillian guilty. He had been heard in two trials, convicted of crimes, and he had not denied that he gave himself over to disgusting doctrines, that he had led nocturnal assemblies of immoral women, and that he had customarily prayed naked.[233] He placed Priscillian in custody until his case could be presented to the emperor. When these matters were brought to the palace, the

emperor decided that Priscillian and his associates ought to be sentenced to death.

CHAPTER 51

Priscillian found guilty and executed;
many of his followers are exiled

1. Ithacius, seeing how unpopular he would be among the bishops, if, as the prosecutor, he was present at the final trial of a capital case (for it was necessary to repeat the trial), withdrew from the trial. He was, needlessly, clever now that the wickedness had been brought to a conclusion. Maximus appointed a certain Patricius prosecutor; he was an agent of the treasury.[234] 2. On Patricius's insistence, Priscillian was sentenced to death; he was joined by Felicissimus and Armenius, who recently, although they were priests, had broken away from the Catholics to become followers of Priscillian. Latronianus also, and Euchrotia, were put to death by the sword. Instantius, who, as I said above, had been condemned by the bishops, was deported to the island of Scilly, which lies beyond the British Islands.

The following judgments were handed out to the rest: Asarivus and the deacon Aurelius were sentenced to death, Tiberian had his possessions confiscated and was sent to the island of Scilly. Tertullus, Potamius, and John were deemed less important and worthy of mercy, because they had betrayed themselves and their confederates before the questioning began; they were sentenced to temporary exile in Gaul.

3. In this manner, the men who were unworthy of the light were either executed, setting a terrible precedent, or were punished with exile. Initially, Ithacius defended these decisions as being commensurate with the law of the courts and by their great importance to the public welfare. Later, having been disturbed by the reproaches and proven wrong in the end, he tried to deflect the blame back onto those magistrates who had rendered the decisions he had sought. Nevertheless, he was the only one to be expelled from his bishopric. For Hydatius, though less guilty, had freely abdicated his bishopric; he did this wisely and with humility, but later he tried again to acquire the post he had relinquished.

4. Moreover, after Priscillian was killed, not only was the heresy that had originated with him not suppressed, but it strengthened and spread widely. For his followers, who initially had honored him as a saint, afterward began to worship him as a martyr. The remains of the executed men were brought back to Spain, and there funerals were celebrated with magnificent ceremonies. As a matter of fact, it was believed that the most binding form of an oath was to swear by Priscillian.

5. Among us there arose a war of perpetual discord. Stirred up by these shameful dissensions, it has raged fifteen years[235] and no one has been able to calm it. At that time, it can be seen that everything was stirred up and mixed up by disturbances among the bishops, and because of them, everything was corrupted by hatred or prestige, fear, inconstancy, envy, factionalism, pleasure, avarice, arrogance, somnolence, and inactivity. Ultimately, the many, with insane decisions and perverse eagerness, were taking action against the few who were offering sound counsel. Amid all this, the people of God and every person who tried to do good were held up for shame and derision.

DIALOGUES

BOOK I

CHAPTER 1

Postumianus, returning from the East,
meets Sulpicius and Gallus

1. When Gallus and I had met[1] in a certain place—Gallus is a man who is most dear to me, both because of the memory of Martin (for he was Martin's disciple) and also because of his own merits—my friend, Postumianus, interrupted us. He had just returned, for our sake, from the East, having abandoned his own land three years earlier. 2. I embraced this most affectionate man. I kissed his knees and his feet. For a minute or two, first dumbfounded, and then crying with joy, we walked, and then, spreading our sackcloth robes on the ground, we sat down.

3. Then Postumianus, looking intently at me, said, "When I was in the remote places of Egypt, it pleased me to proceed all the way to the sea; there I found a cargo ship that was preparing to cast off, bound for Narbonne. That same night, you appeared to stand before me in a dream, and taking me by the hand, you led me to board that ship. Shortly thereafter, when the darkness had been sundered by the dawn, I rose from the place in which I had slept, and thinking more about the dream that was still in my mind, I was suddenly overcome with so great a desire for you that I did not hesitate to board the ship. On the thirtieth day, I landed at Marseilles and ten days later reached you here—so successful a passage assisted my pious desire. In return, yield yourself to me so that I might embrace you and enjoy your company, away from all others, because I have crossed so many seas and have hurried across so much land for your sake."

4. "Yes," I replied, "even when you were staying in Egypt, I was passing the time with you always in my heart and mind, and your kindness was leading me to think about you day and night. You cannot imagine that I will be inattentive to you for even a moment of time: I will hang on your every word, gaze at you, listen to you, speak with you, and no one will be admitted inside our secret place, which this remote cell provides for us. Nevertheless, I think that you will not mind the presence of Gallus with us. For, as you see, he celebrates your arrival with joy, just as I do."

"It is clearly right," said Postumianus, "that Gallus should be retained in our company. 5. It is true that I do not know him very well, but because he is most dear to you, he will also be dear to me, especially since he is a disciple of Martin. Nor will I refuse to speak with both of you together, as you ask, because I have come in order to devote myself to a long, long conversation with my Sulpicius, who has been missing me"—and here he grasped both of my hands.

Chapter 2

Postumianus agrees to tell stories about the ascetics he had met during his travels; Sulpicius's former friend

1. "To be sure," I said, "you have demonstrated how much a pious love can accomplish. For our sake, traveling over so many seas and such a great extent of lands, you have come from the farthest lands or, as I might say, the farthest point, from where the sun rises in the east to where it sets among us. 2. And so come—we are not busy, we are by ourselves here, and we ought to have time for your words— please tell us the entire story of your travels. What sort of faith in Christ flourishes in the East? What is the peace of the saints? What are the practices of the monks? How many signs and deeds does Christ produce among his servants? For since life has become distasteful to us in these lands, in the circumstances among which we live, we will gladly hear from you whether it is permitted to live as Christians even in the desert."

3. Then Postumianus replied to my words, "I will do what I see that you wish me to do. But first I would like to learn from you

whether all of those priests[2] whom I left behind here are still of the same character as they were before I departed."

4. Then I said, "Do not ask me about these matters, for either, as I believe, you already know what I know, or if you do not know, it would be better to hear nothing about them. I am unable to keep silent about the fact that not only have those men you are asking about not become any better than what you once knew, but actually that one man—who once loved us, in whom we were accustomed to seek shelter from those who were persecuting us—has become harsher toward us than he ought to have been. But I will not say anything cruel against him, because I cared for him as a friend, and I loved him even when he was considered an enemy. 5. Nevertheless, as I was turning these thoughts over silently in my mind, this grief pricked me to the limit, that we nearly were deprived of the wisdom and love of such a devout man. Let us abandon these topics that are filled with grief; let us listen to you instead, as you promised a moment ago."

6. "Let it be so," said Postumianus. After he said this, we all sat silently for a few minutes. Then he moved the sackcloth upon which he sat closer to me and began to speak.

CHAPTER 3

The voyage to the East: Carthage and Cyrenia

1. "Three years ago, I said goodbye to you, Sulpicius, before leaving here and setting sail on a ship from Narbonne. After five days, we reached a port in Africa. 2. The voyage, by the will of God, was very successful. It pleased my spirit to reach Carthage so that we might visit the sites associated with the saints and, most importantly, worship at the tomb of the martyr Cyprian.[3] After fifteen days, we returned to the port and sailed on into the high seas, heading for Alexandria. While fighting a southerly wind, we were nearly forced onto Syrtes.[4] The cautious sailors were on their guard against this, and they checked the ship by throwing out the anchors. 3. Now the mainland was in sight, and we landed on it from our boats; when we saw that it was entirely free from human civilization,[5] I, for the sake of exploring the lands, eagerly advanced a greater distance. Approximately three miles from the shore, I saw a small hut among the

sand dunes whose roof was, as Sallust wrote, shaped like the keel of a ship. It reached down to the ground and was decked with very solid boards.[6]

4. "The houses are built this way, not because the people of this land fear the power of any rainstorms—which have never even been heard to occur there—but because the power of the winds is so great that whenever a breeze, even from the calmest sky, begins to blow a bit, the destruction in those lands is greater than on any sea. No seedlings or crops grow there because of the instability of the ground: the parched sands give way to every movement of the winds. 5. But where the winds are resisted, turned back by certain promontories near the sea, the land is somewhat more stable and it produces a sparse, rough vegetation that is useful enough to be food for sheep. The inhabitants live on sheep's milk. Those who are cleverer, or, I should say, wealthier, enjoy barley bread. This is the only crop grown there, as it springs up quickly because of the nature of the soil and thus usually evades destruction by the savage winds, 6. because it is said to take only thirty days from planting to harvest. There is no reason for people to live there, apart from the fact that they are all free from paying tribute. In fact, this is the outermost boundary of the Cyrenians, adjoining that desert that lies between Egypt and Africa through which Cato once led an army when he was fleeing from Caesar."

Chapter 4

Postumianus meets a Cyrenian; the gluttony of the Gauls

1. "I headed for the hut that I had seen from a distance. There I discovered an old man in a skin garment, turning a millstone by hand. 2. He received us with kindness when we greeted him. We explained that we had been driven onto that shore and were unable to return to our journey immediately, detained by waiting for a calm sea. Consequently, we had come ashore and, as is the custom of the human character, wanted to learn about the nature of the region and the manner of life of those who lived here. Since we were Christians, we principally wanted to discover whether there were any Christians in these lonely places.

3. "Then the old man, weeping with joy, threw himself down before our knees. He kissed us repeatedly and then invited us to prayer. Then, spreading sheep skins on the earth,[7] he made us lie down. 4. He served a lunch that was naturally very rich: half a loaf of barley bread. We were four in number and he himself made five. He also produced a small bundle of herbs whose name I have forgotten, but they were similar to mint, with abundant leaves, and were superior to the flavor of honey. We were completely delighted by the charm of the plant's sweetness, and our appetites were fully satisfied."

5. At these words, smiling at my Gallus,[8] I said, "What do you say, Gallus? Doesn't a lunch consisting of bundles of herbs and bread divided between five men sound satisfying?"

Then that very shy man, blushing a little as he endured my teasing, said, 6. "You follow your custom, Sulpicius, from which you never deviate on any occasion that offers you an opportunity to torment us about gluttony. But you act inhumanely, you who would compel us Gauls, mere men, to live like angels—although I, who have an enthusiasm for eating, do believe that even the angels eat. For I would fear, even alone, to taste that divided barley loaf. 7. But allow that man of Cyrene to be contented with it; for him it is either a necessity or his nature to go hungry. Finally, let those visitors be content, for I believe that seasickness had made them willing to abstain from the bread. We are a long way away from the sea and, as I am constantly telling you, we are Gauls. Now allow Postumianus to continue to explain more of the history of his Cyrenian acquaintance."

Chapter 5

The Cyrenian reveals that he is a priest;
the superior qualities of Cyrenian Christians

1. "To be sure," said Postumianus, "I will take care after this not to mention anyone's abstinence, to ensure that a difficult example does not completely offend the Gauls. 2. Nevertheless, I had determined to report the dinner of that Cyrenian and the banquets that followed, for we were with that man for seven days. But I will refrain from this so that Gallus will not believe that I am tormenting him.

3. "Still, the next day, when certain people from among the residents of that land began to congregate in order to meet us, we discovered that our host was a priest, a fact that he had hidden from us
with great dissimulation.[9] 4. Next, we went with him to a church,
which stood about two miles away and was cut off from our sight by an
intervening hill. The church was woven together from insignificant
twigs, not much better than our host's tent; a person could not stand
up in it without stooping.

5. "When we asked about the customs of these people, we
learned this very clearly: they neither bought nor sold anything;[10] they
did not know the meaning of either fraud or theft; they neither had,
nor wished to have, gold and silver, which men believe to be of greatest importance. 6. When I offered ten gold coins to that priest, he ran
away, testifying with loftier wisdom that the church was not built up
with gold, but rather was destroyed.[11] We were able to give him a small
amount of clothing."

CHAPTER 6

The Origenist controversy in Alexandria

1. "After he had courteously received our gift, the sailors called
us back to the sea and we departed. After a favorable voyage, we
reached Alexandria on the seventh day.[12] There, the bishops and
monks were engaged in disgraceful battles. The reason or cause of this
conflict was that the priests, who often met together as one, appeared
to have decreed in their frequent synods that no one should read or
possess the books of Origen, who was considered the most skillful com-
mentator on the Sacred Scriptures. 2. The bishops mentioned certain
outrageous passages in his books; his supporters did not dare defend
those texts but, rather, claimed that they had been deceitfully inserted
by heretics.[13] Therefore, they asserted, the rest of his works should not
be condemned on account of those passages that deservedly were censured. The faith of those reading was easily able to exercise discrimi-
nation, so that they would not follow forged ideas and yet would retain
those things treated in accordance with the Catholic faith. It should
not be a surprise, they claimed, if in these modern books and recent

writings, heretical fraud had been at work, since, in certain places, it had not been afraid to attack gospel truth.[14]

3. "The bishops, struggling quite obstinately against these ideas, were doing their utmost to compel even the correct doctrines to be condemned as a whole along with the errant and even the author himself, because the books that the church had accepted were more than sufficient. The reading of his works was to be strongly rejected because it would harm the foolish more than it would profit the wise.

4. "Nevertheless, after going quite carefully into some points from these books,[15] I found many things that were very pleasing, but discovered some passages in which there is no doubt he had some erroneous opinions[16]—which his defenders claim were forged. 5. I marvel that one and the same man was able to be so inconsistent that, in one part, which is approved, he has no equal after the apostles, but in another, in which he is justly found to be at fault, no one is known to have erred more grievously."

CHAPTER 7

Origen's view that Satan will be rehabilitated;
the dispute leads to violence and exile in Alexandria

1. "For although there was much in what the bishops picked out from those books that admittedly read as being in conflict with the universal faith, one place actually stirred up the greatest controversy. This was where the published reading was that the Lord Jesus, just as he came in the flesh for the redemption of humanity, enduring the cross for the salvation of humans, and had tasted death for the immortality of humans, would also, through the same order of suffering, even redeem the devil, because this would be consistent with his goodness and piety, so that he who had reformed ruined humanity would also free the fallen angel.[17]

2. "After the bishops advanced this idea and others of a similar nature, a dissension arose from the factionalism of the groups. When the authority of the priests proved inadequate to curb this uproar, in a perverse precedent, the city prefect was summoned to govern the discipline of the church.[18] Fearing this, the brothers were dispersed,

the monks became fugitives throughout various lands, and edicts were issued that prevented them from settling anywhere.

3. "Nevertheless, what made a very deep impression upon me was that Jerome, a man who is thoroughly Catholic and highly skilled[19] in sacred law, was believed at one time to have followed Origen. This same man now was leading the way in actually condemning all of Origen's writings.[20] Truly, I would not presume to judge anyone lightly; nevertheless, the most excellent and learned men were said to disagree in this conflict. 4. Whether Origen's opinion is an error, as I think, or heresy, as is believed, not only was it impossible to restrain it through the many condemnations of the priests, but there is no way it could have spread itself so widely unless it had become known through controversy.[21]

5. "That, then, was the kind of disturbance that was battering Alexandria when I arrived. The bishop of that city welcomed me in a very kindly manner that was better than I expected, and he tried to keep me with him. 6. But I had no mind to stay in a place where recent anger about the defeat of the brothers was seething. For even if, perhaps, it seemed they ought to have been obedient to the bishops, such a large number, living under the creed of Christ, should not have been crushed, especially by bishops."

CHAPTER 8

Postumianus reaches Bethlehem; the priest Jerome

1. "Next, we departed from that place and set off for the city of Bethlehem, which is six miles away from Jerusalem and stands sixteen stages of travel from Alexandria. 2. The priest Jerome rules the church[22] in that place, for it is a parish of the bishop who holds Jerusalem. I had already encountered Jerome during an earlier trip, and he had easily convinced me that I should not look for anyone other than him. 3. For apart from the merit of his faith and his endowment of virtues, he has been trained not only in Latin and Greek but also in Hebrew literature, so that no one dares to compare themselves to him in any field of learning. I would be amazed if you had not learned of him through the many works that he has written, books that have been circulated throughout the entire world."

4. "He is far too well-known to us," said Gallus, "for five years ago, I read a certain book[23] written by that man, in which he most violently chastised and cut to pieces the entire tribe of our monks. 5. Since this work, our Belgian friend is accustomed to rage at Jerome, because he said that we are accustomed to fill our bellies to the point of vomiting. Nevertheless, I forgive that man and believe that he was discussing the characteristics of eastern monks more than those of the West. For vigorous eating is gluttony among the Greeks, but it is simply human nature among the Gauls."

6. Then I said, "Gallus the Rhetor![24] You defend your people, but let me ask you, does this book condemn these vices only among the monks?"

"To the contrary," said Gallus, "he overlooked nothing; he cut to pieces, tore up, and exposed all our faults. He principally attacked avarice, but he also went after vanity. He also wrote many things about pride and not a few things about superstition. I admit that he seems to have depicted the vices of many people."[25]

Chapter 9

Discourse on Jerome

1. "But as for the other abuses, how truly and powerfully he argued about the familiarities between virgins, monks, and even clerics. Because of this attack, it is said that he is not loved by certain people whom I am unwilling to name. 2. For just as our Belgian friend was angered that we were condemned for excessive eating, in the same way, those men are said to complain loudly when they read in that little book that he wrote, 'The virgin despises her unmarried brother and hunts for a brother who is a stranger.'"[26]

3. To these charges, I replied, "You go too far, Gallus. Take care or someone who is practicing these things may hear you and, along with Jerome, you also will become unloved. Because you are a rhetor, it will not be considered unwarranted for me to warn you with a verse of the comic poet: 'Indulgence attracts friends, truth attracts hatred.'[27] 4. It would be better for us, Postumianus, if the oration on the East that you have begun was resumed."

"I," he said, "as I had begun to say, was with Jerome for six months. During this time, his ongoing war and perpetual struggle against evildoers stirred up the hatred of the lost. The heretics hate him because he does not stop attacking them; the clerics hate him because he attacks their way of life and their crimes; 5. but clearly, all of the good people admire and appreciate him. Those who consider him a heretic are insane. Let me speak truthfully: the knowledge of the man is Catholic, his learning is sound. He is always either reading or buried in his books; he does not rest, day or night: he is either reading something or writing something. I would not have wanted to spend even the shortest amount of time away from so great a man, except that I had already set my heart and, as I said earlier, had vowed to God that I would go to the desert.

6. "And so, I delivered and entrusted all of my things to that man, including my family members, who were holding me back against my will by following me. Having been completely relieved in a way from such a heavy burden and now finally set free, I returned to Alexandria. After visiting the brothers there, I aimed for the Thebaid, which is upriver from Alexandria, that is, at the farthest boundary of Egypt. 7. They say that many of the monks live there, in the vast, exposed solitudes of the desert. It would take a long time if I wanted to tell all that I saw, so I will only touch lightly on a few points."

CHAPTER 10

Postumianus enters the Egyptian desert;
two boys overcome an asp

1. "Not far from the desert, near the Nile, there are many monasteries. For the most part, they contain one hundred monks[28] in each place, for whom the highest law is to live in accordance with the command of the abbot,[29] to follow their own judgment in nothing, and to subordinate themselves to his will and power. If there are any among those monks who conceive in their mind a higher form of virtue and desire to take themselves into the desert to pursue a solitary life, they do not leave unless the abbot permits it. This is their first virtue, to obey the command of another. 2. Bread or some other kind

of food is provided for those who have gone out into the desert by the order of the abbot.

"By chance, during the days when I had arrived there, there was a certain man who had recently withdrawn to the desert and had established a tent for himself not more than six miles from that monastery. The abbot had sent bread to him by two boys, the elder of whom was fifteen years old and the younger twelve. 3. On the way back to the monastery, they encountered an asp of astonishing size. Running into this snake did not terrify them:[30] when it came before their feet, it lowered its dark blue neck as if enchanted by incantations. The younger of the boys seized the snake in his hand and began to carry it, wrapped up in his robe. Then he entered the monastery like a conqueror.

"When he met the other monks, filled with boastful pride, he opened his robe and put down the captive animal as they looked on. 4. Although the others praised the children's faith and courage, the abbot acted by a higher counsel. To prevent the immature boy from becoming proud, he punished both boys with a beating and scolded them sternly because they had misrepresented what the Lord had worked through them. He said that the work had not been a result of their own faith, but one of divine power. They should learn to prefer to serve God in humility rather than to take pride in signs and powers, because a knowledge of weakness was better than power with vanity."

CHAPTER 11

A humble monk and abbot fed with bread from heaven

1. "When that monk heard this, that the children had been endangered by meeting the serpent and that they, through their victory over the serpent, had earned a beating as a penalty, he begged the abbot to send him no more bread or any food after this. 2. Now eight days had already passed during which the man of Christ had placed himself in danger of starvation; his limbs were withering through his fasting, but his mind, reaching out to heaven, could not yield; starvation was wearing out his body, but his faith was enduring firmly. 3. Meanwhile, the abbot had been warned through the spirit that he should visit his disciple, and he became curious, because of his pious concern, about what life-giving substance was sustaining the

faithful monk, the man who no longer wanted to be supported with bread from men.[31] The abbot set out to investigate this matter.

4. "The monk saw the old man coming from a distance, and he hurried out, gave thanks, and led him into his cell. When the two men entered the cell together, they saw a basket woven from palm leaves, filled with warm bread, attached by the doors, hanging from the door post. 5. First, they perceived the smell of warm bread, and in fact, when they touched it, it seemed as if it had just been snatched from the oven.[32] Nevertheless, this bread did not appear to have the shape of Egyptian bread. 6. The two monks were amazed and realized that this was a gift from heaven.[33] The monk declared that the gift had been presented because the abbot had come, while the abbot attributed the gift more to the faith and virtue of the monk. Then the pair broke the celestial bread with great exultation.

7. "When the old man, after he returned to the monastery, told this story to the brothers, the fervor of all their souls was increased so greatly that they hurried to go out into the desert and the holy solitudes, deeming themselves miserable because they had settled for so long in the gathering of many, where they had to suffer close contact with other humans."

Chapter 12

A discourse on anger

1. "In that monastery, I saw two old men who already had spent forty years there, and consequently, it was said that they had never left that place. I do not think I should overlook them, since in fact I heard their virtues celebrated by the testimony of the abbot himself and in the words of all the brothers. One of them said that the sun had never witnessed him feasting; the other said that the sun had never seen him angry."[34]

2. At these words, Gallus looked at me and said, "Oh, if only that friend of yours—I don't want to mention his name—was here now. I would like him to hear this example; too often have we experienced his violent anger against many people. Nevertheless, because I hear that recently he forgave all of his enemies, if he should hear this story, he might be strengthened more and more by the precept it presents:

that it is a shining example of virtue not to burst out in anger. 3. I will not deny that he had just reasons for being angry, but where the battle is harder, there the crown is more glorious. For this reason, if you will grant it, I believe that a certain man ought to be justly praised, because, when his ungrateful freedman deserted him,[35] he was sorry for him rather than pursuing the fleeing man. Nor did he get angry with the man who seems to have led his freedman away."

4. I replied, "Unless Postumianus had produced this example of anger being mastered, I would have been very angry with the flight of that fugitive; but, because anger is not permitted, we should do away with all mention of those things which incite us to anger. Let us rather listen to you, Postumianus."

5. "I will do," he said, "what you command, Sulpicius, as long as I see that you are still so eager to hear me. But remember that it is not without an expectation of interest that I deposit this speech with you: I cheerfully carry out what you demand provided that in a little while you will not deny me what I will demand."

6. "But we," I said, "have nothing by which we are able to repay the loan to you, even without interest. Nevertheless, command whatever you think, provided that you satisfy our desires, as you have begun to do, for we are greatly delighted by your speech."

7. "I will not cheat you out of what you are so keen to receive," said Postumianus, "and because you have recognized the virtue of one of the hermits, I will relate a few stories about the rest of them to you."

Chapter 13

An old monk and his cow make the desert bloom;
Postumianus and the visiting monks encounter a lion

1. "The desert where I first entered was around twelve miles from the Nile. I was accompanied by one of the brothers, an experienced guide to those places. We came to a certain old monk who was living at the base of a hill. He had a well there, which was most rare in those places. 2. He had one cow whose only job was to produce water by turning the wheel of a pump, for the well was said to be a thousand feet deep or more. There was a garden there that flourished with many vegetables. This definitely went against the nature of the desert,

where everything is parched, scorched by the burning sun, and there are no types of seeds able to produce even a slight root.

3. "But, in fact, this amazingly fertile garden was provided by the work the monk shared with the cow and also his own industry. Frequent irrigation with water gave such a richness to the sands that the plants we saw in this garden were green and bearing fruit in a remarkable manner. 4. And so, utilizing these plants, the cow and its master were living in that place. The holy man gave us dinner from his bounty. I witnessed there, what you people, Gallus, will scarcely believe: the jar that contained the plants from which our dinner was prepared boiled without a fire. The power of the sun is so great there that it suffices for all kinds of cooking, even for the delicacies of the Gauls.

5. "After dinner, with twilight beginning to fall, he invited us to a palm tree that stood at a distance of about two miles away, and whose fruit he customarily used. 6. These are the only trees the desert contains, although they are rare. I do not know whether skilled men procured them in antiquity, or if it is the nature of the soil that produces them. Or did God, knowing in advance that the desert would at some time be inhabited by these holy men, prepare these trees for his servants? 7. For the most part, those who dwell in those remote places are nourished by the fruit of these trees, since no other seeds are able to survive there.

"When we went to that tree to which our host was kindly leading us, we ran into a lion. At the sight of the animal, my guide and I began to tremble, but that holy man approached without hesitation. We, although afraid, followed him. 8. The beast retreated respectfully (for you would discern that this had been commanded by God), and it stood by, while the monk tore off clumps of fruit from the lower branches. When he offered a hand filled with dates, the lion approached and accepted them as freely as any domestic animal. Then, when it had eaten, it withdrew. We watched this, still trembling, and could easily assess how great the faith was in him, and how weak the faith was in us."

CHAPTER 14

The monk and the penitent wolf

1. "We saw another, equally distinctive man, living in a small hut that was only able to admit one person. One story about this man

claimed that a wolf used to stand by him at dinner, and the beast never failed to meet him at the lawful dinner hour, waiting for a long time before the doors until the old man offered the bread left over from his light dinner. Afterward, the wolf usually licked his hand, and then, almost as if it had carried out its duty by making its greeting, the animal would depart.

2. "One night, by chance, the holy man was absent for a long time while he escorted a departing brother who had visited him, and he did not return until nightfall. Meanwhile, the beast, according to its custom, had come to meet the monk at dinner time. When the wolf perceived that the cell was empty and her friend, the patron, was absent, she became curious and entered the cell to find where its inhabitant was. By chance, a small palm basket, filled with five loaves of bread, was hanging within reach. 3. The wolf took a loaf from this basket and devoured it. Then, after committing this wicked act, it departed. When the hermit returned, he saw that the little basket was broken and no longer contained the same number of loaves. He perceived the loss of his private property and recognized the fragments of the stolen bread near his doorway. 4. There was little doubt in his mind about which person had committed the theft. Consequently, when in the subsequent days the beast did not come, eschewing its normal custom—no doubt aware of the bold thing it had done, and giving up her visits to the man she had harmed—the hermit was suffering painfully, having been deprived of the comfort of his pet.

5. "Finally, after seven days had passed, the wolf came, as was its custom, at dinner time, summoned by the prayer of the old man. One would have easily made out the shame of penitence, as it did not dare approach the old man and kept its eyes cast down to the ground in profound shame, and one would have clearly understood that it was appealing for a certain kind of forgiveness. The hermit, feeling pity for the animal's confusion, ordered it to come near and he stroked the head of the sad animal with a soothing hand. Then he fed the guilty animal with two loaves. 6. Thus, having attained his forgiveness, she resumed the custom of her social call that had been dropped in her grief.

"Let us consider, I beg you, the virtue of Christ in this episode, in whom everything that is stupid becomes wise, in whom everything that is savage becomes mild. 7. The wolf performed a social obligation; the wolf acknowledged the crime of theft; the wolf was bewildered by the awareness of its shame. Having been called, it came, it offered its head and received the sense that forgiveness had been granted to it, just as it had borne shame because of its mistakes. 8. This virtue is yours, O Christ! These miracles are yours, O Christ! For those things that are done in your name by your servants are yours, and we groan over the fact that wild beasts know your majesty, but men do not respect it."

Chapter 15

An anchorite heals a lioness's cubs

1. "Should this perhaps appear incredible to someone, I will recall some greater incidents. The faith of Christ is present so that I will not make up anything, and I will not narrate widely spread stories from uncertain authors, but I will lay out those stories that I learned through the most reliable men. 2. Many live in the desert without any tents; these men are called anchorites. They live on the roots of herbs and never stay in any fixed place to avoid being visited by large crowds of people. When night compels them, they sit down to rest where they are.

3. "Two monks from Nitria came to a certain anchorite who was living in this manner and by this law. It was a long way off, but nevertheless, because he had once been a dear friend in association with them in their monastery, they had heard of his virtues and looked for him in the desert. After searching for him for a long time, at last, in the seventh month, they discovered him lingering in that extreme desert that lies adjacent to the Blemmyes. It was said that he had already lived in those forsaken lands for twelve years. This man, who was obviously avoiding contact with any people, nevertheless did not avoid them; he recognized them and did not refuse these most beloved men his company for three days.

4. "On the fourth day, he accompanied them a little way, escorting them as they were leaving. Then they saw a lioness[36] of startling size coming toward them. The beast, after discovering the three, had no uncertainty about which man she sought. She fell prostrate before the feet of the anchorite, and laying there with a kind of weeping and lamentations, was revealing her state of mind through her groaning

and equally by her begging. This moved all of the monks and especially the anchorite whom the lion had known to look for, so they followed her as she led. Occasionally lagging behind, occasionally looking back, it was very easy to understand what she wanted: the anchorite should follow where she would lead.

5. "To cut a long story short, he arrived at the beast's cave, where she was suckling five nearly full-grown cubs that had been badly born, since they came blind from their mother's womb, consigned to perpetual darkness. The mother placed each before the feet of the anchorite, bringing them out, one at a time, from the floor of the cave. 6. Then, at last, the holy man understood the animal's request, and after invoking the name of God, he touched the closed eyes of the cubs with his hand. Immediately the blindness was driven away and the newly opened eyes of the beasts were exposed to the light that had been denied to them for so long.

"As a result, these brothers, having seen the anchorite whom they wished to visit, returned with a very fruitful reward for their labor. For they, having been admitted as a witness of such great virtue, saw the faith of the holy man and the glory of Christ, which they testified about themselves. 7. Here is something even more marvelous: five days later, the lioness returned to the author of such a great benefit and gave the same man the pelt of a rare animal in payment. Generally, that holy man wears this skin as a mantle, since he does not disdain to wear a gift that came from a beast, but rather has understood it to have come from another source."

CHAPTER 16

A monk saved by an ibex

1. "There was another anchorite who had an illustrious name in those regions. He was living in the part of the desert that is in the region of Aswan. This man, when he had first gone out to the desert, had planned to survive on the roots of the herbs, which, sweet and of exceptional taste, the sands sometimes produced; but ignorant of the kinds of shoots he was selecting, he was often picking harmful plants. It was not easy to discern the potency of the root by taste because all the plants were equally sweet, but many had a hidden nature that

concealed a lethal poison. 2. And so this hidden power began to torment him as he was eating the plants: all of his organs were battered with incredible pains, frequent vomiting was tearing apart the very seat of his spirit with tortures that could not be borne, and his stomach was becoming worn out. Afraid of everything that he had been eating, he began a seven-day fast. He was close to fainting 3. when an animal called an ibex came to him. It stood close to him, and he tossed it a bundle of herbs that he had collected but did not dare touch. The animal used its mouth to scatter those plants that were poisonous, and then selected those that it knew were harmless. Thus the holy man learned through the animal's example what could be eaten and what should be rejected.[37] Consequently, he evaded the danger of hunger and avoided the poisonous plants.

4. "But it would take a long time to recount the stories of all those men who occupy the desert, whom we met or heard about. I spent nearly nineteen months in the desert, more as an admirer of the great virtue of others than as one who could have undertaken such an arduous and difficult way of life; in fact, I frequently stayed with that old man who had the cow and well."

CHAPTER 17

A visit to the two monasteries of Saint Antony; the hermit of Mount Sinai

1. "I visited the two monasteries of the blessed Antony that today are occupied by his disciples. I also approached the place in which the most blessed Paul, the first hermit,[38] had stayed for a short time.

2. "I saw the Red Sea and the ridge of Mount Sinai, whose peak is so close to heaven that it cannot be climbed by any means. 3. An anchorite was said to live among its caves; I searched diligently for him for a long time, but was unable to see him. Nearly fifty years earlier he had withdrawn from human society. He did not wear any clothing, and as his body was covered with stiff hair, he became unaware of his own nudity through a divine gift.[39]

4. "Whenever religious men wished to come see this man, he ran off into the wilderness and avoided human contact.[40] It is said that he had shown himself to only one person in the preceding five years, a

man whose powerful faith, I suppose, had earned him the right to have a meeting. When, during their discussions, he was asked why he avoided other humans so diligently, it is said that he responded that those who are visited by humans are unable to be visited by angels.[41] 5. On account of this, a rumor spread that this holy man was visited by angels, and this belief was accepted by many.

6. "Next, I left Mount Sinai and returned to the Nile River, whose banks are lined with numerous monasteries, and I walked along on both sides. I saw that most monasteries, as I said a short time ago, have one hundred monks in each place, but it is known that there are two or three thousand monks in certain villages.[42] 7. You should not believe that the virtue of the monks staying there in the guest houses, among the crowds of monks, is less than what you know is the case among those monks who had removed themselves from the crowds of humans. 8. Obedience, as I already said, is the most important, fundamental virtue there. No one coming to one of the monasteries is received by the abbot until he has first been tested and approved,[43] so that he will never object to an order from the abbot, however hard, difficult, and unworthy of toleration."

CHAPTER 18

A novice's obedience is tested by walking into flames

1. "Let me tell you about two very great miracles of incredible obedience, although I have many similar stories in mind. In order to incite people to emulate virtue, there is no point telling many stories to those for whom a few do not suffice.

2. "When a certain man, having renounced the business of the world, entered a well-ordered monastery and asked to be received, the abbot began to detail the numerous obstacles facing him: the works of that particular monastic discipline were burdensome, his orders were severe, and it was certainly not easy to carry them out patiently; he would do better to look for a different monastery where the rules were easier; he should not try to enter into what he was unable to finish. 3. But the man was unmoved by the description of these terrors, and he promised that his obedience in everything would be so great

that if the abbot commanded him to walk into a fire, he would not refuse to enter.

"When the master received this declaration, he did not hesitate to test the man who had made it. 4. By chance, an oven was burning nearby; it had been kindled with a great fire in preparation for cooking bread. Fire was gushing out from the open ovens, and among the hollows of that furnace the flames were in complete control. The master ordered that newcomer to enter this space. He did not hesitate to obey the command; with no delay he walked into the middle of the flames, which were quickly conquered by such a courageous faith, and they withdrew from him as he came, just as they had for those Hebrew youths.[44] Its nature overcome, the fire withdrew. 5. The man who one might believe would be burned up was surprised to find himself bathed in a kind of cold dew.[45]

6. "But is it really amazing, O Christ, that the fire did not touch your novice, so that the abbot did not regret issuing such a hard command, nor did the disciple regret having obeyed the order? On the day in which he arrived, although he was tested in his weakness, he was found to be perfect. Deservedly happy, deservedly glorious, his obedience was tested, and he was glorified through his trial."

CHAPTER 19

A novice's obedience is tested by carrying water for a dead twig

1. "In the same monastery, it is reported that what I am about to tell happened in recent memory. In the same manner, a certain man who wanted to be admitted came to the same abbot. First the law of obedience was placed before him, and he promised to obey, to the limit, everything forever. By chance, the abbot was carrying a rod of storax[46] in his hand that had dried out long before. 2. He drove this rod into the ground and ordered the man who had come to carry out the following task: he was to care for the rod by bringing water, as long as it took, until that which went against all nature occurred, namely, that the withered stick turned green in the dry ground.

3. "The new arrival subjected himself to the command of this hard law, and carried water daily on his own shoulders, which was brought from the Nile river, about two miles away. A year passed and

his labor brought the end of his task no closer. There could be no hope from the fruit of this labor, but nevertheless he endured in the work through the power of his obedience. The following year also mocked the vain labor of the afflicted brother.

4. "Finally, in the third successive year, when neither by night nor day had the worker stopped bringing water to the rod, it blossomed.[47] 5. I saw the small tree that was produced from this rod. Today it is green with branches in the atrium of the monastery, standing as a testimony that shows what obedience deserved and how much faith can achieve. 6. But this day would be exhausted before I ran out of stories about the various miracles that were told to me concerning the powers of the holy men."

Chapter 20

A monk chooses possession by a demon in order to cure himself of vainglory

1. "Still, I will relate two splendid stories to you: the first is an exceptional warning against the swelling up of wretched vanity; the second will serve as a significant teaching against false righteousness.[48]

2. "A certain holy man, endowed with an incredible power of expelling demons from the bodies of the possessed, was performing unprecedented signs every day. For not only was he curing possessed bodies in person with only a word, but occasionally at a distance as well by sending only fringes from his robe or letters.[49] Consequently, to an amazing extent, this man was attended by people who were coming to him from all over the world. 3. I will keep quiet about the lower orders, but prefects, counts, and judges of varying power often prostrated themselves before the doors of that man. The holiest bishops also set aside their priestly authority and were humbly asking him to touch and bless them, for with good reason they believed that they were sanctified and illuminated with a divine gift as often as they touched his hand or garment.

4. "He was said to always abstain from every drink and from bread—let me whisper this in your ear, Sulpicius, so that Gallus will not hear it—he was sustained by only six figs. 5. Meanwhile, as his reputation grew on account of his virtue, so too did vanity begin to sneak

into the holy man because of his reputation. When he noticed that that evil was advancing in him, he worked long and hard in an attempt to destroy it, but he was unable to drive it out. Even as he was persevering in virtue, he was silently aware of his vanity. 6. Everywhere, demons were acknowledging his name, and he was unable to separate himself from the people coming to him. Meanwhile, a secret venom was spreading in his heart; by his will, the demons were fleeing from the bodies of others, but he was unable to purge the secret thoughts of vanity from himself.[50]

7. "Finally, having been transformed by all of his prayers, it is said that he prayed to God that he might be permitted to spend five months under the power of the devil, so that he might share the experiences of those whom he had cured. 8. Why should I drag this story out? That powerful man, that man who was famous for his signs and powers throughout the entire East, that man to whose doors people had formerly flocked, before whose doors those possessing the greatest powers of this world had prostrated themselves, that man was seized by a demon and he was bound in chains. 9. Having suffered all of the agonies that the possessed are accustomed to bear, in the fifth month, he was purged not only of the demon, but what was even more useful and desirable for him, of vanity."

Chapter 21

The shortcomings of Gallic clerics

1. "But when I reflect upon these things, our own unfaithfulness and weakness present themselves. For who is there among us, if offered respect by one of the humble poor or praised by the silly and fawning words of a woman, is not immediately swollen with pride, is not at once puffed up with vanity? Even if he is not familiar with sanctity, nevertheless, because he is said to be a saint, either through the adulation of the foolish or perhaps erroneously, he will believe himself to be extremely holy. 2. And then[51] if large amounts of money are sent to him, he will assert that he is being honored by the munificence of God, when it is simply mundane gifts that are being conferred upon him while he is asleep. But if even in the most modest

way some signs of some virtue were to attend him, he would believe himself to be an angel.

3. "Should a man undistinguished in either work or virtue be ordained a priest, he will immediately widen the fringes of his robes, rejoice in the greetings of others, become swollen up by those who come to meet with him, and will hurry around everywhere. 4. Having been previously accustomed to travel on foot or by donkey, the proud priest is now carried by foaming horses; once content to live in an insignificant cell, he now erects lofty, paneled ceilings, builds many rooms, carves doorways, and paints bookcases. He rejects crude clothing and desires a soft tunic. He demands these be assigned to dear widows and household virgins, so that the former are to weave a stiff hood while the latter produce a flowing cloak.

5. "But let us leave these things to be described more bitingly by that blessed man Jerome; I will return to my theme."

"But I do not think that you," said my Gallus, "have left anything for Jerome to dispute; you have covered all of our practices in your short summary, with the result that these few words of yours, if they are received with equanimity and pondered patiently, will greatly aid their readers, so that in the future, they will no longer need the books of Jerome to coerce them. 6. But you must continue to offer more of these stories that you have begun, and you must produce that story that you promised you would tell about false righteousness. For, to tell the truth, we are afflicted with no greater evil here in the Gallic provinces."

"I will do so," said Postumianus, "and keep you in suspense no longer."

Chapter 22

A monk who tries to return to his family is seized by a demon

1. "There was a certain young man from Asia who was extremely wealthy, of the best family, and he had a wife and young son. When he was the tribune in Egypt, engaged in frequent battles against the Blemmyes,[52] he came in contact with places in the desert. He also had seen a fair number of the huts of the saints, and he had received a word of salvation from that blessed man John.[53] 2. He did not hesitate to condemn his useless military service with its vain honor, and having

entered the desert with resolve, in a short amount of time, he stood out as one who was perfected in every type of virtue. Strong in fasting, conspicuous for his humility, firm in faith, his desire for virtue easily equaled the ancient monks.

"Meanwhile, he was attacked by a thought, introduced through the devil, that he would be living more correctly if he returned to his country and his only son, in order to save his entire household together with his wife.[54] This would be more acceptable to God than if he was content to save only himself from the world and neglect, with considerable impiety, the salvation of his own family.[55] 3. He was conquered by that type of false righteousness, and after nearly four years, the hermit abandoned his cell and profession.

"When he reached a nearby monastery that was occupied by many brothers, he confessed both the reason for his departure and his plan to those who asked. Although he was opposed by all and primarily restrained by the abbot of that monastery, he was still unable to discard the idea that had been evilly lodged in his mind. 4. And so, rushing out with unhappy stubbornness, he separated from the brothers, with unhappiness on both sides. Scarcely had he departed from their sight when he was filled with a demon who caused a bloody froth to pour from his mouth and made him tear himself with his own teeth. He was carried back to the same monastery on the shoulders of the brothers. When they could not control the unclean spirit in him, the brothers were compelled to restrain him; he was bound with interlocked chains, feet chained to his hands. This was a punishment worthy of a fugitive: the man who could not be held by faith was held by chains.

5. "After nearly two years, through the prayers of the holy men, he was set free from the unclean spirit and shortly thereafter returned to the desert, the place from which he had come. This monk, having been corrected, should be an example to others, so that no one might be duped by the shadow of false righteousness. Nor should wavering fickleness compel someone through useless frivolity to abandon the task that has been started.

"Let it be enough for you to know these things about the powers of the Lord that he has performed among his servants, so that these acts of power might be imitated or feared. 6. But because I have satisfied your ears, although perhaps I have been more long-winded than I ought to have been, in the same way"—Postumianus now spoke to me—"you must repay the debt with interest. As you are accustomed, let us hear you tell many stories about your Martin, to fulfill my burning desire."

CHAPTER 23

A description of how far the Life of Martin *has spread*

1. "What?" I said. "Doesn't my book about Martin suffice for you? You know that I wrote in that volume about his life and his virtues."

2. "I know it very well," said Postumianus. "This book is never out of my right hand. For if you recognize it, here it is!" He took out the volume that had been concealed in his robe. "This book has been a companion to me on land and sea; it was my companion and comforter on every journey. 3. But let me tell you clearly where this book has spread: there is nearly no place in the entire world that does not have a published copy of such a happy history. 4. Paulinus,[56] a man who is most enthusiastic about you, was the first to bring it to the city of Rome; then, when the entire city was fighting to get copies, I saw the booksellers exulting because they didn't have any book that was more profitable, no book that sold more quickly or for a greater price. 5. This book was well ahead of me on my journey. When I reached Africa, it was already being read in all of Carthage. Only that priest of Cyrene lacked a copy, but I loaned him mine, and he copied it.

6. "Now what should I say about Alexandria, where nearly all the people know it better than you do? This book crossed Egypt, Nitria, Thebais, and the entire kingdom of Memphis. 7. I saw it being read in the desert by a certain old man; when I told him that I was your close friend, he and many of the brothers laid this injunction upon me: if I ever returned to these lands and found you unharmed, I should compel you to supply those stories about the virtues of that blessed man that you said you passed over in silence in your book.[57] 8. So come on! I do not want to hear those stories that you have already written enough about. Many people are demanding, along with me, that you relate those stories that you passed over, those you omitted, I suppose, because you worried about boring your readers."[58]

CHAPTER 24

Martin is greater than all the eastern ascetics

1. "Indeed, Postumianus," I said, "just now while I was listening intently to you speaking about the virtues of the saints, I was going back quietly in my thoughts to Martin and realizing that all the deeds that were carried out by various individuals were easily completed by that man alone. 2. For although you recounted lofty deeds—permit me to say this while retaining peace with those holy men—there was nothing I heard from you in which Martin appeared inferior. For just as I acknowledge that their virtue should never be compared to the merits of that man, it is also appropriate to realize that it is unfair to compare that man with the situation of the hermits and also the anchorites. For they, freed from every impediment, are taught to perform admirable deeds with only heaven and angels as witnesses. 3. Martin lived in the middle of a crowd and with various peoples, among disagreeing clerics, among savage bishops, pressured from every side by near-daily scandals. Nevertheless, rooted in impregnable virtue, he stood against all adversaries, and not even those men we just heard about who are or were in the desert were able to do as much as he did.

4. "And even if those hermits had performed equivalent deeds, what judge would be so unjust that he would not declare them to be of lesser merit? For suppose he was a soldier who fought in a disadvantageous position and yet proved to be the victor; they, on the other hand, need to be compared with soldiers who fought from an equal or even superior position. 5. What follows from this? Even if all had won the same victory, the share of glory would not be the same for all. In any event, when you related these splendid deeds, you did not say that anyone had revived someone from the dead; from this one action, at any rate, it must be acknowledged that no one should be compared to Martin."

CHAPTER 25

The case for Martin's superiority over the desert fathers

1. "For even if one should admire that flames did not singe that Egyptian monk, Martin commanded fires quite frequently. If you

should repeat how the wildness of beasts was conquered and submitted to the anchorites, Martin was familiar with animals and he restrained the anger of beasts and the poisons of snakes. 2. But if you should produce that man who was curing those possessed by unclean spirits with a word of command or even by the power of the fringes of his robe, there are many examples to illustrate that Martin was not inferior even in this area.

3. "Even if you were to submit that man who was covered with his own hair in place of a robe, the man who was believed to be visited by angels, well, angels spoke with Martin daily. 4. But then, facing vanity and bragging, he bore such an unconquerable spirit that no one was more steadfast in rejecting those vices, although indeed, from a distance, he cured many who had been touched by unclean spirits, and he ordered the spirits to depart, not only from friends and high-ranking officials, but even from kings themselves. 5. This was the least significant of his powers. You must also believe that no one fought more powerfully against not only vanity but also the causes and occasions that produce vanity. I will speak about a small thing that should not be omitted, because he should be praised who, endowed with the greatest power, still displayed such a scrupulous will in offering reverence to the blessed man.

6. "I remember the prefect Vincent, an uncommon man. There was no one in the Gallic provinces who was able to outdo him in every type of virtue. When he came to Tours, he frequently asked Martin to offer him a meal in his monastery. To support this request, Vincent cited the precedent of the blessed bishop Ambrose, who was said to feed consuls and prefects at times. But Martin, a man of loftier spirit, refused lest any vanity or sense of self-importance creep in from this practice. 7. Consequently, you must acknowledge that the virtues of all of those men whom you enumerated were in Martin, although the virtues of Martin were not in all of them."

Chapter 26

Postumianus also views Martin as superior to the eastern monks

1. "Why do you say these things to me?" asked Postumianus. "As if concerning that man I do not feel the same as you and had not

always felt the same. I, for as long as I live and have my wits around me, will commend the monks of Egypt; I will praise the anchorites; I will marvel at the hermits, but I will always consider Martin to be special. I dare not compare any of the monks, and certainly none of the bishops, to him. 2. Egypt acknowledges this fact, as does Syria, and Ethiopia is learning of it. India has heard it, Parthia and Persia know it, Armenia is aware of it, the far-removed Bosphorus has learned of it, and finally, anyone who visits the Fortune Islands or the frozen ocean knows it.

3. "So how much more miserable is this land of ours, which, although it had so great a man close at hand, did not deserve to know him? I will not include the common people in this indictment; only the clerics, only the priests are ignorant of Martin. It was not without reason that they chose not to recognize him, because, if they had acknowledged his virtues, they would have been forced to face their own vices.[59]

4. "I dread repeating what I heard recently: someone (I do not know him) said that you had written many lies in that book of yours. This is not the voice of a man, but rather the voice of the devil. This claim takes nothing away from Martin, but rather, it drains faith from the Gospels. 5. For when the Lord himself has attested that those types of works that Martin performed were to be done by all the faithful, the person who fails to believe that Martin did these things also disbelieves that Christ said they would be done.[60]

6. "But the unfortunate, the degenerate, and the sleepy, those who are unable to do these things, are embarrassed by the miracles that he performed, and they prefer to deny his virtues rather than confess their own sluggishness. 7. But let us move on to other topics, and leave behind the memory of all these things. I would rather that you, as I have been looking forward to for some time now, tell us about the rest of Martin's deeds."

"But I," I replied, "believe that this is something that should be more properly asked of Gallus, 8. who clearly knows more stories—for the disciple could not ignore the deeds of his master—and he deservedly owes a recompense, not only to Martin, but also to us, because I already wrote the book, and you, until now, have been speaking about the accomplishments of the eastern monks. Let Gallus recount that history at last through an obligatory discourse, because, as I said, he owes us and our Martin a turn speaking, and I believe he will do something for Martin by showing no hesitation to recount his deeds."

CHAPTER 27

Gallus pleads his inadequacy in the face of a demand for stories about Martin

1. "Although I certainly am unequal to so great a task,"[61] said Gallus, "nevertheless I am compelled, by the examples of obedience that Postumianus related earlier, not to excuse myself from this service that you have imposed on me. 2. But when I think about myself, a Gallic man, telling stories among men from Aquitaine, I become afraid that I might offend your sophisticated ears with my uneducated speech. Still, you must listen to me as a man of Sancerre, one who says nothing in a pretentious or lofty style. 3. For if you concede that I am a disciple of Martin, you also must concede that his example permits me to reject empty, flashy speeches and verbal ornaments."

4. "You," replied Postumianus, "may speak either Celtic, or if you prefer, Gallic, provided that you speak about Martin. But I believe that even if you were speechless, you would not lack words to say about Martin with an eloquent tongue, just as Zacharias had his speech restored to give his son the name of John.[62] 5. Moreover, as you are a rhetor, you are making this artful plea for yourself like a rhetor,[63] since you, a man abounding in eloquence, beg our pardon for your lack of skill. But it is not proper for a monk to be so cunning nor a Gaul to be so skillful. 6. It would be better for you to begin and explain what remains for you: for we wasted too much time earlier discussing these other matters, and already the shadow of the declining sun grows longer and reminds us that little remains of the day before night begins."

7. Then, after we had all sat silently for a few minutes, Gallus began to speak. "It seems to me in the first place that I must take care not to repeat the examples of Martin's virtues that Sulpicius commemorated in his book. Following this principle, I will skip over his earliest acts while in the military, nor will I touch on the things he did while a layman or a monk. 8. Nor will I speak about what I heard from others, but rather I will tell you what I witnessed myself."[64]

BOOK II

CHAPTER 1

Martin gives his garment to a poor man

1. "Immediately after I abandoned my studies, I joined that blessed man. After a few days had passed, we were going to church. On the way, a poor man met him who was half-naked in those winter months, and he begged Martin to give him a garment. 2. Then Martin sent for the archdeacon[1] and commanded him to clothe the cold man without delay.

"Next, entering a private chamber and sitting down alone, as was his custom (for he retained this solitude for himself even in the church, a freedom granted to the clergy; the priests sat in another room, having time for morning receptions or remaining occupied with hearing about business affairs).[2] Personal solitude was enfolding Martin until that hour in which custom demanded that he celebrate the sacred rites for the people.

3. "I must not neglect to mention that when sitting in his private chamber, Martin never used a chair. In fact, no one ever saw him sit in church. Recently—and I swear this before God, with a great deal of shame—I saw a certain man resting on an elevated throne in church, as if on the platform of a king. Martin sat on a rustic stool, 4. the kind that is used by servants, which we rustic Gauls call *tripeccias*, but you rhetors, or at least you who come from Greece, call tripods.

"When the archdeacon had put off giving the tunic to him, that poor man watched the separate chamber of the blessed man and then rushed in, complaining that the cleric had neglected him, crying bitterly that he was still cold. 5. Without delay, the holy man, unseen by the pauper, secretly drew the tunic from beneath his robe, clothed the poor man, and ordered him to depart.

"A short time later, the archdeacon entered Martin's room and told him that the people waited in the church in accordance with custom, and that Martin needed to go out to perform the liturgy. 6. Martin responded to him by saying that it was necessary for the poor man first to be clothed—although he was speaking about himself—and that it was impossible for him to go into the church unless the poor man had received clothing. 7. The deacon was unaware of what had happened and was unable to see it because Martin was covered on the outside with his robe, but underneath he was nude. Consequently, he excused himself by saying that the poor man was not there.

"'Bring me the clothing that has been prepared,' said Martin, 'and the poor man will not fail to appear to put them on.'

8. "Then at last the archdeacon, compelled by this requirement, his anger now aroused, snatched a Bigerrian garment from a nearby shop that was short and hairy and cost five silver pieces. Angrily, he threw it before Martin's feet. 'Here is the garment,' he said, 'but there is no poor man.' 9. Martin, remaining motionless, ordered the archdeacon to wait a little while outside his doors and, having obtained privacy, he covered his naked body with the garment, utilizing all of his powers to keep his actions secret. But when do the actions of holy men remain hidden to those who are inquiring?[3] Whether they wish it or not, all their deeds are revealed. And so Martin proceeded out in this clothing to offer the sacrifice to God."

CHAPTER 2

Flames of fire erupt from Martin's head; Martin heals Evanthius and then a servant who had been bitten by a snake

1. "On that same day—I am about to tell you something amazing—when he was blessing the altar, as is customary, we saw a ball of fire shoot out from his head,[4] and as the flame climbed toward heaven, it produced a long tail of fire. 2. And although we saw this happen on an important feast day among a great throng of people, only a woman from among the virgins, one priest, and three of the monks saw the fire. I am not able to judge why the others did not see it.

3. "At about the same time, when my uncle, Evanthius, a man who, although occupied by the business of the world, was very much a Christian, had begun to be hard pressed by a most serious illness and was in imminent danger of death, he called Martin. Martin set out immediately, without hesitation. Nevertheless, before the blessed man had traveled more than half of the journey, the sick man felt the power of the approaching saint. Immediately restored to health, he himself came out to meet us as we arrived.

4. "On the next day, Evanthius retained Martin, who wanted to return home, with a great prayer; while he was there, a serpent struck a boy from the household, leaving a lethal wound. The power of the venom had brought the boy close to death when Evanthius carried him in on his own shoulders and placed him before the feet of the holy man. Evanthius then declared that there was nothing that was impossible for Martin to do. By this time, the serpent's venom had spread throughout the boy's limbs. 5. You could see that the skin had swollen along all of his veins and his vital organs were stretched tight like a water bottle. Martin touched all of the boy's limbs with an outstretched hand, and then he poked a finger near the small wound through which the snake had injected its poison.

6. "Then, in truth—I am about to tell you something amazing— we saw the venom summoned from every part of the boy's body as it converged on Martin's finger. Then the poison crowded through that small hole, accompanied by some blood, in the same way that large quantities of milk flow in long streams from the udders of goats or sheep when they are squeezed by the herdsman's hand. 7. The boy arose, unharmed. We, dumbfounded by such an amazing miracle, were acknowledging what truth compelled us to say, namely, that there was no one under heaven who was able to imitate Martin."

CHAPTER 3

Martin and the treasury guards

1. "In the same way, at a later time we were making a trip with him while he was visiting his dioceses. I do not remember what necessity delayed us, but he had gone on a little ahead. 2. Meanwhile, a coach filled with men who were treasury guards was coming along the public highway. When the nearest mules saw Martin standing on the side of the road in his hairy black garment and wrapped in his dangling cloak, the frightened animals lurched somewhat in the other direction. 3. Their reins became entangled and they mixed up those long harnesses that are used, as you often see, to group the miserable animals together. The difficult task of untying the animals was delaying the men who were in a hurry.

"Angered by this mishap, the guards quickly jumped to the ground. 4. Then they began to poke Martin with their whips and rods, and when he, silent and with incredible patience, surrendered his back to the blows, he provoked greater madness in those unfortunate men. Their anger was stoked by the fact that Martin seemed to pay no attention, like a man who did not even feel their blows. 5. We, following close behind, found him horribly bloodstained and every part of his body lacerated; he was stretched out, unconscious, on the ground. We immediately placed him on his donkey and departed quickly, cursing the place of that bloodshed. Meanwhile, the soldiers had vented their rage and now returned to the coach. They ordered the mules to set off in the direction in which they had been traveling.

6. "Those animals stood rigid, all of them fixed to the ground as if they were bronze statues;[5] the screams of the masters mounted higher, the whips cracked on this side and that, yet the mules were completely unmoved. Then all the guards arose en masse to beat the animals; the punishment of the mules wore out their Gallic flails. 7. The animals were beaten with all the tree limbs torn from a nearby forest, but their cruel hands produced no result. Every mule stood in the same spot, fixed like statues. The unfortunate men did not know what they should do, and by this time they, although as brutal as you please, were unable to pretend any longer that they did not know they were in the grip of a divine power.

8. "And so, returning to their senses, they began to ask about the man whom they had beaten in that place a little earlier. The investigators learned from some who were passing by that it was Martin whom they had so cruelly beaten. Then the cause of their misfortune became apparent to all; they were unable to ignore the fact that they were immobilized because of the injury done to him. 9. They pursued our party at a rapid pace. Conscious of what they had done and of their guilt, bewildered with shame, weeping, their heads and mouths covered with dust with which they had disfigured themselves, they groveled on their knees before Martin, begging forgiveness and requesting that they might be allowed to continue on their way.

"It was enough, they said, that they had been punished by their conscience alone, and enough to have realized that the earth might have swallowed them alive. They also realized that they might have been deprived of their senses, frozen in the rigid nature that is characteristic of stones, and thus fixed to those spots in which they had seen their mules stand. They prayed and begged that he might extend forgiveness for their wickedness and restore their ability to depart. 10. The blessed man had already perceived that they were immobilized, and he had told us about it before they came. He forgave them graciously, and permitted them to depart with their animals restored to them."

CHAPTER 4

Martin restores a pagan child to life;
this miracle converts many pagans

1. "Sulpicius, I often remember that Martin was accustomed to tell you[6] that he did not have nearly the same power available while a bishop as he recalled that he had before his elevation.[7] If this is true, or rather, because it is true, we are able to speculate about how great those deeds were that he did as a monk, those things he did alone with no witness, when we saw so many proofs made by him during his episcopacy with everyone watching. 2. Many of his earlier acts became well-known in the world as they could not be concealed, but there are said to be innumerable deeds that, as he avoided bragging, he hid, and did not permit them to come to human attention. Clearly he, a man who had surpassed human nature and was treading upon the glory of the world in the knowledge of his own power, was enjoying the witness of heaven.

3. "We are able to estimate what was true, either from those deeds that we discovered or from those that could not be hidden. In fact, before his episcopacy, he restored two corpses to life, which you recounted in your book,[8] but during his episcopacy, he only revived one person, a story that I am surprised you omitted. I was a witness of this event, assuming that you have no qualms about the adequacy of my testimony. Nevertheless, I will tell you what happened, just as it occurred.

4. "We were on our way to the town of Chartres for some reason. On the way, while we were passing by a certain village, inhabited by a very large population, an enormous crowd of people who were all pagans came out to meet us. No one in that village had any knowledge of Christianity. But a multitude had joined the flood of those standing

in every field due to the fame of so great a man. 5. Martin sensed that something needed to be done, and having been forewarned by the Spirit, the whole man began to groan. He was not speaking as a man, but was proclaiming the word of God to the Gentiles, groaning often, because such a large crowd did not know the Lord, the Savior.

6. "Meanwhile, just as the incredible multitude had encircled us, a certain woman, whose son had died a little before, extended her hands and began to offer the lifeless body to the blessed man, saying, 'We know that you are a friend of God; restore my son to me, because he is the only one I have.' The rest of the crowd joined in and were shouting their approval of the mother's entreaties. 7. Then Martin accepted the dead body into his own hands, understanding that for the benefit of those who were watching, as he told us later, he could obtain power.

"With everyone watching, he bent his knees, and when he stood up after finishing his prayer, he returned the revived boy to his mother. 8. Then the entire multitude offered a great shout to heaven, acknowledging that Christ was God. Finally, all the people, in a body, began to throw themselves down at the knees of the blessed man, faithfully demanding that he should make them Christians. 9. Without hesitation, even though they were in the middle of a field, he placed his hands upon each person and made them catechumens. When he returned, he told us that it was not unreasonable for catechumens to be made in that field where martyrs had customarily been consecrated."

CHAPTER 5

The stories about Martin have surpassed the stories of the eastern monks; Martin and the Emperor Valentinian

1. "You have conquered, Gallus," said Postumianus, "not me, at any rate, since I am a great champion of Martin, and I have known and always believed all these stories about him; rather you have conquered all the hermits and anchorites. 2. For none of them as your Martin—or more precisely, our Martin—gave orders to dead bodies. Sulpicius rightly compares Martin to the apostles and prophets; the strength of his faith and the works of his powers demonstrate that

Martin was just like them. 3. But I beg you to continue! Although we will be unable to hear anything more magnificent, nevertheless, go on, Gallus, because even now there is more to be said in a discourse about Martin. My spirit is anxious to learn even the smallest deeds or daily routines of Martin, for there can be no doubt that even the least of his actions was greater than the greatest deeds of others."

4. "I will do so," said Gallus. "But I did not witness[9] what I am about to tell you, for this happened before I joined Martin. But what happened is well-known since it was spread by the conversation of the faithful brothers who were present.

5. "At around the time Martin was first elevated to his bishopric, it became necessary for him to go to the imperial court. Valentinian[10] held power then. This emperor, when he discovered that Martin was bringing requests that he was unwilling to grant, gave orders to keep him outside the doors of the palace. For in fact, his wife, Arriana, had stirred up his cruel and proud spirit and turned the emperor completely against the holy man, so that he would not show him any of the respect that was due.

6. "And so Martin, after he attempted to approach the haughty prince once or twice, reverted to his familiar methods: he wrapped himself in sackcloth, sprinkled himself with ashes, abstained from food and drink, and remained in prayer, day and night. 7. On the seventh day, an angel appeared near him and commanded him to go to the palace with confidence. The palace gates that had been closed would be standing wide open of their own accord and the proud spirit of the emperor would be softened. 8. Having been strengthened by the reassuring words of the angel who had appeared, and confident of assistance, Martin returned to the palace. The gates stood open; no one opposed him. Ultimately, he made his way to the king with no one hindering him. 9. When Valentinian saw Martin coming from a distance, he began gnashing his teeth, asking why Martin had been admitted. He refused to honor Martin, who stood nearby, by rising from his throne, until fire engulfed the chair and the flame scorched the king in that part of his body upon which he sat. Thus, the proud man was ejected from his seat and, against his will, rose in the presence of Martin.

"He heartily embraced the man whom earlier he had decreed should be rejected, and having been improved, he freely acknowledged that he had felt divine power flowing through his body. He did not wait for Martin's requests, but rather, he agreed to everything before Martin asked. 10. He often invited Martin to a discussion or to dinner. Finally, as the bishop was leaving, he offered him a great deal of money, but the blessed man, as always, rejected all the money without hesitation so that he might protect his own poverty."[11]

CHAPTER 6

Martin and the wife of Emperor Maximus

1. "And because we have now entered the palace, it is only appropriate that I append an account of the deeds accomplished in the palace at various times. It would not be right to omit the example of a faithful queen's admiration for Martin.

"At that time, the Emperor Maximus[12] was governing the state; 2. he was a man whose entire life would have been said to be worthy, if he had been permitted to reject the crown that a rebellious army had improperly imposed on him, or if he had abstained from civil wars. But it is dangerous to reject a great empire, and it is impossible to retain it without military force.[13] 3. Maximus honored Martin with great respect, summoning him often and receiving him in the palace. Martin discussed everything with him in conversations about present events, the future, the glory of the faithful, and the eternity promised the saints.[14] Meanwhile, the queen was hanging on the words of Martin through the days and nights. She was not inferior to that example found in the Gospel, of the woman who washed the feet of the Holy One with her tears and dried them with her hair.[15] 4. Martin, who never had any contact with a woman, was unable to evade her persistence or, rather, her slavish devotion. She was not considering the wealth of the monarchy, the dignity of the empire, her crown, or her purple robe. She lay prostrate at Martin's feet and it was impossible to tear her away. Finally, she asked her husband—saying that the two should compel Martin—to dismiss all the other servants and allow her, alone, to serve him a meal.

5. "The blessed man was unable to fight back too stubbornly. The chaste offering prepared by the hands of the queen was set out; she arranged the chair, brought out the table, washed his hands with water, and put the meal that she had cooked herself before him. Then she, while he was eating, stood immobile in one place at a distance, adhering

to the discipline of a slave, demonstrating in all her actions the modesty appropriate to a serving girl, the humility of a servant. She mixed his drink and brought it to him. 6. When the meal was finished, she collected the fragments and crumbs of the bread that remained, faithfully preferring those leftover crumbs to imperial banquets.

"Blessed woman, who deserves to be compared in terms of her great piety to that queen who came from the ends of the earth to listen to Solomon[16]—if in fact we are to follow simple history. 7. But the faiths of the two queens should be compared, assuming that I may be allowed to suggest a distinction in the greatness of what is a mystery: the first queen wanted to listen to a wise man; the second was not content to hear wisdom—she deserved to serve wisdom."

CHAPTER 7

A discussion of whether the story of Martin and the queen provides a precedent for clerics dining with women

1. After these words, Postumianus said, "For some time, while listening to you speaking, I have been admiring the queen's faith deeply. But what is the source of the story that claims that no woman was allowed to stand near Martin? 2. Look, this queen not only stood near him but she even served him, and I am afraid that those men who mingle with women might employ this story as something of a precedent for their conduct."

3. Then Gallus said, "What? Do you not know that rhetors customarily teach the place, the time, and the person? Place before your eyes the man caught in the palace, hemmed in by the prayers of the emperor, coerced by the faith of the queen, limited in action by the necessity of the moment,[17] compelled to act in order to free those locked up in prison, bring back those sent into exile, and restore goods that had been confiscated. Do you believe that all these factors should have been deemed important enough for the bishop to relax his customary rigor for a short time in order to secure them?

4. "You believe that some will use this precedent badly, but men will be fortunate if they do not depart from the teaching contained in this example. For they should perceive the fundamental facts: it only happened once in his life; he was already a septuagenarian;[18] she was

not an unattached widow or a frisky virgin, but rather a woman living under a husband, and her husband had requested this from Martin as well; she was a queen who served and waited on Martin as he ate and who did not take her place with the dinner guest, nor dare to partake of the meal, but simply offered her service.

5. "So learn from this teaching: let a married woman serve you, but do not let her command you; and she should serve rather than recline at the table. In this manner Martha served the Lord, but she was not admitted to the meal; in fact, Mary,[19] who chose to hear the word, was preferred to the one who served the meal. In the case of Martin, this queen accomplished both ends: as Martha, she served, and as Mary, she listened. 6. Thus, anyone who would like to use this example should ensure they grasp all the details. Let the cause and person be the same, let the service and meal be the same, and let it happen only once in a person's life."

Chapter 8

The Gallic priests are guilty of intermixing with women;
the monks and virgins of Gaul hate Sulpicius;
straw collected from Martin's bed heals a demoniac

1. "Excellent," said Postumianus. "Your speech prevents those among us from going beyond the precedent set by Martin. But I confess to you that these ideas will be heard by deaf ears. 2. For if we were to adopt Martin's ways, we would never have to plead cases involving kissing, and we would be free from all the reproaches of unfavorable opinion. But, as you are accustomed to say when you denounce gluttony, 'We are Gauls';[20] thus we in this region will never be corrected by the example of Martin or through your arguments. 3. Nevertheless, as these things were being discussed by us for such a long time, I have been wondering: why are you remaining so stubbornly silent, Sulpicius?"

"In fact," I said, "I am not only silent, but once I resolved to keep silent about these matters. For once I had to rebuke a certain unstable, flashy, extravagant widow who was living a licentious life. I also had to deal, in the same manner, with a virgin who was clinging indecently to the body of a teenage boy. This boy was dear to me, and I heard that she was speaking publicly about her love for him—although complaining about others who were doing the same things. After this, a great hatred of me was stirred up among all the women and the monks, with the result that both armies have taken the field, sworn to wage war against me.

4. "Because of this I ask you to keep quiet, so that what you are saying will not be reported and increase the hatred toward me. But let us put aside all of these thoughts of them and return to Martin. 5. You, Gallus, as you have undertaken, continue the work you have begun."

Then he said, "Indeed, I have already told you about such great works that my discourse ought to have satisfied your desires. But because I am not permitted to refuse to humor your wishes, I will speak as long as the day remains. 6. For actually, since I see that straw is being prepared for our beds, a story comes to mind, about straw in which Martin lay, that produced an act of power. 7. This is what happened: the village of Clion is on the border between Bourges and Tours; the church there is well-known for the devotion of its saints and made no less glorious by its multitude of holy virgins. And so, Martin, when passing through, had a room in a private place in the church.

8. "After he left the village, all the virgins rushed into that private room. They touched the individual places where the blessed man had either sat or stood; even the straw in which he had lain was divided among them. 9. One of these virgins, a few days later, suspended a portion of the straw[21] that she had collected for herself as a blessing around the neck of a possessed man who was being tormented by a spirit of error. Without any delay, no sooner said than done, the demon was expelled and the person was cured."

CHAPTER 9

Martin heals a demon-possessed cow;
Martin saves a rabbit from the dogs

1. "At around the same time, a cow that was stirred up by a demon met Martin as he was returning from Trier. This cow had abandoned its own herd and was moving among humans; it had gored many people with its dangerous horns. When the animal approached

us, those who were following it at a distance began to warn us in a loud voice to be on our guard. 2. When the frenzied cow came closer to us with a grim light in her eyes, Martin met her with a raised hand and ordered the cow to stop. Immediately, the cow responded to his command and stood frozen.

3. "Meanwhile, Martin saw the demon sitting on top of the cow's back, and he rebuked it, saying, 'Leave this cow, polluted one. Stop bothering this harmless animal.' The bad spirit complied and departed. 4. The cow did not lack perception, and it knew that it had been liberated. Peace had been restored to the animal, and she prostrated herself before the feet of the holy man. Then, ordered by Martin, she returned to her own herd and blended in, more placidly than a sheep, with the other cows of the herd.

5. "This happened around the same time as when he had been placed in the middle of the flames and did not feel the fire. I do not think it is necessary to tell this story since Sulpicius, although omitting it from his book, nevertheless revealed it later in a letter to Eusebius, who, then a priest, has now become a bishop.[22] I believe that you, Postumianus, have read this letter, or if you do not know it, whenever it pleases you, you may readily procure a copy from this chest. I shall relate those things that Sulpicius left out.

6. "At a certain time, when he was visiting his dioceses, we ran into a band of hunters. Their dogs were following a rabbit. By that time, the little animal was exhausted by the long course. Finding no hiding place anywhere in the open fields, it was on the point of being caught, although it was deferring death by repeated swerves. The blessed man, his pious mind feeling pity for the rabbit's peril, ordered the dogs to stop chasing and allow the rabbit to slip away. The dogs were frozen at the first word of his command. You would have believed that they were bound, or rather tethered, and frozen in their own footprints. Thus the little rabbit safely evaded its restrained persecutors."

CHAPTER 10

Martin's notable spiritual sayings

1. "Nevertheless, it is also worthwhile to recount some of his familiar sayings that are spiritually salted. 2. When he had seen a sheep

that had been recently sheared, he said, 'This animal has fulfilled the command of the Gospel: she had two tunics; she has generously given one of them to the person who has none. You also should do this.'

3. "Likewise, when he saw a swineherd, cold and nearly naked in a skin garment, he said, 'Look! Adam, having been ejected from paradise, is feeding hogs in a skin garment; but let us, having set aside the old garment that remains on this man, choose to put on the new Adam instead.'

4. "In another place, cows had eaten part of the meadow grass, and pigs also had rooted around some; the remaining part of the grass that survived unharmed was blossoming, as if it had been painted with a variety of flowers. Martin said, 'That part that has been given to cattle for food offers an example of marriage: even if it has not completely lost the loveliness of the grasses, nevertheless it does not possess the full excellence of the flowers. But that part that a filthy herd of pigs has despoiled represents foul fornication; as for the rest, that portion that has felt no injury represents the glory of virginity: it flourishes rich in grasses, the fruit of hay abounds in it, and, decked with flowers beyond all beauty, it glows as if decorated with sparkling jewels. Blessed is this beauty and worthy of God! Nothing is to be compared to virginity. 5. There is also wrath stored up for those who compare marriage to fornication, and thus make a terrible mistake. Moreover, those who think marriage and virginity are equivalent states are thoroughly wretched and fools.[23] 6. But this distinction must be held by the wise: marriage belongs among the acts that may be forgiven, virginity tends toward glory, and fornication is assigned to punishment, unless it is atoned for by making amends.'"

Chapter 11

Martin counsels a monk
who wants to live with his wife

1. "A certain soldier had rejected his military vocation in a church and taken the vows of a monk. He had erected a cell for himself in a remote spot, at a distance from the church, so that he might live as a hermit. Meanwhile, the cunning enemy was stirring up his

animal instinct with various thoughts, with the result that, having
changed his mind, he decided that he wanted his wife, whom Martin
had taken into his convent of young women, to live with him.

2. "The resolute hermit came to Martin and confessed what he
had in mind. But Martin strongly forbade that a woman should be
joined in this inappropriate manner to a man who was now a monk,
not a husband. Then the soldier insisted, affirming that there would
be nothing harmful in this proposal, that he only wanted the comfort
of his spouse, and furthermore, there should be no fear that they
would turn and revert to their former way of life; he was a soldier of
Christ, and she also had been sworn in by the same military oaths; the
bishop should allow them to fight side by side as holy people, since
the strength of their faith allowed them to pay no attention to their
gender. 3. Then Martin said (and I will give you his exact words), 'Tell
me: Were you ever in a battle? Did you ever stand in a battle line?'

"That soldier responded, saying, 'I have often stood in a battle
line, and was often in a battle.'

4. "At these words, Martin said, 'Then tell me: In that battle line,
in which arms were prepared to go into battle, or were already fighting against a hostile army with the foot soldiers engaged in hand-to-
hand combat, their swords unsheathed, did you ever see a woman
standing there or fighting?'

5. "Then the confused soldier finally blushed in shame, and gave
thanks that he had not been given permission to indulge his error, but
had been corrected—not with a harsh scolding of words, but rather
through a true and reasonable comparison that made sense to a military person.

6. "Then Martin, turning to us as he often did when crowds of
brothers had surrounded him, said, 'A woman should not go to the
men's camp; the battle line of the army should stand apart. Let the
woman, spending time in her own tent, be kept far away, at a distance,
for it produces a contemptible army if crowds of women are allowed
to mix with the cohorts of men. 7. Soldiers belong in the battle line,
soldiers are to fight in the field; a woman ought to be confined
behind defensive walls. She has her own glory if she will guard her
chastity in the absence of her man, and the first sign of this, as well as
the completed victory, is to avoid being seen.'"

CHAPTER 12

The virgin who refused to receive Martin

1. "But I believe that you, Sulpicius, remember that story by which we were touched; it was when you also were present in person, and he praised that virgin who had completely removed herself from the sight of all men, to such an extent that she would not even admit Martin himself into her presence when he wanted to visit her on official business. 2. For when he was passing near the plot of land on which the chaste woman had confined herself many years earlier, since he had heard of her faith and virtue, he turned aside so that, as a bishop, he could honor out of religious duty a woman of such illustrious merit.

3. "We who were following believed that virgin would be glad that she would have as a testimony to her own virtue the fact that a priest of such a well-known name, with his own rigorous rule set aside, had come to her. 4. But she would not relax those chains of her most formidable discipline, not even to see Martin. Consequently, the blessed man, after receiving her laudable excuse from another woman, departed joyfully from her doors, which had not been opened to allow him to see and greet her.

5. "O glorious virgin who did not allow herself to be seen, even by Martin! O blessed Martin, who did not take her rejection as an insult to himself, but rather, he made much of her virtue through his delight, and he was rejoicing at the example that was uncommon at least in these regions. 6. When the approaching night forced us to stop not far from her little farm, that same virgin sent a gift to the blessed man; Martin did what he had not done before, for he never accepted any gift, never took any money. Nevertheless, he refused nothing from those things that the venerable virgin had sent, saying that the blessing of a woman who was to be preferred to many priests should certainly not be refused by a priest.

7. "I hope that the virgins hear of this example, so that they also might close their doors—even to the good—if they want to resist evil. In order to prevent the wicked from accessing them freely, they should not fear to exclude even priests. 8. Let the entire world hear of this: the virgin who did not allow Martin to see her! It was not just that she drove some common priest away from herself, but this girl

would not even allow herself to be seen by this man who brought salvation to those who saw him. 9. Moreover, what priest would not have counted this as an insult to himself, except for Martin? What feelings, what great anger, would he have conceived against that holy virgin? He would have judged her a heretic and would have ordered that she should be anathematized.

10. "For in fact, he would have preferred to that one blessed spirit those virgins who everywhere scurry around in crowds and show themselves, face-to-face, to priests. He would have preferred those who arrange lavish meals, those who recline at the table alongside him.[24] 11. But where is my speech taking me? This freer manner of speaking ought to be curbed a little, lest it run into giving offense to others. For words of correction will be of no use to the faithless, but this example will satisfy the faithful. I, consequently, will praise the virtue of that virgin, without taking anything away from those who often came to see Martin from distant regions, since in fact angels, from the same impulse, also frequently visited that blessed man."

CHAPTER 13

Martin converses with heavenly visitors; he speaks with an angel about the results of a synod

1. "For the rest of what I will tell you"—here he looked at me—"Sulpicius, I call you as a witness for this. On a certain day, this man Sulpicius and I were standing guard outside Martin's doors; already we had been sitting there for several hours in silence, in great awe and trembling, as if we had been commanded to serve as sentries before the tent of an angel, although Martin did not know that we were there, as the door of his cell was closed. 2. While we waited, we heard the murmur of conversation; we were enveloped with a certain sense of awe and bewilderment, and we were certainly aware that some divine event had taken place.

3. "Martin came out to us after nearly two hours. Then that Sulpicius (as there was no one who spoke more familiarly in his presence) began to plead that he should indicate to such pious seekers[25] what that thing of divine awe had been that we admitted we both had felt, or with what beings he had been speaking in his cell: for clearly

we had both heard the low sound of almost unintelligible conversation through the doors. 4. Then Martin hesitated for a time, but there was nothing that Sulpicius could not get out of him, even against his will. Perhaps what I am about to say may seem very incredible, but with Christ as my witness, I am not making it up, unless someone is so sacrilegious that they would believe that Martin had told a lie.

5. "'I will tell you,' he said, 'but I ask you to tell no one else: Agnes, Thecla, and Mary[26] were with me.' Then he told us about the appearance and dress of each. 6. And he confessed to us that they frequently visited him, not just on that day. Nor did he deny that he often saw Peter and also Paul, the apostles. He was also rebuking the demons, whenever any came to him, with their own names. He was suffering greatly from troublesome Mercury, and he said that Jupiter was brutish and stupid.[27]

7. "These things will seem incredible even to those who were living in that same monastery,[28] nor do I have confidence that all who hear these things will believe. For unless Martin had led this inestimable life and displayed such power, he would not be regarded as so glorious among us. Nevertheless, it would not be at all surprising if weak humans doubted the works of Martin, when we see many today who do not even believe the Gospels.[29] But Martin often saw angels face-to-face, and we sensed and experienced it.

8. "I will speak about a matter that is very small, but nevertheless, I will tell it. A synod of bishops was held near Nîmes, to which, in fact, he had refused to go. Nevertheless, he wanted to know what had been done there. By chance, this Sulpicius was sailing with him, but as always, Martin was staying in an area of the ship that was apart from the others. There, an angel announced to him what had happened at the synod. Later, we carefully inquired about the time the council had been held, and learned for certain that it had been convened on the same day, and the decrees that had been issued there were those that the angel announced to Martin."

CHAPTER 14

Prophecy about the return of the antichrist and Nero

1. "Moreover, when we were asking him about the end of the age, he told us that Nero and the antichrist must come first; Nero

would rule in the western area after subduing the ten kings, and he would initiate a persecution so severe that it would force the people to worship the pagan idols. 2. But the rule of the East would first be seized by the antichrist, who would have his throne and the center of his rule in Jerusalem; he would rebuild the city and the temple.

3. "In the future persecution of the antichrist, people would be compelled to deny that Christ is God and to affirm, rather, that he, the antichrist, is Christ; and he would order that all men be circumcised in accordance with the law. Then the antichrist would destroy Nero, and the entire world and all of the nations would be subdued under his power, until the impious one is overthrown by the return of Christ.

4. "There should not be any doubt that the antichrist, conceived by the spirit of evil, had already been born and, already a young man, was waiting to assume power at the appropriate age. Eight years have passed since we heard these things from Martin. Judge for yourself how close we are now to those things that are feared for the future."

5. Gallus was in the middle of speaking these words, and he hadn't had time to explain what they meant, when a house servant entered and announced that the priest Refrigerius was standing at our doors. 6. We began to doubt whether it was better to continue to listen to Gallus or to hurry out to greet that best of men who was visiting us on official business.

7. Then Gallus said, "Even if our discussion had not been interrupted by the arrival of this most holy priest, night itself compels us to end my speech at this point.[30] 8. But because I have not, by any stretch of the imagination, told you everything that could be said about the virtues of Martin, let these things that you have heard today suffice. We will speak about his remaining deeds tomorrow." Thus, having received this promise from Gallus, we got up together.

BOOK III

CHAPTER 1

The discussion resumes; a number of prestigious visitors arrive;
the common people are turned away

1. "The day is dawning, Gallus—time for you to get up. For, as you see, Postumianus is here, as is the priest who missed the lecture yesterday, and he is waiting for you to unfold, as you promised, the stories about Martin that you put off for today. 2. For he, in fact, is aware of everything that must be mentioned, but knowledge is sweet and pleasing even to one who is going back over what he knows. In fact, it was established by nature that anyone who knows that his knowledge, certified by the testimony of many people,[1] is not uncertain will rejoice in what he knows.

3. "For this man also, a follower of Martin from his youth, knows many stories indeed, but he will gladly hear again these stories that he knows. For I admit to you, Gallus, I have often heard about the virtues of Martin, obviously because I have entrusted many stories about him to my literary works; but through my admiration for his deeds, these stories that center on him are always new for me, even though I have heard them many times. I am very happy that Refrigerius has been added to your audience, since through him, Postumianus, who is in a hurry to carry these stories to the East, will more readily be able to accept the truth certified by you, like witnesses in a court of law."

4. While I was saying this, and as Gallus was ready to begin speaking, a crowd of monks rushed in: the priest Evagrius, Aper, Sabbatius, and Agricola; and not far behind them entered the priest Aetherius with the deacon Calupion and the subdeacon Amator; finally the priest Aurelius,[2] a man who was most dear to me and had come the farthest, rushed in, out of breath.

5. "What brings you," I said, "so suddenly and unexpectedly, and from such diverse places, to gather here so early?"

"We," they said, "learned that yesterday Gallus had told stories about the virtues of Martin for the entire day, and that he had left the remaining stories for the next day only because night had stopped him. Therefore we hastened here as a group to join the audience for a speech about so great a topic."

6. Next, it was reported that many laypeople were standing outside the doors. They did not dare enter, but were requesting that they be admitted as well. Then Aper said, "By no means should they be allowed to enter and mix with us, because they come to hear more from curiosity than from religious sentiment."

7. I was upset on behalf of the people who were not to be admitted, but I did manage, with difficulty, to arrange it so that the former deputy of the praetorian prefect, Eucherius, and that man of consular rank, Celsus, were admitted; the rest of the people were turned away. Then, we placed Gallus on a chair in the middle of the audience. 8. He, after maintaining silence for a short period out of his well-known modesty, finally began to speak:

CHAPTER 2

Martin heals a mute girl

1. "You have come," he said, "you holy and learned men, in order to listen to me; but I imagine that you have brought ears that are more religious than learned, to hear me as a faithful witness, rather than as a speaker of rich oratory.[3] Nor will I repeat those stories that were told yesterday; those who did not hear them will discover them from the transcripts.[4] 2. Postumianus expects new stories that he will tell in the East, so they will not prefer themselves over the West in comparison with Martin. The first thing that I am anxious to tell is a story that Refrigerius whispered in my ear.

3. "This happened in the city of Chartres. A certain father began to offer his twelve-year-old daughter, mute from the time of birth, to Martin, asking that the blessed man use the merits of his holiness to untie her bound tongue. 4. In deference to the Bishops Valentinus and Victricius, who were then walking on either side of him, Martin declared that he was unequal to so great a task, but nothing was impossible for the bishops, as they were even more saintly.[5]

5. "But the bishops, in a tone of supplication, joined their pious prayers together with the father in order to beg Martin to accomplish what was hoped. Hesitating no longer—for he was distinguished by both his demonstration of humility and his reluctance to rebuff piety—he ordered the multitude of people who were standing around

to be removed; only the bishops and the father were allowed to remain. He then stretched himself out in prayer, as was his custom. 6. Next, he blessed a bit of oil with the formula for exorcism, and then he poured the sanctified fluid into the mouth of the girl while he held her tongue with his fingers.[6] 7. The result did not disappoint the holy man: he asked the name of her father and she quickly responded. The father cried out with both rejoicing and tears and seized Martin's knees. Then he announced to all the astounded men standing around that this was the first time he had heard the voice of his daughter. 8. If, perhaps, this seems too incredible to anyone, Evagrius, who is present, will offer testimony that this is a true story, for he was there when the deed was done."

CHAPTER 3

Avitianus's wife and the overflowing vase of oil;
Sulpicius's jar of oil preserved through a miracle;
a barking dog silenced in Martin's name

1. "There is a story that I learned recently from Arpagius, the priest, who told me; it is a small matter, but I don't think it should be passed over. 2. The wife of count Avitianus[7] sent oil to Martin so that he would bless it, as is the custom, because it was useful in various cases of sickness. The glass bottle was the type that is round at the bottom with a long neck. The hollow of the protruding neck was not filled, because small bottles are customarily filled so as to leave the upper end free for the insertion of a stopper.

3. "The priest testifies that he saw the oil expand under Martin's blessing, so much so that it flowed abundantly over the top and then flowed in different directions;[8] the same oil, while the bottle was being returned to the wife, boiled with power. 4. For in the hands of the boy who carried it, the oil continued to overflow everywhere, with the result that every part of his garment was covered with an abundant shower of liquid. Nevertheless, the woman received a bottle that was full, right up to the lip, so that, as this priest affirms to this day, there was no space to insert a cork at the top of the bottle, as people normally do to preserve things that need to be kept with extra care.

5. "This reminds of another marvel, which happened to this man"—here Gallus looked at me. "He had placed a glass bottle of oil that Martin had blessed in one of his higher windows. A servant carelessly pulled off the cloth that was covering it, not realizing the bottle was there. The bottle fell upon a floor that was paved with marble, and everyone was terrified that the blessing had been lost. The bottle was found to be unharmed, just as if it had fallen upon the softest feathers. 6. This miracle must be attributed less to chance than to the power of Martin, whose blessing could not be destroyed."

"And what about this, which was done by a certain man whose name must be suppressed, because he is present and he has forbidden that he should be revealed, but at that time, Saturninus here was also present. 7. A dog was barking at us in a most annoying manner. 'In the name of Martin,' this man said, 'I order to you be quiet.' The dog became silent; the barking stuck in its throat and you might believe its tongue had been cut out. 8. So it is not enough that Martin himself performed acts of power: believe me that other people too did many things in his name."[9]

Chapter 4

Martin overcomes Avitianus and protects the people of Gaul from his brutality

1. "You were familiar with the extreme barbarity and the cruel ferocity that went beyond all others, of Avitianus, a former count. This man, in an angry spirit, entered the city of Tours, accompanied by lines of chained men[10] who had a miserable appearance; he ordered that various punishments should be prepared to destroy his captives. He arranged for the fearful work to be carried out on the following day; the city was appalled. 2. When Martin discovered this, a little before midnight, he set off alone for the headquarters of that beast. But with everyone asleep in the deep silence of the night, it was impossible to enter through the bolted doors; consequently, he stretched out before those cruel steps.

"Meanwhile, Avitianus, buried in a deep sleep, was struck by an angel who rushed into his chamber. 'The servant of the Lord,' said the angel, 'lies upon your steps and you sleep?'

3. "The man was driven from his bed[11] dismayed by the voice he heard, and summoning his servants, the frightened man announced that Martin was in front of the doors; they must go immediately and open the locks, so that the servant of God would not be injured.

4. "But these men, in accordance with the nature of all servants, barely went out to the top of the stairs, laughing about their master because he had been deceived by a dream. They returned and said that there was no one outside the doors, concluding from their own experience that no one would be able to stay awake at night, nor did they believe a priest lay before a stranger's steps in the chill of that night. Avitianus was easily persuaded, and once again he slipped back into sleep.

"Soon he was struck by a greater power and cried out that Martin was standing before his doors and that, as a result, his body and spirit were allowed no rest. 5. The servants were not quick enough, and he went all the way to the outside stairs. There, just as he had sensed, he discovered Martin. The miserable man was struck hard by the manifestation of such power.

6. "'Why,' he asked, 'have you done this to me, lord? It is unnecessary for you to speak. I know what you desire. Leave immediately, so that the wrath of heaven does not consume me on account of the wrong done to you. Let the punishment I have already suffered be enough. Believe that I have not made the decision lightly about how I should proceed.'

7. "After the holy man left, Avitianus summoned his officials and ordered them to free the prisoners; shortly thereafter, he departed Tours. Thus, with Avitianus put to flight, the city rejoiced and was liberated."

Chapter 5

Witnesses adduced for the story about Avitianus; Sulpicius defends his practice of naming witnesses for each story

1. "These events were revealed after Avitianius told many people; then, recently, the priest Refrigerius, whom you see here, heard the story from Dagridius, a faithful man from the tribunate. Under an

invocation of divine power, Dagridius swore that Avitianius had told him this story."

2. Now I do not want you to be surprised that I am doing today what I did not do yesterday,[12] in joining the names and personalities of the witnesses to each one of these displays of power; if any listener should be incredulous, let him go to these witnesses who are still in the flesh. 3. The disbelief of quite a number of people required this, those who are said to waver about the things we discussed yesterday.[13] And so let them receive these witnesses who are still alive and well, and let them believe these witnesses more, because they have doubts about our reliability. If they are truly unbelievers, then I declare they will not believe even these witnesses.

4. Nevertheless, I marvel that any person who possesses even the slightest sense of religion should want to commit so great a sacrilege by thinking that someone could lie about Martin.[14] 5. Let that suspicion depart from anyone who lives under the rule of God: Martin does not need to be supported by lies. We lay the trustworthiness of our words completely before you, O Christ; we have not spoken of any deeds—nor will we speak of any—other than what we ourselves have seen, or what we have learned from well-known sources, or often from Martin himself.

6. But even if I have adopted a type of dialogue in which the reading is varied to alleviate the boredom of the reader, I still declare, in good conscience, to be producing the truth of history. The disbelief of a certain number of people has compelled me to insert these off-topic comments, not without sadness on my part.

7. Let us return to our discussion as we sat together: in this discussion, when I saw that everyone was listening to me so attentively, I acknowledged that it was appropriate for Aper to have done what he did—refusing to admit unbelievers to our discussion—as he had judged that only those who believed ought to listen.[15]

CHAPTER 6

Martin and the demoniacs

1. "My spirit is exasperated, if you will believe this, and I am driven mad by such grief: Christians do not believe in Martin's powers,

which were acknowledged by demons! 2. Two miles separated the monastery of that blessed man from the city. But whenever he was coming to the church and he stepped over the threshold of his cell, you would have seen, throughout the entire church, the demon possessed beginning to bellow.[16] It was almost as if the judge was arriving and the prisoners were driven by fear of condemnation. Consequently, the wailing of the demons would signal to the clerics that the bishop, who they did not know was coming, was on his way. I saw a man who, when Martin approached, was snatched up into the air, suspended with his arms stretched upwards, so that he did not touch the ground with his feet at all.

3. "When Martin was engaged in the work of exorcising demons, he touched no one with his hands, he scolded no one with speeches—contrary to the flood of words employed by the clerics—but rather, when demon-possessed persons were brought to him, he would order the others to depart, and with the doors bolted, wrapped in sackcloth and sprinkled with ashes, he would pray, stretched out on the floor in the middle of the church.

4. "Then you would have heard the miserable people being tormented in various ways: some were snatched up by their feet into the air, as if they hung from a cloud, although their robes did not hang over their face, so that they were not shamed by having part of their body exposed. Among a different group, you might have seen some who had been shaken—without interrogation—and were confessing their crimes. They were even giving their names without being asked: this one confessed that he was Jupiter, that one Mercury.[17] 5. Finally, you would have seen all the ministers of the devil tormented along with the source himself, so that it must be acknowledged that what was written had been fulfilled in Martin: 'The saints will judge the angels.'"[18]

CHAPTER 7

Martin protects a region from hail;
that protection lapsed with his death

1. "Hail was troubling a certain village near the Seine every year. Compelled by these extreme troubles, the inhabitants asked Martin

for help; a quite trustworthy embassy was sent by the prefect Auspicius. The winds customarily ravaged his fields more seriously than others. 2. Subsequently, after praying in that place, Martin freed the entire region from the oncoming destruction, so that in the twenty years that followed during which he remained in his body, no one endured hail in that area. 3. To ensure that this was attributed to the power of Martin and not to chance, in the same year he died, the land was oppressed again with the returning storms. The world felt the death of that faithful man to such an extent that it mourned the death of one whose life it had justifiably enjoyed.

4. "But if a weaker listener demands witnesses for what I have said, I will produce not one man, but rather many thousands, and I will call upon the entire region around the Seine to testify about the power they have experienced.

5. "And I am sure that you also, priest Refrigerius, remember a conversation that was held among us recently about this event, together with Romulus, the son of the well-known Auspicius. He was telling us about these events as if they were unknown and, when he expressed fear for future harvests because of the ongoing damage, as you yourself saw, he began lamenting to himself that Martin had not been saved for these times."

CHAPTER 8

Martin drives a demon out of Avitianus; a pagan temple is miraculously destroyed in Amboise

1. "But to return to Avitianus, who left unspeakable reminders of his own cruelty in every place and town, leaving only Tours unharmed: even that beast who used to feed on human blood and the deaths of the unfortunate behaved calmly and tranquilly in the presence of that blessed man. 2. I remember a certain day when Martin came to see him. When Martin entered his chamber, he saw an incredibly large demon sitting behind Avitianus's back. Martin blew out (to use a word that is not good Latin, which I must) on this demon from afar, and Avitianius, thinking that Martin was blowing on him, said, 'Why are you doing this to me, holy man?'

"'Not to you,' said Martin, 'but to him, that revolting creature who is lying on your neck.'

3. "The devil stopped and relinquished the bench where it usually sat. It is an established fact that, after that day, Avitianus was milder, either because he understood that he had always done the will of the devil that was sitting beside him, or because the unclean spirit, which Martin sent fleeing from its seat near him, had been stripped of its power to attack him; in any event, the subordinate was ashamed by the demon, and the demon no longer pressured its subordinate.

4. "In the village of Amboise, the old fortress that is now inhabited by crowds of brothers, you know that there was the temple of an idol, constructed on a large scale. With the smoothest stones, the massive structure was built up into turrets, which, rising to a lofty point, was preserving superstition in that place because of the impressiveness of the craftsmanship.

5. "The blessed man had often commanded Marcellus, who had taken the position of priest in the same place, to destroy the temple. Returning after a short amount of time, Martin scolded the priest, asking why that structure devoted to an idol still stood. 6. He offered as his excuse that it would be virtually impossible to tear down such a great structure with a band of soldiers and the power of a multitude of people; so why should Martin so readily believe that it could be attended to by feeble clerics and infirm monks? 7. Then Martin returned to his well-known resources: he remained in prayer throughout the entire night. In the morning, a storm arose that leveled the idol's temple, right down to its foundation. Let Marcellus confirm these words!"

CHAPTER 9

A column falls out of the sky and destroys the base of an idol; a woman's bleeding healed; a serpent driven away

1. "I will present another of his deeds that demonstrates similar power in a similar type of work, a story that is supported by Refrigerius. He was preparing to overthrow a column of great weight that supported an idol, but there was no apparent way to bring this about. Consequently, he resorted to his customary practice of prayer. 2. At that point, the people saw a column of a roughly equal size fall from

the sky, which, having struck the idol, smashed the entire impregnable structure into powder. Naturally, it would not be saying much if he had employed the powers of heaven invisibly, but the powers themselves were seen to serve Martin in a way that was visible to human eyes.

3. "Refrigerius is also a witness for me in the case of a woman who was suffering from a flow of blood; when she touched Martin's robe, following the example of the woman in the Gospels,[19] she was healed at that very moment.

4. "Once, when a serpent was swimming, traversing a stream toward the bank on which we were standing, Martin said, 'In the name of the Lord, I command you to go back.' Quickly the evil beast twisted itself around and crossed back to the opposite shore, as we watched. When all of us regarded this deed with wonder, Martin groaned deeply and said, 'Serpents hear me, but men do not.'"

CHAPTER 10

The miracle of the fish; Arborius's vision

1. "It was his custom to eat fish on the days of Passover, and a little before the dinner hour, he asked whether any was available. 2. Then the deacon Cato, who was concerned with running the monastery and was a skillful fisherman, reported that he had been unable to catch any fish for them that day. Moreover, none of the fisherman who usually sold them fish had brought them any at all."

3. "'Go,' said Martin, 'cast your line, and you will succeed in capturing fish.'[20]

"Our monastery, as Sulpicius has described, is near a stream. We all went out so that, as is natural on holidays, we might watch the fisherman. We were all hoping that his attempts—trying to catch fish through the authority of Martin and for his use—would not be in vain.

4. "At the first cast, the deacon pulled out a giant salmon in his very modest net, and hurrying joyfully to the monastery, no doubt, as the poet said (I do not know whom; I am employing a learned allusion because I am conversing with the learned), 'He carried the captive boar to the admiring Argos.'[21]

5. "Truly this disciple of Christ demonstrated that Christ was working in him through his emulation of the miracles performed by

the Savior, which he produced as an example for his holy monks. Christ, glorifying his holy man in every conceivable situation, was conferring the rewards of his various graces on this one man.

6. "Arborius, from the prefecture, has testified that he saw Martin's hand while offering the sacrifice clothed with the most valuable gems and shining with purple light, and when Martin raised his right arm, he heard the sound the gems made as they rattled against each other."

CHAPTER 11

Martin opposes the bishops
who conspired against Priscillian

1. "I come now to that well-known story that, on account of the times, he always concealed; but he was unable to hide it from us. This story concerns a miracle in which he spoke face-to-face with an angel. 2. Emperor Maximus, who before this time had been reasonably good,[22] was corrupted by the counsel of the priests;[23] after the death of Priscillian, he employed his royal power on behalf of bishop Ithacius, Priscillian's accuser, and others of his party—it is not necessary to name them, in order to prevent anyone from holding it against him for being part of the group responsible for Priscillian's condemnation.[24]

3. "Meanwhile, Martin, compelled to travel to court by the many serious cases of those who were suffering, fell into the very winds themselves of this whole tempest. The bishops, who were in daily communication with Ithacius and had joined in common cause with him, had assembled and were being held in Trier. When it was unexpectedly announced to them that Martin was coming, they were shaken in their spirits and began to grumble and be afraid. 4. For long before, the emperor had ratified their decision and sent tribunes armed with the highest power to the Spanish provinces; they were to search for heretics and deprive those they caught of both life and possessions.[25]

5. "There was no doubt that this storm would also ravage the great crowds of saints, for the tribunes were hardly able to discriminate between the classes of men: the tribune would judge by his eyes

alone, with the result that a man would be deemed a heretic more for his ashen appearance and robe than for the faith he professed.

6. "The bishops knew that these plans would never please Martin, and on top of their bad conscience, their most troublesome concern was that when he arrived, he would refuse to enter into communion with them. There would be no shortage of others who would follow the steadfastness of such a great man, once his authority had been placed before them.

7. "Then they formed a plan with the emperor: imperial representatives would be sent to meet Martin. They would forbid him to come any closer to the city unless he declared that he would be at peace with the bishops who were in session there. Martin cleverly thwarted these officials by stating that he was arriving in the peace of Christ. 8. Later, after entering the city at night, he went to the church, only for the purpose of prayer. The next day, he went to the palace. It would take too long to detail all the requests he brought, but the following were his principal petitions: for Count Narses and Governor Leucadius, as both men had belonged to the group that had supported Gratian;[26] in fact they had been too stubborn in their fervor for Gratian (but this is not the time to explain this), and they had incurred the anger of the victor.

9. "More important was his request that tribunes not be sent to the Spanish provinces with the power of the sword. For Martin's pious concern was that the emperor should free not only Christians, who would be harassed under this pretext, but even the heretics themselves.

10. "But on the first day and then the next, the clever emperor kept Martin in suspense, making it unclear whether he was considering the matter carefully or whether, because submissive to the bishops, he was opposed to the good, or possibly, as many thought then, he was fighting back avarice, since in fact he was greedy for the goods of the condemned. 11. For although endowed with many good qualities, he is said to have subordinated nothing to his avarice except the necessity to maintain his reign. Clearly, with the treasury of the republic exhausted by earlier emperors, he lived always in expectation and ready for civil wars, so that anyone would readily excuse him for having taken any opportunities to strengthen his rule."[27]

CHAPTER 12

Martin and
Emperor Maximus

1. "Meanwhile, Martin had not joined the communion of the bishops, and they hurried in fear to the king, complaining that they had been condemned already. Their position had already been undermined if Martin's authority was arming the stubbornness of Theognitus, who alone had condemned them in a well-publicized sentence; Martin should not have been admitted within the walls; already he had proven to be not only a defender of heretics but their avenger as well; nothing good would come from the death of Priscillian if Martin was allowed to attain revenge for him.

2. "Finally, after they had prostrated themselves with tears and lamentations, they begged the palace to use its power against this one man. The emperor was nearly driven to consign Martin to the fate of the heretics. But he, although he demonstrated that he was clearly subservient to the bishops by giving them far too much support, knew that Martin stood above all mortals in faith, holiness, and virtue. The emperor chose a different path to defeat the holy man.

3. "First, he sent for him and addressed him in coaxing terms: the heretics, he said, had been condemned under the law, by the decision of public trials rather than through persecuting priests;[28] he should not believe that this was a suitable reason to condemn the communion of Ithacius and the others of his party; Theognitus had created the division, more from his hatred than for any good reason, and it was only that man who, in the interim, had separated himself from communion with the bishops; nothing new had been done by those who remained.

"Furthermore, a few days earlier, a synod had decreed that Ithacius was guiltless in this affair. 4. When Martin was little moved by these words, the king's anger flared up, and he quickly took himself out of Martin's sight. Immediately, assassins were sent against the men for whom Martin had interceded."

Chapter 13

Martin is compelled to enter into communion with Ithacius;
Martin flees Trier afterward and meets an angel on the road

1. "When Martin discovered this, he rushed into the palace, even though it was already night. He promised that if he was shown mercy, he would join himself in communion, only let the tribunes who had been sent to destroy the churches in the Spanish provinces be brought back. Without delay, Maximus granted all of his wishes. 2. The next day, the ordination of Felix to the bishopric was prepared; he was certainly a most holy man, and he deserved to have been ordained to his priesthood in a better age. Martin entered into their communion on this day, believing that it was more important to yield for the moment than to disregard the sword that was threatening the necks of the Spaniards.

3. "The bishops struggled mightily with him so that he might attest to the fact that he had joined their communion with his signature, but they were unable to force him to give it. The following day, he fled the city, and when he returned to the road, he was groaning gloomily because he had allowed himself to be mixed up with that guilty communion even for a moment. He sent his companions ahead of him, and then sat down not far from the town that is named Niederanven,[29] where the recesses of the forests extend over a vast solitude. He began mulling over the cause of his grief and what had been done, his thoughts alternately accusing and defending his actions.

4. "Suddenly, an angel appeared next to him and said, 'It is right, Martin, for you to feel compunction, but you were unable to escape this in any other way. Regain your virtue, resume your constancy, or it will be your salvation, not your reputation, that is in danger.'

5. "Consequently, from that time onward, he took great care not to associate with the communion of Ithacius's faction. Moreover, when he was curing certain possessed men more slowly and with less grace than was customary, he wept and acknowledged to us that he perceived a reduction of his power because of the evil of that communion to which he had joined himself for only a brief moment, through necessity rather than for a spiritual reason.[30]

6. "After this event, he lived sixteen years[31] and never attended another synod; he removed himself from all episcopal gatherings."

CHAPTER 14

A demoniac healed; a storm stilled by invoking Martin's name;
Lycontius's household is healed by Martin's prayers;
Martin refuses money from Lycontius; the monk and the stove

1. "But clearly, as we have experienced, he regained the favor that had been diminished at that time, and his reward was multiplied. I saw afterward a demon-possessed man being led to the side door of the monastery itself, and before he could even touch the doorway, he was cured.

"I heard a certain man testifying recently that when he was sailing on the Tyrrhenian sea[32] on that course that would bring him to Rome, the ship was caught in a sudden waterspout and extreme peril threatened the life of all aboard. 2. Then, when a certain businessman from Egypt, who was not yet a Christian, cried out in a loud voice, 'God of Martin, deliver us!'[33] the tempest quickly became calm, and the ship held the desired course across undisturbed, completely tranquil seas.

3. "Lycontius, a former deputy and a man of the faith, experienced an extreme infection that was troubling his household slaves, and when, in an unprecedented example of disaster, sick bodies lay throughout his entire house, he begged for Martin's assistance in a letter. 4. At this time, the blessed man predicted that a healing would be difficult to bring about, for he was sensing in his spirit that that house was being battered by a divine power. Nevertheless, he did not give up, continuing in prayer and fasting for a total of eight days and nights before what he had been asked to pray for was granted.

5. "Soon, Lycontius, having experienced divine blessings, sped to Martin, announcing (and at the same time giving thanks) that his household had been freed from every danger. He offered one hundred pounds of silver, which the blessed man could neither refuse nor accept. 6. Before that mass of silver could touch the threshold of the monastery, Martin decided that it should be used to ransom captives. When some of the brothers suggested to him that a portion of

the silver should be held back to meet the expenses of the monastery (for all were suffering from hunger and many lacked clothing), Martin said, 'We should be fed and clothed by the church, provided that we do not appear to have acquired anything for our own use.'

7. "The great miracles of that man come to mind in this place, which I am more easily able to admire than to speak about. You realize, of course, what I am referring to: many of his feats cannot be explained. There is, for example, this story, which I do not know if it is possible for me to explain exactly what happened. 8. When one of the brothers (you are familiar with his name, but his identity should be concealed so that we do not embarrass a holy man) had discovered an abundance of coal in his stove, he moved his stool near it and, spreading his legs around the fire, he settled down with his groin exposed. Immediately, Martin perceived that something harmful was occurring beneath the holy roof, and he proclaimed in a loud voice, 9. 'Who is defiling our dwelling by baring his groin?' When the brother heard Martin's voice and his conscience recognized that he was the one being scolded, he ran to us immediately, terrified, and confessed his shame, thanks to Martin's power."

CHAPTER 15

Bryce, goaded by demons, abuses Martin

1. "On a certain day, in the same way, while he was walking in the very small space around his hut, he had sat down on that wooden stool that all of you know, and he perceived two demons in those high cliffs that tower over the monastery. They stood together on the cliff and from there, briskly and gleefully, they hurled their voices, filled with encouragement of this kind: 'Come on, Bryce! Come on, Bryce!' I believe that they sensed the miserable man approaching from a distance and were aware of the great anger they had stirred up in his spirit.

2. "Without delay, the frenzied Bryce[34] burst in. There, overflowing with madness, he spewed out a thousand charges against Martin. Martin had scolded him the day before, for Bryce, who had nothing before he had become a priest—clearly because he had been raised in the monastery by Martin himself—was keeping horses and buying

slaves. At that time, many people were denouncing him for buying not only barbarian boys but also girls with pretty faces. 3. Because of all this, the utterly wretched man was stirred up by an insane poison—I believe that he was primarily driven by the goading of those demons—with the result that as he approached Martin, he could barely control his hands. On the other hand, the holy man, with a placid appearance and a tranquil mind, was trying to check the folly of that unfortunate man through his calming words.

4. "But a wicked spirit was overflowing in Bryce, to such an extent that he did not even have his own wits, no matter how impotent, about him. With trembling lips, with an uncertain expression on his face made pale by his rage, he was hurling sinful words, asserting that clearly he, who from his earliest years had lived among the sacred disciplines of the church, was holier than Martin, who had raised and educated him. Martin, he said, was unable to deny that as a young man he had soiled himself with military service, and now that he had grown old, he was filled with empty superstitions and visions of ghosts amid frankly laughable delusions. 5. After Bryce spewed out these insults and many others that were even bitterer and are better left unstated, he departed with his anger finally satiated, as if he had finally vindicated himself and was hurrying back in the direction from which he had come.

"Meanwhile, (and I believe this happened through Martin's prayers), the demons were sent fleeing from Bryce's heart. Once he returned to penitence, he quickly returned and threw himself down before Martin's knees. He begged forgiveness, he acknowledged his error, and he confessed that without the demon [he would not have talked like that, and that][35] he was in a healthier state of mind.

6. "Then the holy man revealed to Bryce and to all of us as well how he had perceived that Bryce had been driven by demons; he himself had not been shaken by the abuse, words that had harmed Bryce more than the one they had been aimed at. 7. Later, when that same Bryce was often accused by many people of great crimes, it was not possible to force Martin to remove him from the priesthood, in case it might seem that he had taken revenge for the injury Bryce had done to him. Frequently, Martin said, 'If Christ endured Judas, why should I not suffer Bryce?'"

Chapter 16

An angry man who should learn from Martin's example of forbearance

1. Postumianus said in response, "Let that man from our neighborhood hear that story. That man who, though he is wise, pays no attention to the present or the future, but should he become slightly offended, he raves, lacking control of himself:[36] he is brutal toward the clerics, he attacks the laity, and he disturbs the entire world with his vengeance. He has pursued this continuously for the past three years, and neither time nor reason has brought him rest. 2. We should pity and grieve over his condition, even if this was the only incurable disease that oppressed him. You should have kept reminding him about those examples of patience and tranquility, Gallus, so that he would learn not to be angry and how to forgive.

3. "If, perhaps, he should become aware of my words spoken against him and interpolated into this discourse, let him know that I have spoken, not with the mouth of an enemy but with the spirit of a friend, because if it was possible, I would wish for people to say that he was more like Bishop Martin than the tyrant Phalaris.[37] 4. But let us move beyond this, the remembrance of which is not very attractive, and return, Gallus, to our Martin."

Chapter 17

Sulpicius concludes the conversation and lays a charge upon Postumianus

1. Then, when I perceived by the declining sun that evening was at hand, I said, "The day departs, Postumianus, and it is time to get up. Moreover, we should provide dinner for such keen listeners. You should not expect that there could be any end to talking about Martin; he transcends anything that could ever be encompassed in a discussion.

2. "Meanwhile, you must carry these stories about that man to the East, and as you return and pass various coasts, places, ports, islands, and cities, spread the name and glory of Martin among the

people. Most importantly, remember not to skip Campania. 3. Even if this detour might take you right off your track, you should count as inconsequential this diversion or even the expense of great delays if you get to visit Paulinus, who is illustrious and praised by the entire world. I ask you to unroll for him, before anyone, the transcript of what we accomplished yesterday and what we said today. 4. Tell him all the stories, recite everything to him, so that through him, Rome will learn about the holy glory of Martin just as with our first book, which Paulinus spread not just through Italy but throughout all of Illyricum as well. 5. Paulinus is not jealous of Martin's glory. Rather, he most dutifully honors the glorious and holy powers in Christ, so that he does not refuse to compare our Martin's religious preeminence even to his own Saint Felix.[38]

"From Campania, if perhaps you should cross the sea to Africa, carry what you have heard to Carthage, even though, as you have already said, that city knows Martin. Nevertheless, now let it learn more about him so that they will not admire only Cyprian, their martyr, in that city, although he did consecrate the place with his holy blood.

6. "Then if, heading north a little, you enter the left side of Achaia, let Corinth understand, let the Athenians know that Plato was not wiser in his Academy nor was Socrates braver in his prison. Greece is blessed indeed as it deserved to hear the preaching of the apostles, but the Gallic regions have by no means been abandoned by Christ, since he gave them the gift of Martin. 7. When you reach Egypt, although that place takes pride in the number and virtue of its holy men, remember that Egypt should not disdain to hear how, in Martin alone, Europe concedes nothing to them, or even to all of Asia."[39]

Chapter 18

Sulpicius asks Postumianus to visit the grave of Pomponius

1. "But when you leave there for Jerusalem, placing your sails before the winds again, I inflict our mournful business on you: if you ever come near the coast of the illustrious Ptolemais,[40] make careful inquiries about where the tomb of our brother Pomponius[41] may be found, and do not disdain to visit his bones that are interred in foreign

soil. 2. Shed many tears in that place, as much from your own disposition as from our inmost feelings, and although an empty gift, sprinkle his grave with purple flowers and sweet-smelling herbs. At the same time, forgive his having been deceived and feel pity for his flight. Say that the Lord has been placated on his behalf, and pray for an indulgent judgment for him, exposed as he was to such great errors. Say to him, however—not harshly though, not bitterly, but rather address him with compassion and not reproaching him with a list of charges— 3. that if he had ever chosen to listen to you once, or to me constantly, and if he had elected to emulate Martin rather than that man whom I do not want to name,[42] then he never would have separated from me so cruelly, been covered with the unfamiliar sand of North Africa, and suffered the death of a shipwrecked pirate in the middle of the sea, with the result that his body barely achieved burial ashore.

4. "Let them see this as his own work, those who wanted to harm me in order to gain vengeance for him; let them see their glorious achievement and, even now, let them abandon their attacks against us, for they have had their punishment."

5. I groaned over these words with a very tearful voice, and tears were generated in all the listeners by these laments. We departed with great admiration for Martin, of course, but the grief produced by our weeping was no less.

NOTES

INTRODUCTION

1. P.-Nol. *Ep.* 5.4; Clare Stancliffe, *St. Martin and His Hagiographer* (Oxford: Oxford University Press, 1983), 15, suggests AD 355.

2. Paulinus noted that Sulpicius's father had cut him out of his inheritance when Sulpicius renounced the world and became an ascetic (P.-Nol. *Ep.* 5.6).

3. Gennadius asserted that Sulpicius was distinguished in his birth (Gennad. *Vir.* 19), but Paulinus also mentioned that Sulpicius's inheritance was less of a burden than his own (P.-Nol. *Ep.* 5.5).

4. Gennad. *Vir.* 19. Gennadius also asserted that Paulinus of Nola had a sister, and that he had written her many letters and a treatise on the contempt of the world; one wonders if Gennadius has mixed the two men up (Gennad. *Vir.* 49).

5. P.-Nol. *Ep.* 1.1. For the date and translation of this letter, see Peter Walsh, *Letters of St. Paulinus of Nola*, vol. 1 (New York: Newman Press, 1966), 211.

6. Ibid., 5.6 (trans. Walsh).

7. Ibid., 5.4.

8. See Catherine Conybeare, *The Irrational Augustine* (New York: Oxford University Press, 2006), 20, for a discussion of Augustine's *otium ruris*, which served as a backdrop for the production of his first literary work.

9. See Cassian *Inst.* 1.2.2 and the discussion at Richard Goodrich, *Contextualising Cassian: Aristocrats, Asceticism, and Reformation in Fifth Century Gaul* (Oxford: Oxford University Press, 2007), 117–150.

10. A short list of similarities includes the assertion that both Hilarion and Martin were born to pagan parents (Hier. *Vit. Hil.* 2, Sulp.-Sev. *Mart.* 2.1). Both boys aimed at divine service from their youth. Hilarion took no pleasure from secular shows, but rather, his whole pleasure came from the assemblies of the church (Hier. *Vit. Hil.* 2); Martin was always thinking carefully about either the monasteries or the church (Sulp.-Sev. *Mart.* 2.4). Hilarion heard about Antony and set off into the desert to see him (Hier. *Vit. Hil.* 3); Martin

251

longed for the desert, but since he was only twelve, he was too young to go (Sulp.-Sev. *Mart.* 2.4). When Hilarion was eighteen, a band of robbers searched for him to steal his possessions or scare him. They could not find him until the morning, and when they did, they asked him what he would do if he encountered robbers. He replied that he did not fear robbers because he was not afraid to die (Hier. *Vit. Hil.* 12); Martin, traveling back to his home-land to preach the gospel to his parents, also encountered a band of robbers. Captured and asked if he was afraid, Martin replied that he had never felt so safe because he knew the mercy of God would protect him in times of trial. He then preached the gospel to the robber and converted him (Sulp.-Sev. *Mart.* 5.4–6). Finally, both Jerome and Sulpicius brought up the great Homer in their works; Jerome claimed that Homer would envy him his theme or prove unequal to it (Hier. *Vit. Hil.* 1), and Sulpicius asserted that Homer would be unable to document all of Martin's superior qualities (Sulp.-Sev. *Mart.* 26.3).

11. P.-Nol. *Ep.* 11.11 (trans. Walsh).

12. Following the argument of Clare Stancliffe, *St. Martin,* 71–72. Martin died in November 397, and in the dream/vision Sulpicius reported in his *Epistle* II, Saint Martin appeared, holding a copy of the *Life* in his hands. This means that the book had been completed before Martin's death, and indeed, had he died before its release, it would have been very odd for Sulpicius not to have mentioned it. Another piece of evidence is found in Paulinus's letters: his *Epistle* V, written in the summer of 396, did not mention the book, but *Epistle* XI, written in spring 397, does (P.-Nol. *Ep.* 11.11). This means that Sulpicius must have sent the book to Paulinus in the fall of 396.

13. See discussion at Stancliffe, *St. Martin,* 98–101.

14. For a treatment of this subject, see J. Scourfield, *Consoling Heliodorus: A Commentary on Jerome, Letter 60* (Oxford: Clarendon Press, 1993), passim.

15. For the dating of this letter, see Peter Walsh, *Letters of St. Paulinus of Nola,* vol. 2 (New York: Newman Press, 1967), 321.

16. P.-Nol. *Ep.* 28.5 (trans. Walsh).

17. For dating, see Walsh, *Letters of Paulinus,* 2: 327.

18. See discussion at Stancliffe, *St. Martin,* 80.

19. See the discussion at G. K. Van Andel, *The Concept of History in the Chronicle of Sulpicius Severus* (Amsterdam: Adolf M. Hakkert, 1976), 61–69.

20. See ibid., 69–83.

21. See ibid., 72.

22. See ibid., 77–79, for a list of Sulpicius's emphases when treating these men. The notion that rule by a monarch was an undesirable form of government was a commonplace in Greek and Roman political theory and was also expressed by Sulpicius at Sulp.-Sev. *Chron.* 1.31.1.

23. For a discussion of Sulpicius's apocalyptic theme in the *Chronicles*, see Van Andel, *Concept of History*, 117–138.

24. See discussion at ibid., 132–135.

25. See ibid., 135–138.

26. See discussion of dating at Stancliffe, *St. Martin*, 81.

27. Hier. *Ezech.* 11.36.1/15.

28. Greg.-T. *Hist.* 2.9; see discussion, John Drinkwater, "The Usurpers Constantine III (407–411) and Jovinus (411–413)," *Britannia* 29 (1998): 288.

THE LIFE OF SAINT MARTIN

1. Clare Stancliffe, *St. Martin and His Hagiographer* (Oxford: Oxford University Press, 1983), 50, has suggested that this Desiderius served as a link between Sulpicius, Paulinus of Nola, and Jerome. A friend and fellow monk with Sulpicius, he may also have been the recipient of a letter from Paulinus of Nola (P.-Nol. *Ep.* 43), and the man who, with Riparius, stirred Jerome to write against Vigilantius (Hier. *Vigil.* 3). A preface was often used to secure the patronage of the wealthy and more powerful, men who could support a budding author's career (see Catherine Conybeare, *The Irrational Augustine* [New York: Oxford University Press, 2006], 14–20, for a discussion of Augustine's use of dedications in his preface to attract the interest of a patron). The fact that Sulpicius only mentions Desiderius once, and names no other potential patrons in his other prefaces, might suggest a financial security that required no outside funding.

2. This preface is entirely conventional. See Tore Janson, *Latin Prose Prefaces: Studies in Literary Conventions* (Stockholm: Almquist and Wiksell, 1964), 134–138, for a discussion of these elements, as well as the page numbers placed in parentheses. This chapter includes such stock elements as the reluctance to allow anyone to see a written work and that the dedicatee should be the only reader (148); a plea that the author lacks stylistic ability because of both a lack of training and the length of time that has passed since he was taught (130–133); the assertion that a reader (Desiderius) has over-ridden Sulpicius's hesitation and compelled him to release the work (117–120); and the hope that future readers will judge the work on content rather than presentation (133–134), coupled with a reminder that God used rustic fishermen rather than orators to spread his message (128–129).

3. Sulpicius's preface enters into a dialogue with Sallust's *Catiline Conspiracy*. See discussion at Stancliffe, *St. Martin*, 73–74; Jacques Fontaine, *Sulpice Sévère: Vie de Saint Martin. Tome II: Commentaire* (Paris: Les Éditions du Cerf, 1968), 393–422; and in the following notes.

4. Contradicting Sal. *Cat.* 1; Sallust had argued that bodily strength was transitory, but what could be achieved through the intellect (writing history)

was everlasting. Sulpicius approaches this from a Christian perspective that sees all human accomplishment as transitory; only God is eternal.

5. One of the primary goals of the ancient historians was to offer *exempla*, positive and negative examples of human actions from the past that would assist readers to make the best choices in their own lives. Sulpicius, by proffering Martin as a pattern of virtue (see introduction), follows this model.

6. Sulpicius draws on some common New Testament themes: true wisdom (1 Cor 2:6–7), service as a soldier for Christ (2 Tim 2:3–4), and the call to embrace divine excellence (2 Pet 1:3–4).

7. Another contrast with Sal. *Cat.* 1, in which the historian looked forward to the secular renown he would win for the composition of his work.

8. Sulpicius will repeatedly point to his own sins and shortcomings (see Sulp.-Sev. *Ep.* 2.1–5), but here there is an implied hope that he might make some amends for his sinful life and win favor with God by offering this account. That this might be possible was suggested by Paulinus of Nola, who wrote that the *Life of Martin* was Sulpicius's fleece, a reference to the cloak that Martin had divided to clothe a beggar and ultimately win Jesus' approbation (see 3.2–4; P.-Nol. *Ep.* 11.11; Stancliffe, *St. Martin*, 76).

9. Sulpicius here melds a standard humility trope and a biblical injunction: Martin did all of his work in secret, because he did not desire the praise of men (Matt 6:1). For an example of Martin working in secret, see Sulp.-Sev. *Dial.* 2.1.2–9.

10. Stancliffe, *St. Martin*, 88, suggested that this might be an allusion to Cic. *Orat.* 2.62: no historian should dare to speak anything false. Any discussion of this needs to be considered in light of A. J. Woodman, *Rhetoric in Classical Historiography* (Kent, England: Croom Helm Ltd., 1988), 70–83, who has argued that the truth discussed in this passage might not mean what a modern audience thinks it means.

11. Modern Szombathely, Hungary.

12. Constantius II, one of Constantine's three sons, was emperor 337–361. He is portrayed as a weak emperor, a pawn of the Arian bishops in Sulp.-Sev. *Chron.* 2.36–45.

13. Julian was a cousin of Constantius. He served as Caesar under Constantius 355–360 and was emperor 360–363. He was an opponent of the growing Christian movement and would later be dubbed *the Apostate*.

14. Sulpicius has a significant problem to solve here: Martin spent a considerable portion of his life in the army, and there were many who believed military service disqualified a person from being a saint. An example of this point of view can be found at Sulp.-Sev. *Dial.* 3.15.4, where Bryce claimed he was holier than Martin because Martin had spent his youth in the army. Because of this, it was important for Sulpicius to establish that Martin's tenure as a soldier was not his choice; to the contrary, he was always more interested in the spiritual life, as the rest of this paragraph suggests.

15. Metaphorically speaking; Sulpicius continues to emphasize Martin's unwillingness to be a soldier.

16. An allusion to John 13:1–9, the story in which Christ washes his disciples' feet, with a further allusion to Mark 9:35, where Christ reminds the disciples that whoever wants to be first must be a servant to all.

17. An allusion to Matt 25:35–36. This line artfully foreshadows the next chapter, in which Martin is depicted clothing the naked.

18. In other words, Martin had given away all of his money and possessions to take care of the disadvantaged.

19. This rounds out the analogy begun at 2.8; Sulpicius set the scene with an allusion to Matt 25:31–46, the parable of the sheep and the goats. Now Martin performs the actions that Christ had praised, demonstrating that he was one of Christ's sheep; those who moaned deeply are the equivalent of the goats, those who chose not to care for the less fortunate among them and earn Christ's condemnation (Matt 25:41–46).

20. Matt 25:40.

21. An allusion to 2 Cor 12:1–5.

22. Another suggestion that military life was incompatible with the life of a baptized Christian; see 254n14.

23. The Vangiones were a Germanic tribe; their city is Worms.

24. Stancliffe, *St. Martin*, 63–64, notes that this encounter with Julian has been cast in the form of typical martyrdom accounts. This suggests that Sulpicius had an extensive familiarity with this genre.

25. Martin was discharged in 356 (Stancliffe, *St. Martin*, 22). This creates a chronological problem: if he was twenty years old when he was discharged, how could he be in his seventies when he has dinner with the Emperor Magnus Maximus and his wife (Sulp.-Sev. *Dial.* 2.7.4) in the 380s (Maximus ruled 383–388)? See Stancliffe, *St. Martin*, 119–133, for an examination of the evidence, which ultimately leads her to conclude that the reference to his age in Sulp.-Sev. *Dial.* 2.7.4 should simply be understood to mean that he was old, rather than offering a precise age.

26. Sulpicius cast Bishop Hilary of Poitiers (350–368) as one of the central figures in the western resistance to the Arians in Sulp.-Sev. *Chron.* 2.42–45.

27. There is a chronological problem here: Hilary was sent into exile by the Synod of Beziers (which met June 356), and Martin was not discharged from the army until July or August of 356. Stancliffe, *St. Martin*, 134–137, argues that if Hilary did not immediately go into exile, there might have still been a month when the pair could have been together in Poitiers.

28. A man's resistance to the honor of ordination is entirely conventional, a standard humility trope in ecclesiastical *Lives* (see Paulin. *Vit. Ambr.* 3; Possid. *Vit. Aug.* 4; and the warning that a monk should not be ordained at

Cassian *Inst.* 11.18). Stancliffe, *St. Martin*, 137, suggests that with Hilary headed into exile, Martin may not have wanted to be tied to the church in Poitiers.

29. See Sulp.-Sev. *Dial.* 1.22.2–5, where the desire of a young monk to return to preach the gospel to his family is regarded as a sin and is labeled "a type of false righteousness."

30. A very similar story is found at Hier. *Vit. Hil.* 12.

31. Luke 23:43: "Truly, I say to you, today you will be with me in paradise."

32. Heb 13:6.

33. Martin plays no role in Sulpicius's account of the battle against Arianism found in Sulp.-Sev. *Chron.* 2.35–45.

34. Bishop Auxentius of Milan (355–375) was a supporter of Arianism and the predecessor of Bishop Ambrose. Sulpicius mentions him at one other point, noting that he was selected to fill the See of Milan when the Nicene bishop, Dionysius, was driven into exile (Sulp.-Sev. *Chron.* 2.39.3).

35. Hilary was allowed to return to Poitiers in 360; at Sulp.-Sev. *Chron.* 2.45.2, Sulpicius ascribed this to imperial irritation rather than penitence; Hilary was characterized as a "breeding ground of discord and a disturber of the East."

36. Martin's first monastery was at Ligugé, five miles from Poitiers; see Stancliffe, *St. Martin*, 23, for a description of the excavated site.

37. This story resembles 1 Kgs 17:17–24, in which Elisha restores the widow's son to life.

38. The power of holy prayer to effect a change in a person's eternal destiny after death was also illustrated in *Pass. Perp.* 2.3–4, which recorded the outcome of Perpetua's intercession for her dead brother, Dinocrates.

39. Another account that seems to be based on 1 Kgs 17:17–24, although the ending resembles the restoration of Jairus's daughter (Matt 9:18–25).

40. Martin became the bishop of Tours around 371 (Stancliffe, *St. Martin*, 24).

41. A lack of concern with one's grooming was a badge of sanctity among some monks. Jerome, for instance, suggested that female ascetics should not bathe, as they should not want to see themselves undressed, and a holy squalor would quench the fire of vanity (Hier. *Ep.* 107.11); on the other hand, he does advocate a middle road when it came to clothing, counseling Eustochium to wear a robe that was neither too neat nor too slovenly (Hier. *Ep.* 22.27).

42. Ps 8:2. The Latin word *defensorem* (Defender) was taken as a prophetic allusion to the man who opposed Martin's election.

43. Compare this economy with the behavior censured at Sulp.-Sev. *Dial.* 1.21.3–4: a newly ordained priest will immediately widen the fringes of his robe and order the widows and virgins to weave new clothing for him.

44. Stancliffe, *St. Martin*, 24–29, locates Sulpicius's description of the monastery at Marmoutier in the broader context of eastern asceticism and the attempt by western Romans to integrate the ascetic impulse into their own lives.

45. This statement recalls the idealized, communal model of the early Jerusalem church (Acts 4:32); Cassian claimed that the renunciation of possessions was a core value of eastern monasticism (Cassian *Inst.* 4.3–4).

46. See Hier. *Ep.* 22.33, for Jerome's account of the brother in Nitria who earned money by weaving linen; when he died, the other monks discovered that he had left behind a hundred silver pieces. Uncertain of what to do with this illicit wealth, they elected to bury it with his body, as he had condemned himself by working and hoarding money.

47. See Hier. *Ep.* 22.35.

48. Jerome described a very similar arrangement among the coenobites (Hier. *Ep.* 22.35). The importance of solitary prayer in the cell for eastern monks is exemplified in sayings like *Apophth. Patr.* Moses 6: "Go, sit in your cell, and it will teach you everything!"

49. Jerome advocated daily fasting, followed by a small meal that avoided satiety (Hier. *Ep.* 22.17).

50. Jerome, in his famous letter to Eustochium, advised her to avoid wine, as it tended to inflame lust. The only exception to that would be drinking wine if she was ill, as the apostle had permitted (Hier. *Ep.* 22.8; 1 Tim 5:23).

51. Sulpicius now opens a block of four chapters (12—15) that depict Martin's antipagan activities.

52. Martin mistakenly believed that he was witnessing a lustration, a Roman religious ritual in which the people would circle their fields or lands in a procession and then sacrifice animals within the boundaries that had been marked out to purify the area or win protection from malevolent forces.

53. See Sulp.-Sev. *Dial.* 2.3.6–7, where the mules pulling the cart of the treasury agents (who have brutally beaten Martin) are frozen in one spot.

54. As Stancliffe, *St. Martin*, 364, notes, there is a similar story about Abba Apollos in the *Historia monachorum* (*Hist. mon.* 8.25–29). The *Historia monachorum* was composed after the *Life of Martin*; it is possible that Sulpicius had heard an oral version of a story that was later written down in the *Historia*. In an interesting difference, the pagans in the *Historia* convert to Christianity, whereas they do not seem to alter their religious affiliation here.

55. Martin made the sign of the cross; this sign was also a powerful tool in the hands of the eastern ascetics; see Ath. *Vit. Anton.* 35.

56. This miracle will provoke one of Sulpicius's critics to ask why, if Martin could control fire, he had been scorched in a fire in a church. Sulpicius's *Epistle* I was the response to this skeptic.

57. The traditional weapons of Martin, employed when he encounters opposition that his own power is unable to overcome. See also Sulp.-Sev. *Dial.* 2.5.6.

58. The Aedui were a Gallic people who lived in what would become central France, the region now located between Saône and Loire.

59. John Matthews, *Western Aristocracies and Imperial Court: A.D. 364–425* (Oxford: Clarendon, 1975), 156, argues that Martin forged relationships with Gallic aristocrats like Tetradius to advance his evangelistic agenda. The support of prominent landowners was crucial in the war against rural paganism.

60. In the desert tradition, when a demon was defeated, it often left a foul stench in its wake (see Ath. *Vit. Anton.* 63, and further 24.8).

61. The cure of lepers was a biblical staple; see 2 Kgs 5:1–19; Matt 8:1–4; Luke 17:11–19. Christ had commanded his disciples to heal the sick and cleanse the lepers (Matt 10:8), so this healing miracle serves to locate Martin among the men with apostolic power.

62. This demonstrates that Martin truly was of apostolic stature; see Acts 19:11–12, where handkerchiefs and aprons touched by Paul also effect miraculous cures, and Sulp.-Sev. *Dial.* 2.8.8–9, where straws from the bed Martin had lain upon drive out demons.

63. Arborius was a nephew of the Gallic poet Ausonius. In 380, he was the prefect of Rome (see Matthews, *Western Aristocracies*, 70–71).

64. A form of malaria in which the fevers recur at three-day intervals.

65. Paulinus, bishop of Nola (410–431), was a senatorial aristocrat, a former governor of Campania, and a good friend of Sulpicius. In 395, he and his wife, Therasia, established a shrine to Saint Felix in the Italian town of Nola. He would remain there until his death, writing poetry and corresponding with the major ecclesiastical figures of his day (Jerome, Augustine, Rufinus, and Sulpicius).

66. Magnus Maximus ruled the western half of the Roman Empire 383–388. He had been a general, commanding the armies in Britain, under Emperor Gratian, but had led a revolt and ultimately displaced Gratian. He was responsible for the death of Priscillian and played a major role in Sulpicius's works (see Sulp.-Sev. *Chron.* 2.49–51; Sulp.-Sev. *Dial.* 2.6–7; 3.11–13).

67. The inappropriate conduct of the bishops who seek royal favor is a major theme in all of Sulpicius's works; see p. 11.

68. A possible allusion to Hilar. *Contra Const.* 5–6. See Stancliffe, *St. Martin*, 65–66, for a discussion of Hilary's influence on Sulpicius, especially with regard to his condemnation of bishops who sought imperial patronage; see previous discussion at chapters 16—19 for Sulpicius's association of Martin with the apostles through his miracle stories.

69. Maximus's usurpation had deprived both sons of Valentinian I: his older son, Gratian, had been killed by Maximus's master of horse in August 383; his younger son, Valentinian II, had been allowed to live, but was driven out of Italy in 387.

70. Flavius Euodius was Maximus's praetorian prefect. He held the consulship in 386. He also presided over the trial of Priscillian (Sulp.-Sev. *Chron.* 2.50.2–3).

71. Sulpicius emends this description at Sulp.-Sev. *Chron.* 2.50.2 to "a man both harsh and severe."

72. Maximus invaded Italy in 387. Valentinian II fled to the East to secure help from Emperor Theodosius. Theodosius then led his troops into the West in 388.

73. Maximus was killed in Aquileia on August 28, 388.

74. One of the powers of Satan and the demons is the ability to appear to humans in a variety of forms in order to mislead and deceive them. A monk cultivated discernment in order to gain protection against these forms of deception; failure to do so could be very dangerous (see Cassian *Coll.* 2.5, for the story of an old monk named Heron, who was misled and ultimately killed himself because he lacked discernment). The ability to recognize Satan, no matter what form he took (see also 22.1; 23.9–10) attested to this quality in Martin.

75. See also Sulp.-Sev. *Dial.* 2.13.6; 3.6.4.

76. This claim depends on a view advanced by Origen (Or. *Princ.* 3.6.5–6). Origen had argued that God's mercy was so all-encompassing that in the fullness of time, even Satan and the demons would be restored. Shortly after the *Life of Martin* was released, the controversy over the works of Origen exploded, leaving Sulpicius with a problem: if this sentiment of Origen's was considered heretical, then, by extension, Martin was also a heretic. Sulpicius would address this issue obliquely at Sulp.-Sev. *Dial.* 1.6–7 (see notes there as well as a fuller discussion in Richard Goodrich, "Satan and the Bishops: Origen, *Apokatastasis*, and Ecclesiastical Politics in Sulpicius Severus' *Dialogi*," *Adamantius* 19 (2013): 84–96).

77. Sulpicius makes it quite clear that he is not endorsing the view that Satan might eventually be rehabilitated. In fact, even the attribution of this sentiment to Martin has been qualified—at 22.3, Sulpicius noted that this was a secondhand account: "Some of the brothers used to attest..." The story is too good to leave out, since it shows Martin's fervor for evangelization, but there is an element of plausible deniability built into its presentation.

78. Martin was still alive when this work was finished, which means that Clarus died before him. When Sulpicius recounted his vision of Martin's ascension to heaven (Sulp.-Sev. *Ep.* 2.5), he claimed that he saw Clarus, who had recently died, ascend in Martin's wake.

79. It is not clear whether this is the same Bishop Rufus as the man who convinced Maximus to put Priscillian on trial (Sulp.-Sev. *Chron.* 2.50.2); Henry Chadwick, *Priscillian of Avila: The Occult and Charismatic in the Early Church* (Oxford: Clarendon, 1976), 139n1, thinks they are two different men.

80. John the Baptist; presumably his return would usher in the second coming of Christ.

81. A similar justification is found in P.-Nol. *Ep.* 23.4–5, where Paulinus recounts submitting to the ministrations of Sulpicius's courier, Victor.

82. See 19.3.

83. Jerome made a similar claim about Hilarion in his work (Hier. *Vit. Hil.* 1).

84. A possible reference to Bryce, who became bishop after Martin; see Sulp.-Sev. *Dial.* 3.15.

EPISTLES

1. See Sulp.-Sev. *Mart.* 14.1–2.

2. See Matt 27:42.

3. Acts 28:4.

4. A reference to Jonah, who spent three days in the belly of a fish and then preached to the Assyrians.

5. See 2 Cor 11:23–27.

6. See Sulp.-Sev. *Mart.* 26.1.

7. The idea that God protects his servants in times of trial by sprinkling them with dew in the middle of flames is common in both Sulpicius and other monastic literature (see Sulp.-Sev. *Dial.* 1.18.5; *Hist. mon.* 19.8).

8. The epistle is written to a deacon, Aurelius, who may have been the same Aurelius who joined the audience for the third book of the *Dialogues* (Sulp.-Sev. *Dial.* 3.1.4).

9. Martin died in November 387, which establishes the *terminus ad quem* for the production of the *Life of Saint Martin.*

10. One of Martin's disciples, who figures prominently in the story at Sulp.-Sev. *Mart.* 23.1–10.

11. The presence of servants in Sulpicius's monastery at Primuliacum suggests a very unusual ascetic foundation, at least in comparison to the monasteries of the East; see discussion at Richard Goodrich, "Aristocrats and Slaves: Status in Early Western Monasticism," *Studia Anselmiana* 146 (2009): 153–157.

12. See *Hist. mon.* 19.7–8 for the story of the monk Apollonius who was said to have done this.

13. These details may be found in the apocryphal *Ascension of Isaiah*, 5. Clare Stancliffe, *St. Martin and His Hagiographer* (Oxford: Oxford University Press, 1983), 62, suggests that either Sulpicius was familiar with this work, or that the story was well-known in the fourth century, although as Richard Bernheimer, "The Martyrdom of Isaiah," *The Art Bulletin* 34, no. 1 (1952): 22, noted, Epiphanius and Jerome had condemned the text's teaching about the

Holy Spirit, and as a consequence, it would be rejected in the medieval period.

14. Sulpicius's claim to a special relationship with Martin underpins the defense of his literary legacy in the *Dialogues* (see Sulp.-Sev. *Dial.* 2.13.3).

15. Bassula was Sulpicius's mother-in-law, and as this letter makes clear, even after his wife's death, the two maintained a close relationship.

16. Sulpicius's *Epistle* II to Aurelius (see previous).

17. An allusion to Mark 14:27.

CHRONICLES

Book I

1. Sulpicius used far fewer literary topoi in the preface to *Chronicles* (see the discussion of these conventions at 253n2. The plea that a work had been demanded by its readers, however, is entirely conventional (Tore Janson, *Latin Prose Prefaces: Studies in Literary Conventions* [Stockholm: Almquist and Wiksell, 1964], 116–120).

2. See P.-Nol. *Ep.* 28.5, who stated that Sulpicius had immersed himself in trying to work out a chronology of events by reconciling secular histories with the Bible.

3. Although Cardinal James Ussher (1581–1656) was one of the most famous exponents of the young Earth theory, calculating that the Earth had been created in 4004 BC, he was not the first to attempt to date the earth using the Bible: Cyprian (Cypr. *Ad. Fort.* 2, 11), Lactantius (Lact. *Inst.* 7.14.9), and Jerome (Hier. *Ep.* 51.6; 140.8) all asserted that the earth was six thousand years old.

4. Sulpicius hints at an argument that would later be expressed by Augustine in his attempt to explain discrepancies between the Septuagint and the Hebrew text: both were divinely inspired by the same Spirit, and the differences were intended to lead the reader past a literal, historical interpretation, in order to contemplate the higher significance (Aug. *Ciu.* 15.14; 18.43–44). The failure of antiquity, on the other hand, could be a reference to the problem of copyists introducing errors into a text. Sulpicius will rail against their negligence later, at 1.39.1.

5. See Gen 4:17. The Vulgate, Septuagint, and Hebrew versions agree in attributing the construction of the first city to Cain; G. K. Van Andel, *The Concept of History in the Chronicle of Sulpicius Severus* (Amsterdam: Adolf M. Hakkert, 1976), 16, lists this among Sulpicius's inaccuracies. Augustine claimed that the city was named after the founder's son, Enoch (Aug. *Ciu.* 15.9).

6. See Gen 5:3. The Vulgate and Hebrew texts state that Adam was 130 years old when Seth was born. The Septuagint has 230 years, as do the *Vetus Latina* translations of Genesis (see Aug. *Ciu.* 15.10; 15.13).

7. Most English versions of the Bible translate the Hebrew of Gen 6:2 as "the sons of God," but the Alexandrian manuscript tradition of the Septuagint, as well as writers like Tertullian (Tert. *Virg.* 7) and Josephus (Jos. *A.J.* 1.3.1), have "angels of God."

8. This question is discussed by Augustine (Aug. *Ciu.* 15.23), and after reviewing the textual evidence, he concluded that the angels did not engage in intercourse with women, but rather, this was a reference to the corruption of Seth's line (the sons of God). Sulpicius will highlight the dangers of intermingling two races in the following chapters (see 1.7.3; 1.23.1; 2.3.2). See Ghislaine de Senneville-Grave, *Sulpice Sévère: Chroniques*, Sources Chrétiennes 441 (Paris: Les Éditions du Cerf, 1999), 369, for the proposal that Sulpicius was using this biblical emphasis to warn against Roman policies toward the Germanic peoples.

9. A slight variation from Gen 8:4, where the ark comes to rest on Mt. Ararat before Noah begins to send out the birds.

10. "The trees that had been exposed" (*nudari cacumina arborum*) is an allusion to Ov. *Met.* 1.346; see Van Andel, *Concept of History*, 25.

11. More precisely, Noah cursed Ham's son, Canaan. Noah had planted a vineyard, made wine, then proceeded to get drunk and pass out naked in his tent (Gen 9:20–21). When Ham discovered his inebriated father, he summoned his brothers to witness the spectacle. Ham and Japheth acted with appropriate dutifulness toward their father, refusing to look at his naked body, and they protected his modesty with a blanket. Later, when Noah learned of Ham's lack of filial piety, he cursed Ham's son, Canaan, and this cursing explained the later animosity between the Canaanites and Israel. Sulpicius deviated from the biblical text and placed the curse on Ham; Senneville-Grave, *Chroniques*, 354, suggests that Sulpicius intended to forge a link between Noah's curse on the line of Ham and the foundation of the city of Babylon. Augustine (Aug. *Ciu.* 16.2) noted that the curse was not aimed at Ham, but rather was against his activity, the fruit of his life.

12. Nimrod, a mighty hunter, was the most famous son of Cush (Gen 10:8–9) and the founder of Nineveh (Gen 10:11). Sulpicius has again deviated from the Genesis account to emphasize the wickedness of Ham's line: it will produce Babylon, a place of enslavement for Jews during the exile, and the ultimate adversary of Christianity in the end times (Rev 17:18; 18:1–24). See also Aug. *Ciu.* 16.3 for the link between Nimrod and Babylon.

13. It might seem that Sulpicius was a bit sloppy in chapter 4, referring to Abram with the Latin word *Abraham* rather than *Abram*. He does know that there is a difference, as he uses both words when he discusses the alteration of Abram's name at 5.1. Augustine justified this practice in his own work

by noting that although their names were changed, Abraham and Sarah were the forms that were in universal use (Aug. *Ciu.* 16.28).

14. Abram's family went forth from Ur of the Chaldeans to go into the land of Canaan (Gen 11:31). Ur was one of the great Sumerian cities of Mesopotamia. The Chaldeans (ca. tenth to sixth centuries BC) did not arrive in Mesopotamia until centuries after the death of Abram, so this attribution is an anachronism in both the biblical text and Sulpicius.

15. Sulpicius omits Abram's sojourn in Egypt and the Pharaoh's infatuation with Sarai (Gen 12:10—13:1).

16. Although difficult to see in English, the Hebrew lacks vowels, so this alteration is just the addition of one Hebrew letter.

17. See 1 Chr 1:32.

18. Sulpicius here avoids an anachronism found in the Hebrew, Septuagint, and Vulgate versions of the text: these works claim that Abimelech was the king of the Philistines (see Gen 26:1), but the Philistines will not appear in this region until around 1200 BC.

19. Sulpicius again mentions the importance of not intermingling races. See earlier note at 262n8.

20. Migdal Eder (Tower of Eder) in Hebrew. The location of this tower is not known.

21. The Bible does not mention happy Egyptians or a rejoicing king; to the contrary, it would appear that Joseph had to persuade the Pharaoh to allow his family to remain (Gen 46:31—47:6).

22. This detail is not found in the Bible.

23. The name of Moses' second son, Eliezer, is found at Exod 18:4.

24. Sulpicius places the story of Job before Moses' reception of the Law. Augustine (Aug. *Ciu.* 18.47) noted that despite the Jewish claim that no one who lives apart from the Mosaic Law is accepted by God, the Jews still recognize God's acceptance of Job, who was neither Jewish nor a proselyte, a man who lived in the third generation after Israel. Senneville-Grave, *Chroniques*, 362, suggests that Sulpicius's decision to place Job at this point in his chronology reflects a rhetorical decision to contrast the suffering and patience of Job with the suffering, impatience, and discouragement of the Israelites.

25. Job is an example of a man who was righteous because he lived in accordance with what Tertullian labeled the "primordial law," present in all nations and containing the seeds of the law that was fully developed in the Mosaic Law (Tert. *Iud.* 2). There is also an echo here of Paul (Rom 1:18–20; 2:14–15), who writes about the Gentiles who respond to natural law and live righteously.

26. Job is an exception to Sulpicius's fundamental contention that wealth is corrosive and should have no place in the life of the faithful.

27. Sulpicius deviates from the versions of this story found at Exod 7:11 in the Hebrew, Septuagint, and Vulgate versions, where the wise men and magicians are Egyptians. As noted earlier (263n14), the Chaldaeans did not appear in Mesopotamia until the tenth century BC.

28. Sulpicius attributes a unique motivation to the Pharaoh's reluctance to allow the Israelites to depart. The writer of Exodus characterizes this as hardness of heart, although at certain points of the narrative, the Lord is said to harden the Pharaoh's heart (Exod 9:12; 10:1).

29. The Feast of Unleavened Bread, described at Exod 12:14–20 and Lev 23:4–6.

30. Sulpicius here follows the text of Exod 13:17 into another anachronism (see the note on the Philistines at 263n18).

31. The Latin phrase *virilis ac muliebris sexus* is a possible allusion to earlier Latin historians; see Liv. 31.44.4, Tac. *Hist.* 5.13, and Tac. *Ann.* 4.62.

32. In the following chapters, Sulpicius is going to emphasize the rebellious nature of the Jews. Their rebellious nature explained why God's blessing had passed on to the Christians. Nevertheless, his contemporary Christian readers should learn from their example and bring their lives into accord with God's will.

33. Sulpicius is referring to the coriander plant, whose white flowers, when in bloom, cover the land like a winter's frost.

34. Sulpicius indulges in another anachronism, employing Roman military ranks to describe the leaders of the people.

35. Exod 21:22–23 addresses a situation in which two men struggling strike a woman who miscarries; if no further harm comes to the woman, then the man who struck her pays a fine to the husband; if she dies from the miscarriage, then the man is also killed. Sulpicius seems to read this law in the context of a deliberate abortion, rather than an accidental miscarriage. The struggling men are eliminated and an examination of the fetus determines whether the death penalty is applied to the person who caused the abortion. Roman law did not prohibit abortion, so this attack on the practice seems to have been a personal conviction.

36. Another anachronism: Sulpicius is describing the Roman practice of *vindicta*, in which a slave is set free when touched by the rod (cf. Liv. 2.5). The Bible does not mention the staff of manumission (see Exod 21:26–27).

37. The Hebrew, Septuagint, and Vulgate versions of Exod 32:28 state that three thousand men were killed. 1 Cor 10:8 claims that twenty-three thousand men were killed in this incident.

38. Exod 35:4—40:33.

39. In other words, Sulpicius will skip the entire Book of Leviticus. Senneville-Grave, *Chroniques*, 366, attributes this to his reluctance to discuss Jewish rites and rituals.

40. See 1.15.2.

41.   Sulpicius's source for this number is unknown; it is not found in Num 11:31–35.

42.   There is a lacuna in the manuscripts at this point.

43.   Sulpicius calls this town Geth, but the Hebrew, Septuagint, and Vulgate versions refer to it as Ai (see Josh 8:1–29).

44.   Sulpicius fails to mention that the people of Gibeon actually tricked the Israelites by claiming to be from a distant country. After a covenant had been made between the two peoples, the Gibeonites revealed that they were from a nearby city. They were made to carry wood and water for the Israelites as a punishment for this deception (Josh 10:22–27).

45.   This is a theme that Sulpicius wove throughout all of his works: Gallic bishops were far too worldly, more concerned with power, wealth, and standing than their role as shepherds of the church. See pp. 11, 16–17, 20 for discussion.

46.   This line continues the theme that Sulpicius has emphasized throughout this work: the dangers of intermixing different nations (see 262n8).

47.   See Deut 7:1–5.

48.   Judg 3:7–8. After turning to the worship of Ba'al, God allowed the people to be conquered by Cushanrishathaim of Mesopotamia.

49.   That is, Deborah foreshadows the role of the church in releasing prisoners from bondage to Satan.

50.   A brief excursus on the history of Judaism: Christianity was necessary because the Jewish people were unable to learn from their mistakes, no matter how many times the cycle of prosperity and disaster repeated itself.

51.   Judg 10:2; the Hebrew, Septuagint, and Vulgate versions all read twenty-three years.

52.   Judg 10:8; eighteen years in the Hebrew, Septuagint, and Vulgate versions.

53.   Although Sulpicius had enough interest in this story to recount it here, he offers no judgment of the actions of Jephthah. Ambrose cites this story as an example of an instance when a vow should be broken, although clearly it was better to have never made a vow (Ambr. *Off.* 1.50.264). Augustine seems to suggest that the sacrifice of Jephthah's daughter was morally justified, a parallel to the near sacrifice of Isaac (Aug. *Ciu.* 1.21).

54.   Although Sulpicius does not make the point explicitly, it is once again evident that no good comes from this marriage between two nations.

55.   According to the Hebrew text of Judg 15:17–20, Samson discarded the bone he had employed to slay the Philistines. Thirsty, he called upon the Lord, and God split the hillside and created a spring to refresh Samson. The Septuagint and Vulgate, however, state that God broke open a hollow in the discarded jawbone and water flowed from it. Josephus solved this problem by

noting that Samson called the hill where God made the spring *Jawbone,* after the bone he had discarded (Jos. *A.J.* 5.8.9).

56. See Judg 19:1.

57. See, for instance, Jos. *A.J.* 5.9.1 and Hier. *Chron.* 860. Neither of these sources lists any judges between Samson and Eli. In the following chapters, all citations of Eusebius and Jerome's *Chronicle* will employ the number of years since the birth of Abraham as a reference point.

58. The actions of the Benjaminites resemble those of the people of Sodom, described at Gen 19:4–9.

59. At 1 Sam 4:18, the Bible states that Eli judged Israel for forty years.

60. Here Sulpicius follows the Septuagint, which states that Eli was a judge for twenty years (LXX *1 Ki.* 4:18), as opposed to the Hebrew and Vulgate, which have forty years (1 Sam 4:18).

61. The plague of biting mice does not occur in the Hebrew text of 1 Sam 5 but may be found in the Septuagint at LXX *1 Ki.* 5:6; 6:1. Mice that ravage the land are mentioned in the Hebrew text at 1 Sam 6:5, and the Philistines made golden images of both the tumors and the mice to return with the ark as a guilt offering.

62. 1 Sam 6:19. The descendants of Jeconiah failed to rejoice at the return of the ark, and so God killed seventy of them.

63. This is a thoroughly Roman sentiment; the Roman Republic was designed to keep any single man from exercising the power of kingship over the people, and it was not until Julius Caesar and Augustus that this political freedom was lost.

64. God's favor had been transferred from Saul to David (cf. 1 Sam 18:12).

65. The cave of Adullam (1 Sam 22:1).

66. The witch of Endor (1 Sam 28:7–25).

67. Acts 13:21.

68. Eusebius and Jerome state that Samuel and Saul ruled together for forty years, which might have been Sulpicius's source for this idea (Hier. *Chron.* 900).

69. Van Andel, *Concept of History,* 28, regards this as a reference to the work of Julius Africanus.

70. See 1.30.2 and 1 Sam 7:1–2.

71. There is a lacuna in the manuscript at this point.

72. See Hier. *Chron.* 900.

73. There is some confusion about the name of this son; the NRSV form (2 Sam 2:8) has been given here, but Sulpicius has *Isbaal.* The Septuagint renders it Ἰεβοσθὲ, and the Vulgate *Hisboseth.*

74. See 1.30.2.

75. The new king of the Ammonites, Hanun, had shaved David's ambassadors, removing half their beards and also cutting their robes in half at their hips (2 Sam 10:4–5).

76. In the Hebrew, Septuagint, and Vulgate versions, the messenger is the prophet Gad (2 Sam 24:11).

77. The Hebrew and Vulgate report that the final option was three days of plague. Sulpicius is influenced by the Septuagint's "three days of death" (τρεις ήμέρας θάνατον; LXX *2 Ki.* 24:13).

78. The Septuagint has 440 years (LXX *3 Ki.* 5:18), while the Vulgate and Hebrew have 480 (Vulg *3 Reg.* 6:1; 1 Kgs 6:1). Clare Stancliffe, *St. Martin and His Hagiographer* (Oxford: Oxford University Press, 1983), 175, argues that this paragraph shows Sulpicius's critical approach to the text, as he attempted to reconcile chronological differences with reason rather than simply accepting the text's dating without question.

79. Sulpicius has confused Jeroboam with Hadad, who fled to Egypt and married the Pharaoh's sister (see 1 Kgs 11:14–19; Van Andel, *Concept of History*, 16).

80. Sulpicius appears to have added the 120,000 soldiers mentioned in the Septuagint (LXX *3 Ki.* 12:21) to the 180,000 found in the Hebrew and Vulgate to arrive at this number (Vulg *3 Reg.* 12:21, 1 Kgs 12:21).

81. Sulpicius, following the Septuagint, has named this king *Abiud* (Gk: Ἀβιοὺ). I have altered the name to match the spelling found in the NRSV.

82. At 1 Kgs 15:2 and 2 Chr 13:2, Abijam is said to have reigned three years. Jerome and Eusebius also state that he reigned for three years (Hier. *Chron.* 1037). Van Andel, *Concept of History*, 29, suggests that this mistake was imported from Hippolytus's *Chronica*.

83. These three faults are discussed at 2 Chr 16:1–12.

84. According to 1 Kgs 15:33, Baasha ruled twenty-four years.

85. This entire passage bears no relationship to the Hebrew or the Greek: at 1 Kgs 16, Zimri is said to have killed Elah, and then after seven days, the soldiers made Omri, the commander of the army, king (1 Kgs 16:15–16). Zimri then killed himself by burning down the king's house. Van Andel, *Concept of History*, 29, suggests that Hippolytus might again have been the source for Sulpicius's version.

86. Sulpicius's confusion continues here: in the preceding chapter, he mixed up Omri and Zimri, and now he states that Ahab was the son of Ambri. Omri was the father of Ahab (1 Kgs 16:29).

87. Because of Ahab's act of penitence, God said he would not bring evil upon Ahab, but evil would fall upon his descendants (1 Kgs 21:29).

88. Sulpicius has altered the order of events. In the Bible, the story of Naboth's vineyard (1 Kgs 21:1–29) follows the invasion of the Syrian king (1 Kgs 20:1).

89. Sulpicius follows his pattern of deemphasizing the miraculous in his account. The biblical passage (2 Kgs 1:9–14) features three sets of fifty men sent to apprehend Elijah; the first and second group are consumed by fire from heaven. The captain of the third group begs Elijah to spare them and they are not destroyed.

90. Somewhat confusingly, there was a King Jehoram of Israel and a King Jehoram of Judah at this time. The NRSV employs two spellings for this name: *Jehoram* (2 Kgs 1:17) and *Joram* (2 Kgs 8:16). Sulpicius consistently spells this name *Ioram*, which is used here.

91. The Hebrew Bible places the ascension of Elijah much earlier (2 Kgs 2:1–12). Once again, a famous miracle (Elijah's ascension to heaven in a fiery chariot) is downplayed. Josephus (Jos. *A.J.* 9.2.2) is also very circumspect about this incident, stating that Elijah had disappeared and, as with Enoch, nobody knew if he had died.

92. Sulpicius alludes to the miracles of Elisha in a compressed summary: the restoration of the widow's son (2 Kgs 4:18–37); the cleansing of Namaan (2 Kgs 5:1–14); the provision of food during the famine (2 Kgs 4:38–44); the production of water (2 Kgs 3:13–20); and supplying a woman with oil to pay her debts (2 Kgs 4:1–7).

93. The ability of fawning men (courtiers or bishops) to pervert a previously good king is one of Sulpicius's emphases; see pp. 15–17.

94. 2 Kgs 14:2 and 2 Chr 25:1 both state that Amaziah ruled for twenty-nine years. Van Andel, *Concept of History*, 29, notes that one version of Hippolytus's *Chronicon* has the number nine, so perhaps this was the source of Sulpicius's error.

95. This king is called Azariah in 2 Kings (e.g., 2 Kgs 14:21) and Uzziah in 2 Chronicles (e.g., 2 Chr 26:1).

96. Israel (the ten northern tribes) was conquered by the Assyrians in 722; Judah (the two southern tribes) fell to the Neo-Babylonians in 586. In Sulpicius's estimation, the history of Judah is more important than that of Israel.

97. Asshur is called Cush in modern English translations (Gen 10:6, 8), which is based on the spelling of the Hebrew word and also reflected in the Vulgate's *Chus*. Josephus called this man (Jos. *A.J.* 1.6.4) Ἀσσούρας (Asshur), which matches the Septuagint reading: "Asshur came out of that land and built Nineveh" (LXX *Ge.* 10:11). The Hebrew text is slightly ambiguous in identifying the founder of Nineveh; it was most likely Cush, but also could have been his son Nimrod.

98. Ham in modern English translations (see Gen 10:6).

99. See LXX *Jn.* 3:4; the Hebrew text and Vulgate have forty days.

100. An allusion to Lot's sons-in-law, who disregarded Lot's warning that the Lord was about to destroy the city (Gen 19:12–14). The people of Sodom and the Ninevites exhibit a marked contrast in behavior that illustrates a

proper response to a warning. Those who disregard the warning are destroyed; those who amend their ways are spared. Let Sulpicius's readers, living in the last times, pay attention.

101.   The second Pekahiah is called Pekah in the NRSV (2 Kgs 15:25); the Septuagint and Vulgate also differentiate between the two names.

102.   Sulpicius here deviates from the biblical text, which states that Hoshea did what was evil in the sight of the Lord, but that he was not as wicked as the kings who had preceded him (2 Kgs 17:2).

103.   The deportation of Israel took place in 721 BC. The Assyrian King Shalmaneser V (727–722 BC) had died and was replaced by Sargon II (722–705), who, contra Sulpicius, was actually responsible for the deportation of the ten tribes.

104.   A suggestion found in Hier. *Chron.* 1270.

105.   2 Kings and 2 Chronicles offer very different accounts of Manasseh's reign, and it is quite evident that Sulpicius has elected to follow the version found in 2 Chr 33:1–17.

106.   This description of Josiah's suppression of non-Jewish worship is drawn from 2 Kgs 23:4–20, but the description of his death comes from the more detailed account found at 2 Chr 35:23.

107.   The Hebrew (2 Kgs 24:6) and Vulgate versions make a distinction between Jehoiakim and his son, Jehoiachin, but the Septuagint (LXX *4 Ki.* 24:6) does not.

108.   This is Sulpicius's interpretation. Both 2 Kgs 24:9 and 2 Chr 36:9 blame Jehoiachin's evil for the return of Nebuchadnezzar.

109.   Phase one of the Babylonian exile, one of the defining events of Jewish history, began under Nebuchadnezzar on March 16, 597 BC (cf. John Bright, *A History of Israel,* 3rd ed. [Philadelphia: Westminster Press, 1981], 327).

110.   According to 2 Kgs 25:15, Zedekiah was Jehoiachin's uncle (a son of Josiah); his name was Mattaniah before he was made king.

111.   2 Kgs 25:27 places Jehoiachin's release from the Babylonian prison at thirty-seven years after the first deportation.

112.   The following story is drawn from Jer 37:1—38:13.

113.   The cistern of Malchiah (Jer 38:6).

114.   Jer 39:7.

115.   Jer 40:6.

Book II

1.   The story of Susanna is not found in the best Hebrew manuscripts of the Book of Daniel. It is in the Greek version, compiled by Theodotion, and in the Vulgate as Vulg. *Dan.* 13. This chapter does not appear in most English translations of the text, and there was doubt among early Christians

about its canonicity. Its inclusion here would suggest that Sulpicius accepted it as canonical. Discussion of a second addition to the Book of Daniel, the story of the idol Bel, may be found later (2.8.2–3).

2.   Here the term *Chaldean* refers to the Neo-Babylonian Empire. The Chaldeans were a Semitic race who migrated into southeastern Mesopotamia in the late tenth to early ninth centuries BC. Originally under the control of the Assyrian Empire, they joined forces with the Babylonians and defeated the Assyrians in 605 BC. The Chaldeans were assimilated into the Babylonian people. Nebuchadnezzar II (ruled 605–562 BC) was the second and most famous of the Chaldean kings who ruled in Mesopotamia.

3.   At the time Sulpicius was writing this work, the Roman Empire was divided between the two sons of Theodosius. Honorius (ruled 395–423) controlled the West, and his brother, Arcadius (ruled 395–408), ruled in the East. This period was also marked by the revolts of western army generals, including Gildo (397–398) and Marcus (406–407).

4.   Sulpicius alludes to the Roman practice of co-opting Germanic peoples and settling them on the borders of the empire as *foederati*. This attempt to use Germanic tribesmen as a defense against other Germans contributed to the disastrous defeat at the Battle of Hadrianople (378), and ultimately, the misguided policy led to the loss of the Gallic provinces.

5.   Sulpicius's animosity toward the Jewish people, never far from the surface, emerges here: Christians and Jews are like iron and clay; as long as the Jews refuse to acknowledge Christ as the Messiah, the two groups will never come together as one. This chapter looks back to a theme that emerged in book I, the danger of intermingling separate races (see 262n8).

6.   The equation of the dream's stone with Christ is found in earlier Christian exegesis (see Iren. *Haer.* 5.26.2). Josephus noted that although Daniel did explain the significance of the stone to Nebuchadnezzar, he (Josephus) did not think it proper that he should disclose it in his work (Jos. *A.J.* 10.10.4).

7.   Possibly a reference to Ezek 37:1–14, in which Ezekiel is granted a vision of bones that are brought back to life (cf. Hilar. *Trin.* 6.20; 12.47; Ghislaine de Senneville-Grave, *Sulpice Sévère: Chroniques*, Sources Chrétiennes 441 [Paris: Les Éditions du Cerf, 1999], 393).

8.   See 1.53.3.

9.   Jer 42:1 places the ultimate blame for the flight to Egypt on Johanan and Azariah, the leaders of the soldiers who had defeated Ishmael. Sulpicius attributed the decision to ignore Jeremiah's prophecy to the *plebs*, the common mob that cannot be counted upon to do the right thing.

10.   Sulpicius exaggerated the extent to which Nebuchadnezzar's religious views were changed by this experience. At Dan 3:29, Nebuchadnezzar decreed only that anyone who spoke against the God of Shadrach, Meshach, and Abednego would be executed.

11.   See 1.53.3.

12.   The length of time reported at 2 Chr 36:21.

13.   Evil-merodach is not mentioned in 2 Chronicles; he is referred to in 2 Kgs 25:27 and Jer 52:31. Presumably, this is a reference to the *Chronicles* of Eusebius and Jerome, which mentions him at Hier. *Chron.* 1445.

14.   Darius the Mede does not appear outside the Book of Daniel and those works that depend on it. He is not mentioned in the Persian or Babylonian lists of kings. The last king of the Babylonians was Nabonidus, who was defeated by Cyrus of Persia in 539 BC (see Amélie Kuhrt, *The Ancient Near East c. 3000–330 BC*, vol. 2 [London: Routledge, 1995], 658–659).

15.   Astyages was the last king of the Medes, supplanted by Cyrus in 550 BC.

16.   Contra Sulpicius, the Babylonians were under the rule of Nabonidus (ruled 555–539 BC) when Cyrus conquered Babylon.

17.   The story of Bel and Daniel is found in one of the apocryphal additions to the Book of Daniel (Vulg. *Dan.* 14:1–21); see 269n1.

18.   Ver. *Aen.* 1.729.

19.   See 2.8.1.

20.   Sulpicius has made a significant mistake in chronology here by confusing the reigns of Darius I and Darius II (Ochus); see further 2.10.1. The rebuilding of the temple was completed in the sixth year of Darius I (Ezra 6:15), which was 516 BC.

21.   Artaxerxes I ruled Persia 464–423 BC.

22.   King Darius II ruled Persia 424–404 BC.

23.   See above, n14 for a discussion of the belief that Darius the Mede was not a historical figure.

24.   Cyrus II, founder of the Achaemenid Empire, ruled Persia from 559–530 BC (Kuhrt, *Ancient Near East*, 648, 656).

25.   According to Eusebius and Jerome (Hier. *Chron.* 1980), Tarquinius Superbus began to rule in the twenty-fourth year of Cyrus's reign.

26.   Eight years, according to Eusebius and Jerome (Hier. *Chron.* 1987). They also claimed that Cambyses was called Nebuchadnezzar II and the story of Judith (see further, 2.12.1) belongs to this period. Cambyses is actually Cambyses II, and according to Kuhrt, *Ancient Near East*, 648, he ruled from 530–522 BC.

27.   Darius I ruled Persia 522–486. See Kuhrt, *Ancient Near East*, 664–665, for a discussion of the problems associated with his rise to power.

28.   Flavius Stilicho was a famous half-Vandal Roman general who was married to the niece of Emperor Theodosius I. He held a consulship in AD 400.

29.   Xerxes, the son of Darius, ruled 486–465 BC (twenty-one years; see Kuhrt, *Ancient Near East*, 648; 670–671). During his reign, he attacked Greece and defeated the Spartans at Themopylae, but ultimately he lost a

significant portion of his fleet in the Bay of Salamis; later, his army was scattered after the Battle of Plataea (479 BC).

30. Artaxerxes I ruled 465–424/3 BC.

31. Darius II, the son of Artaxerxes, ruled 423–405 BC.

32. When Artaxerxes died in the winter of 424/3, his two sons, Xerxes and Sogdianus (also called Secundianus), fought for control of the empire. Their dispute lasted for several months and resulted in both of their deaths. Ultimately, Ochus, an illegitimate son of Artaxerxes, claimed the throne, and he took the name Darius II (Kuhrt, *Ancient Near East*, 672), ruling from 423–405 BC.

33. As noted previously (271n20), Sulpicius has confused Darius I and II; these stories refer to Darius I, rather than the later Darius II (Ochus).

34. The story of Darius and the three Hebrew bodyguards comes from the apocryphal book of 1 Esdras (LXX *1 Es.* 3:1—4:48). The Persian king in that story is actually Darius I, not Darius II (Ochus) as Sulpicius claimed.

35. Ezra 7:15.

36. Sulpicius's mistaken identification of King Darius continues to lead him into errors. Ezra lived during the reign of Artaxerxes II (405–359 BC), a century after the temple had been rebuilt (515 BC).

37. Ezra 7:1–10.

38. Jerusalem had already been rebuilt by the time of Ezra (Neh 6:15).

39. Nehemiah was the cupbearer for Artaxerxes I, serving him wine (Neh 1:11—2:1).

40. Sulpicius's calculations are once again incorrect, because he has placed Nehemiah in the reign of Artaxerxes II (405–359 BC) rather than Artaxerxes I (465–424/3 BC).

41. Another Roman anachronism: the Latin word *praetor* refers to a provincial governor in the Roman Empire, often a synonym for proconsul or propraetor. In the Vulgate, Jerome used the more ambiguous *dux* (leader) to describe the Persian administrators (Vulg. *2 Esdr.* 2:9).

42. See Neh 4:6.

43. The ten tribes of Israel were deported by the Assyrians; they never returned to the Holy Land. See 1.48.1.

44. Geminus and Rebellius were consuls in AD 29 (see Tac. *Ann.* 5.1).

45. The temple was destroyed by Titus and the Roman army in AD 70.

46. See Dan 9:24–27.

47. Sulpicius is now going to devote five chapters to the relatively obscure Esther and Judith. Noting the connections between the two stories and Sulpicius's emphases, G. K. Van Andel, *The Concept of History in the Chronicle of Sulpicius Severus* (Amsterdam: Adolf M. Hakkert, 1976), 67–68, has argued that Sulpicius devoted so much time to them because the pair represent a typological foreshadowing of the church, the bride of Christ who rescues her people.

48.   Actually, four kings of the Achaemenid dynasty were named Artaxerxes: Artaxerxes I ruled 465–424 BC, Artaxerxes II ruled 404–358 BC, Artaxerxes III ruled 359–338 BC, and Artaxerxes IV ruled 338–336 BC. Sulpicius mentions the first Artaxerxes at 2.9.1 and 2.9.4; the second appears at 2.10.2 and 2.11.1–2. As noted above, 271n26, Eusebius and Jerome placed the story of Judith in the reign of Cambyses. The story of Esther should probably be placed during the reign of Xerxes I (Senneville-Grave, *Chroniques*, 404).

49.   See 272n36, 272n40 regarding Sulpicius's errors in chronology.

50.   The Latin text here evokes Tacitus's famous characterization of the Christians who were arrested under Nero (Tac. *Ann.* 15.44). Sulpicius's use of Tacitus draws out the parallels between these two unjust persecutions, which may have been important for his typological interpretation (see Van Andel, *Concept of History*, 57, 67–68).

51.   The Septuagint is quite explicit in asserting that this Nebuchadnezzar was a king of Assyria (LXX *Ju.* 1:1, 7). It is not clear why Sulpicius felt obliged to link him to the Persian kings.

52.   A possible reference to Julius Africanus (see Van Andel, *Concept of History*, 28, and 266n69). Jerome and Eusebius also claim that Cambyses was called Nebuchadnezzar by the Jews (Hier. *Chron.* 1987).

53.   Jdt 1:1.

54.   Darius II (423–405 BC); see previous notes and discussion, 271n20.

55.   Herodotus attributed this to Cambyses; the Persian king, suspecting that the Egyptians were mocking him, stabbed the young calf that was thought to be the god Apis with his knife, and then derided the Egyptians for worshiping a god whose flesh could be wounded with steel (Hdt. *Hist.* 3.27–29). Van Andel, *Concept of History*, 39–40, suggested that Sulpicius was so obsessed with proving that Nebuchadnezzar was not Cambyses that he inadvertently included this story about Cambyses here.

56.   A man named Bagoas discovered the headless Holofernes in his tent (LXX *Ju.* 14:14–16).

57.   An extremely uncommon name. It occurs in LXX *Ju.* 1:1, 5 and Gen 10:22 as a grandson of Noah.

58.   To make this story fit with Persian history, Sulpicius places it after the return from the Babylonian exile. While LXX *Ju.* 4:9–12 asserts that the people went up to the temple to ask for God's assistance, it does not mention a recent return from slavery.

59.   Sulpicius has introduced another error into his chronology. This Ochus was actually the son of Artaxerxes II, and he took the name Artaxerxes III. He seized power in a brutal bloodbath after his father died (Justin *Epit.* 10.3.1) and ruled 359–338 BC. Egypt was reconquered by the Persians during his reign.

60. A version of this story is found in Diodorus (D.S. *Hist.* 17.5.4). He was killed by a eunuch named Bagoas, who placed his son, Arses, on the throne after him (Kuhrt, *Ancient Near East,* 674–675).

61. Arses, who took the name Artaxerxes IV, ruled 338–336 BC (Kuhrt, *Ancient Near East,* 648, 673). He also was killed by Bagoas (D.S. *Hist.* 17.5.5).

62. Darius III ruled 336–330 BC. He also was placed in power by the machinations of Bagoas, but he managed to kill the eunuch before Bagoas could assassinate him (D.S. *Hist.* 17.5.6). This Darius was the last of the Achaemenids; he was supplanted by Alexander of Macedonia.

63. Son of Philip II of Macedonia, Alexander (356–323) conquered the Persian Empire in 330.

64. Cyrus began to rule in 559; Alexander seized control in 330; the Persian Empire stood for 229 years.

65. Josephus claimed that Alexander treated the priests well and offered a sacrifice to God (Jos. *A.J.* 11.8.5).

66. Alexander's empire was divided among his leading generals: Seleucus, Antigonus, Lysimachus, and Ptolemy.

67. Seleucus I (ruled 312–280 BC) was the founder of the Seleucid Empire, one of the three great Hellenistic kingdoms.

68. Lust, avarice, and a desire to dominate others are themes drawn from Sallust (see, for instance, Sal. *Jug.* 41). The competition for the high priesthood is paralleled in Sulpicius's thought by contemporary bishops who were competing for prestige and power in Gaul; see pp. 16–17.

69. Onias III served as the high priest until 175 BC. He is mentioned at 2 Macc 3:1—4:10 and Jos. *A.J.* 12.4.10. For a discussion of his tenure, see James VanderKam, *From Joshua to Caiaphas: High Priests after the Exile* (Minneapolis: Fortress Press, 2004), 188–197.

70. The seventh ruler of the Seleucid Dynasty, Seleucus IV Philopater ruled 187–175 BC.

71. The sixth king of the Seleucid Empire, Antiochus III ruled 222–187 BC.

72. According to 2 Macc 3:5, Simon told Apollonius of Tarsus that the treasury in Jerusalem was full of money that the king could confiscate. This message was passed on to the king, who sent Heliodorus to seize the money. When Heliodorus attempted to carry out his charge and enter the temple, he was blocked by a powerful horse and rider, accompanied by two strong men who whipped him (2 Macc 3:25–26). Although this prevented the robbery of the temple, Simon later used the incident to turn the king against Onias, which led to his loss of the high priesthood (2 Macc 4:1–6).

73. Antiochus IV Epiphanes was the younger brother of Seleucus IV Philopator, and he ruled 175–163 BC. Trevor Bryce, *Ancient Syria: A 3,000 Year History* (Oxford: Oxford University Press, 2014), 200, suggests that Jason was

a leader of a pro-Hellenic party of Jews and places the initiative for what follows with him.

74. Jason was the high priest 175–172 BC. For an account of his purchase of the office, see 2 Macc 4:7–10. Hier. *Chron.* 1845 noted that Jason was also called Jesus, which matches the name found in Josephus (Jos. *A.J.* 12.5.1). Onias was away in Antioch when Jason managed to buy the office (VanderKam, *High Priests,* 198).

75. Here is another example of how easily kings are led astray.

76. Jason had sent Menelaus to the king with the latest installment of his payment; Menelaus took this opportunity to outbid Jason and won the support of Antiochus. See 2 Macc 4:23–24 and Bryce, *Ancient Syria,* 201.

77. In fact, Menelaus served as high priest for ten years (172–162 BC). When he failed to meet his financial obligations, the king appointed his brother, Lysimachus, deputy high priest (2 Macc 4:29).

78. While Antiochus was occupied in Egypt, a civil war broke out in Jerusalem between the supporters of Menelaus and the deposed Jason. Jason's forces trapped Menelaus and his men in the citadel in Jerusalem. Many members of Menelaus's faction were slaughtered, but Jason was forced to flee Jerusalem. He died in Egypt. See 2 Macc 4:5–10; Jos. *A.J.* 12.5.1; Bryce, *Ancient Syria,* 201; VanderKam, *High Priests,* 209–210.

79. 2 Macc 4:8–10 credits Jason with initiating the hellenization of the Jewish people. Josephus attributed this to Menelaus (Jos. *A.J.* 12.5.1), rather than to Jason. Sulpicius follows Josephus in placing the initiative in the time of Menelaus, but attributes the wicked impulse to the desire of the people. See VanderKam, *High Priests,* 198–200, 209, for a discussion of the variation between II Maccabees and Josephus.

80. Hier. *Chron.* 1844 places this in the fourth year of Antiochus's reign, and states that he had been made to return from Egypt by an order of the Roman senate. Bryce, *Ancient Syria,* 194–196, characterizes this as a defensive war; upon Antiochus's accession, Ptolemy VI had calculated the Seleucid king was weak, which might allow Egypt to regain control of Syria. In fact, Antiochus Epiphanes rose to the challenge and launched a preemptive strike into Egypt in November 170. In 168, the Romans, concerned about the growing power of the Seleucid king, sent a delegation that demanded Antiochus withdraw from Egypt or face the legions.

81. In fact, Antiochus seems to have believed that with the return of Jason, the people of Judea were rebelling against him (VanderKam, *High Priests,* 210).

82. According to 2 Macc 5:11–14, eighty thousand people were slaughtered.

83. Hier. *Chron.* 1848 indicates that three years separated the return from Egypt and the attack on Judaism.

84.   Sulpicius is generally accurate in his calculations, although Seleucus I actually began to reign eleven years after Alexander's death (323 BC) at the Partition of Babylon in 312.

85.   See 2.17.1.

86.   The Battle of Magnesia (see Liv. 37.45). For a discussion of this battle against the Romans and its disastrous consequences for the Seleucids, see Bryce, *Ancient Syria*, 189–190.

87.   The Romans forced the defeated Antiochus III to sign the Treaty of Apamea in 188 BC. The terms of the treaty required him to leave Europe, surrender all of his elephants, offer twenty hostages, and pay an indemnity of fifteen thousand talents (App. *Syr.* 38). This crushing fine was part of the reason Seleucid kings began looting the Jewish temple (see further 2.19.2).

88.   See 2.18.1.

89.   Seleucus was assassinated by a group of conspirators led by a court officer named Heliodorus (App. *Syr.* 45).

90.   Coin evidence suggests that Seleucus's son, a five-year-old boy also named Antiochus, was the next in line for the throne, but that he was displaced by his uncle, Antiochus IV Epiphanes (Benjamin Scolnic, "When Did the Future Antiochus IV Arrive in Athens?" *Journal of the American School of Classical Studies at Athens* 83, no. 1 (2014): 123; Bryce, *Ancient Syria*, 192–193).

91.   See 1 Macc 1:33–35.

92.   2 Macc 6:1–11. See discussion in Bryce, *Ancient Syria*, 202, and VanderKam, *High Priests*, 212–222.

93.   See 1 Macc 3:10–12. Josephus identified Apollonius as a general of the Samaritan armies (Jos. *A.J.* 12.7.1); see discussion of the conflict in Bryce, *Ancient Syria*, 204.

94.   Only three generals are chosen at 1 Macc 3:38 and Jos. *A.J.* 12.7.3.

95.   See 2.21.2.

96.   Antiochus V Eupator ruled 163–161 BC. He appeared to be interested in repealing his father's policies toward the Jews, as is evident in the letter he sent them that is recorded in 2 Macc 11:27–33. Sulpicius does not seem to have noticed this change of policy.

97.   See 2.19.2. Demetrius I Soter ruled 161–150 BC.

98.   Bryce, *Ancient Syria*, 207–208, notes that it was not that the Romans doubted that Demetrius would be a good king; to the contrary, this is what they expected, and they did not want a strong king at the head of the Seleucid Empire to oppose their growing influence in that region.

99.   Antiochus V and Lysias were both executed, apparently on the orders of Demetrius (Bryce, *Ancient Syria*, 208).

100.   A copy of the epistle from the Roman senate is preserved at 1 Macc 8:22–28.

101.   Alcimus (high priest 162–159 BC) succeeded Menelaus.

102.   Judas was killed in this battle; see 1 Macc 9:18.

103.   Alcimus had begun to pull down the inner walls of the temple sanctuary and the works of the prophets (1 Macc 9:54–55).

104.   Alexander I Balas ruled 150–145. According to our sources, he bore a strong resemblance to the assassinated Antiochus V, and he was put forward as another son of Antiochus IV. His claim was supported by the Romans and the Egyptian Ptolemies. At the head of an Egyptian army, he fought and defeated Demetrius in 150, thereby winning the Seleucid throne (Bryce, *Ancient Syria*, 209).

105.   Demetrius II Nicator ruled 145–138, was deposed, and then ruled a second time, 129–126.

106.   He died in Arabia (1 Macc 11:17).

107.   Five years is correct. Hier. *Chron.* 1866 claims that he ruled nine years and ten months.

108.   See 1 Macc 11:39. This is a very confusing passage in Sulpicius. Demetrius continued to rely upon the mercenaries who had helped place him on the throne. These mercenaries were hated by the people, who quickly turned against him (1 Macc 11:38). Tryphon, a former supporter of Alexander, took custody of Alexander's son and advanced the claim that the younger Alexander, rather than Demetrius, was the legitimate king. The supporters of Alexander rallied around Tryphon and the boy king. Jonathan remained loyal to Demetrius and ended up attacking him. Jonathan was killed in an ambush (1 Macc 12:48; see discussion, Bryce, *Ancient Syria*, 211).

109.   Sulpicius fails to note that Tryphon executed the young Antiochus (1 Macc 13:31–32) and seized control of the kingdom, ruling as Diodotus Tryphon (140–138). Later, Demetrius II Nicator, who had been taken prisoner by the king of Persia, would have a second reign (129–126).

110.   See 2.25.1.

111.   Ptolemeus, the son of Abubus, conspired against Simon and killed him at a banquet (1 Macc 16:13–17; Jos. *A.J.* 13.7.4).

112.   This detail comes from Hier. *Chron.* 1892.

113.   This material also seems to have been drawn from ibid., 1913.

114.   According to Josephus, Alexander left behind two sons, but he had made his wife, Salome (called Alexandra by the Greeks), the ruler of Judea (Jos. *A.J.*13.16.1; Hier. *Chron.* 1940).

115.   Hyrcanus and Aristobulus were the two sons of Salome Alexandra. Upon her death, according to Josephus, Hyrcanus became high priest. Having been attacked by Aristobulus, he stepped down from his office and Aristobulus became king (Jos. *A.J.* 14.1.1–3).

116.   Pompey the Great was a famous Roman general and politician. He would later join in the First Triumvirate with Julius Caesar and Marcus Crassus. Ultimately, he was killed in battle against Caesar. At this time, Rome was actively expanding its sphere of influence in the east, so the opportunity to intervene in the squabble between Hyrcanus and Aristobulus was welcomed. As noted at

Hier. *Chron.* 1950, this was the point where Judea would lose its freedom, coming under the control of Roman procurators.

117.   Antipater (d. 43 BC) was the father of King Herod the Great. Josephus claimed that he goaded Hyrcanus into attacking his brother, Aristobulus, after Hyrcanus had stepped down from the high priesthood (Jos. *A.J.* 14.1.3).

118.   King Herod the Great ruled 37–4 BC.

119.   See also Hier. *Chron.* 1978.

120.   Ibid., 1983 developed this idea at length, quoting the prophet Daniel and suggesting that Christ had fulfilled the prophecy found in Dan 9:25: there would be seven weeks and sixty-two weeks from the rebuilding of Jerusalem to the coming of the anointed one. According to Eusebius and Jerome, the sixty-nine weeks was equivalent to the 483 years the Jewish people were under the rule of the anointed ones, the high priests. This line ended with Hyrcanus, clearing the way for the advent of the prophesied Christ.

121.   December 25. Hier. *Chron.* 2015 noted that Christ was born exactly 2,015 years after Abraham.

122.   When Herod I died in 4 BC, his territory was divided between his sons. Herod Archelaus ruled Judea, Idumea, and Samaria 4 BC–AD 6.

123.   Herod Antipas, brother of Archelaus, ruled Galilee and Peraea 4 BC–AD 39. This Herod was responsible for the execution of John the Baptist (Matt 14:1–12), and also questioned Christ during his trial (Luke 23:6–12).

124.   See also Lact. *Mort.* 2.

125.   The Book of Acts concludes with the Apostle Paul under house arrest in the city of Rome (Acts 28:30–31).

126.   The Roman emperor Nero ruled AD 54–68.

127.   A number of early Christian writers named Nero as the first emperor to persecute the growing Christian movement (see Eus. *Hist. Eccl.* 2.25.1–4; Tert. *Apol.* 5; Lact. *Mort.* 2).

128.   See Sulp.-Sev. *Dial.* 2.14.1–4 for Martin's prophecy about the imminent return of Nero and the antichrist, who, there, are said to be two different beings.

129.   Nero's mother, Julia Agrippina, was eliminated because of her opposition to Nero's dalliance with Poppaea Sabina. When the first attempt on her life failed (a boat with a lead roof that was designed to crush her), she was killed by one of Nero's slaves (Tac. *Ann.* 14.3–8).

130.   The description of Nero's wedding to Pythagoras is copied from Tac. *Ann.* 15.37.

131.   The belief that Peter was the first Bishop of Rome is implied in works as early as Iren. *Haer.* 3.2–3, where it is stated that Peter and Paul organized the church in Rome and then passed the leadership on to Linus.

132. At Acts 25:11, Paul invoked his right as a Roman citizen to have his case heard by the emperor, and subsequently, he traveled to Rome.

133. This story is found in the apocryphal *Passion of the Holy Apostles Peter and Paul* (*Pass. Ap. Pet. Paul* 50–56; Clare Stancliffe, *St. Martin and His Hagiographer* [Oxford: Oxford University Press, 1983], 61). Eus. *Hist. Eccl.* 2.13–14 notes that Peter's preaching defeated Simon, but Eusebius did not offer this particular account.

134. The great fire of Rome (AD 64) destroyed ten of the fourteen districts of the city. Nero was immediately suspected of the arson (Tac. *Ann.* 15.38–44).

135. Noted by Tacitus at Tac. *Ann.* 15.39.

136. Sulpicius's description of the brutality extended toward the Christians is drawn directly from Tac. *Ann.* 15.44.

137. Sulpicius misrepresents the Roman position toward the Christians. As noted by T. D. Barnes, "Legislation against the Christians," *Journal of Roman Studies* 58 (1969): 35, "Severus clearly has no knowledge of any specific law or edict against the Christians....The vague plurals show that Sulpicius has simply made an inference from the fact that Christianity was illegal." While this is undoubtedly correct, the belief in a larger persecution under Nero was a commonplace in Christian writing at this time: Orosius, writing slightly after Sulpicius, noted that the persecution that began in Rome during the reign of Nero spread out into the provinces (Oros. *Hist.* 7.7).

138. A similar description of the death of the apostles is found at Eus. *Hist. Eccl.* 2.25.5, Lact. *Mort.* 2, and Oros. *Hist.* 7.7.

139. This would appear to be a mistake; the actual name of the Roman procurator was Gessius Florus (Jos. *A.J.* 20.11.1) or Cestius Florus (Hier. *Chron.* 2084). Both of these sources claim that this man, who governed Judea 64–66, was the direct cause of the Jewish revolt.

140. The future Emperor Vespasian, who ruled AD 69–79.

141. The belief that Nero had not died can be traced to the rumors reported at Tac. *Hist.* 2.8.

142. See Rev 13:3; one of the heads of the beast bore a fatal wound that had been recently healed.

143. The story that Nero's body was never discovered and that he might simply be waiting to return is also found in Lact. *Mort.* 2, although Lactantius characterized this as the view of people with extravagant imaginations.

144. In the year after Nero's death, four Roman generals (Galba, Otho, Vitellius, and Vespasian) fought one another for control of the state. Vespasian emerged as the victor.

145. As Senneville-Grave, *Chroniques*, 428, notes, this is an anachronism; the early emperors did not do this, and the practice probably began with Diocletian.

146.   As Tac. *Hist.* 3.85 makes clear, Vitellius was killed by a Roman mob.

147.   A similar sentiment is expressed at Hier. *Chron.* 2086. This is the end result, in Sulpicius's thought, of centuries of intransigence and a failure to conform to God's will. The rebellious Jews lost God's blessing, which was now transferred to the Christians.

148.   These numbers are from Hier. *Chron.* 2086, which quoted Jos. *B.J.* 6.9.3; cf. Oros. *Hist.* 7.9.

149.   This is a controversial passage; Van Andel, *Concept of History*, 43–48, following Bernays, believes that Sulpicius may have copied this from a lost section of Tacitus's *Histories* 5. Oros. *Hist.* 7.9 also reported this indecision: Titus did not know if he should leave the temple intact as a sign of Roman benevolence; nevertheless, fearing that it might encourage the Jews if he did, he elected to destroy the temple. Orosius attributed the decision to God: with the advent of the Christian movement, the temple was a relic of the past that served no further purpose.

150.   Although appended as a motivation for the destruction of the temple, it is very unlikely that Titus would have considered Christianity enough of a threat at this time to justify this action, and this is simply Sulpicius's interpretation of the subsequent actions; see Van Andel, *Concept of History*, 47–48.

151.   Most early church writers (e.g., Eus. *Hist. Eccl.* 3.17, Lact. *Mort.* 3, Oros. *Hist.* 7.10) regarded the Emperor Domitian (ruled 81–96) as the second persecutor of Christians. As Barnes, "Legislation," 35–36, notes, this is rather unlikely.

152.   Also reported in Hier. *Chron.* 2110; Eus. *Hist. Eccl.* 3.18; Oros. *Hist.* 7.10.

153.   Tertullian (Tert. *Apol.* 2.6) and Eusebius (Eus. *Hist. Eccl.* 3.33) both mention a persecution under Trajan, although, as Barnes suggests, they have no more evidence to support their claim than what was found in the letter of Pliny the Younger (Barnes, "Legislation," 36–37).

154.   The Emperor Trajan ruled 98–117. The investigation that Sulpicius reports should be attributed to Pliny, who, while governor of Bithynia in 112, reported his encounters with Christians to the emperor (see Plin. *Ep.* 10.96). Oros. *Hist.* 7.10 lists Trajan as the third persecutor of Christians, claiming that he ordered Christians should be compelled to sacrifice or be put to death. Pliny is then said to have intervened by noting that Christians did not appear to be doing anything wrong, which led Trajan to moderate the severity of his rescripts against Christians.

155.   Hadrian ruled the Roman Empire 117–138. In 132, the Israelites rose up in the Bar Kochba revolt. Under the leadership of Simon Bar-Kochba, who many believed was the Messiah, the Jews broke free from Roman control for a short period.

156.   Sulpicius takes this from the account of the discovery of the cross written by Paulinus of Nola (P.-Nol. *Ep.* 31.3). Orosius had a rather different

view of Hadrian: he asserted that Hadrian had received instruction in the Christian faith and thus was very familiar with it. His suppression of the Bar Kochba revolt was, to a certain extent, vengeance against the Jewish people who had been oppressing the Christians who were living in Judea. Although Jews were forbidden to live in Jerusalem, the emperor gave permission for the Christians to reside in that city (Oros. *Hist.* 7.13).

157. See Eus. *Hist. Eccl.* 4.6; Hier. *Chron.* 2150.

158. Jerome and Eusebius attribute this decision to the will of God and the Romans (Hier. *Chron.* 2150).

159. According to Eus. *Hist. Eccl.* 4.6, a certain Mark was the first Gentile bishop of Jerusalem.

160. Oros. *Hist.* 7.13 claimed that Hadrian sent a rescript to Minucius Fundanus, proconsul of Asia, that no one should condemn Christians without an accusation and proof of a crime.

161. Sulpicius follows Hier. *Chron.* 2182 in attributing a persecution to Marcus Aurelius (ruled 161–180).

162. Eusebius mentions a Pothinus, who was martyred in Lyons (Eus. *Hist. Eccl.* 5.5.8); Hier. *Chron.* 2183 mentions many martyrs who died gloriously in Gaul. Oros. *Hist.* 7.15 states that the fourth persecution of Christians happened in Asia and Gaul under Marcus Aurelius (his numbering of the persecutions now differs from Sulpicius because he did not count Hadrian as a persecutor).

163. Septimus Severus was Roman emperor 193–211. For martyrdoms during his reign, see Eus. *Hist. Eccl.* 6.1.1; Hier. *Chron.* 2218; Oros. *Hist.* 7.17.

164. Maximinus Thrax ruled the empire 235–238. Eusebius (Eus. *Hist. Eccl.* 6.28) claimed that he ordered a persecution of Christians that targeted the leadership of the church; Oros. *Hist.* 7.19 listed Maximinus Thrax as the sixth persecutor of the church, which brings his count back into line with Sulpicius.

165. Decius, who ruled 249–251, is generally considered by modern historians to have been the first Roman emperor to have launched an official persecution of Christians. According to Orosius, he began his persecution because the emperor he had supplanted (Philip the Arab) had been a Christian (Oros. *Hist.* 7.21). Lactantius, who does not follow the scheme of persecutions adopted by other Christian authors, noted that there were no persecutions between Domitian and Decius (Lact. *Mort.* 4).

166. Valerian, who ruled 253–260, reinstated the persecution of Decius. His efforts at suppressing Christians ended when he was captured by Shapor I of Persia (Lact. *Mort.* 5).

167. Orosius inserted another persecution in this span, that of the Emperor Aurelian (ruled 270–275). This was the ninth persecution of the Christians (Oros. *Hist.* 7.23), which will give him an even ten when the persecution of Diocletian is included; see further, 2.33.2.

168.   Diocletian, who ruled 284–305, launched the Great Persecution, which raged 303–313 (Lact. *Mort.* 10ff., Oros. *Hist.* 7.25).

169.   The Emperor Constantine I ruled the Roman Empire from 306–337. He and his coruler, Licinius, were the first Roman emperors to legalize Christianity.

170.   Eusebius and Jerome's *Chronicle* does not mention a persecution under Licinius (coruler with Constantine 308–324). Eus. *Hist. Eccl.* 10.8.10 does mention a persecution of soldiers who refused to sacrifice, but Sulpicius does not seem to take this very seriously. Orosius, although not discussing the death of Licinius directly, does note that Constantine began to act without apparent cause and executed his own son, Crispus, and his sister's son, Licinius (Oros. *Hist.* 7.28).

171.   Sulpicius alludes here to the ten plagues that struck the Egyptians (Exod 7:8—11:10). Orosius devoted a considerable amount of text to demonstrating the correspondence between those plagues and the experience of the Christians under the persecuting emperors (Oros. *Hist.* 7.27).

172.   As noted above (281n167), Orosius lists Aurelian as a persecutor, and thus enumerates ten persecutions. Consequently, whereas Sulpicius needs a final (future) persecution to make ten, Orosius noted that the number had now been completed. In Orosius, there will be a final persecution, but this is the equivalent of the Egyptians pursuing the departing Jews and then perishing in the Red Sea. The Christians will pass through one more trial before they enter the promised land with Jesus (Oros. *Hist.* 7.27).

173.   The following paragraphs, regarding Helena's archaeological investigations in Jerusalem, are drawn from P.-Nol. *Ep.* 31.

174.   Eusebius credited both Constantine and Helena with the initiative in discovering the holy sites associated with Christ's life and erecting churches in those locales (Eus. *V. C.* 3.25–43). Sulpicius focused exclusively on the role of Helena, excluding Constantine from the following account.

175.   Although the material in this chapter is largely drawn from P.-Nol. *Ep.* 31, Sulpicius has added this paragraph from an unknown source; these two chapters represent a deviation from the work as a whole, for, as Stancliffe notes, Sulpicius has consistently omitted the miraculous from his presentation in the *Chronicles* (Stancliffe, *St. Martin*, 182).

176.   Although this story is found in Paulinus's letter, another version of it may be found in Rufinus, who had returned to Italy with Melania the Elder, and become friends with Paulinus. In his translation and continuation of Eusebius's *Church History*, Rufinus offered an account of Helena's discovery of the three crosses. When uncertain which represented the true cross of the Savior, the people touched them to a dying woman, who was revived by the true cross (Ruf. *Hist.* 10.7–8). The earliest western account of Helena finding the cross is found in Ambr. *Obit. Th.* 40–45; for a discussion of the development of this legend, see Jan Drijvers, *Helena Augusta: The Mother of Constantine*

the Great and the Legend of Her Finding of the True Cross (Leiden: Brill, 1992), 81–117.

177. Sulpicius returns to a Sallustian theme: peace and prosperity breed discord and disaster. For a discussion of Sulpicius's treatment of the Arian controversy, see Van Andel, *Concept of History*, 85–116.

178. Sulpicius is referring to Ursacius and Valens, who emerge as the leaders of the movement in following chapters (Senneville-Grave, *Chroniques*, 437–438).

179. This is an important theme in Sulpicius's works: emperors, who were not theologians by training or interest, were easily led by manipulative bishops to persecute other Christians. See discussion pp. 15–17.

180. The Arian views were first propounded by Arius (256–336), a priest of Alexandria, who, interestingly, is not mentioned in Sulpicius's account.

181. In other words, Jesus was not God but a creature, the first thing God created, predating the creation of heaven and Earth.

182. The Council of Nicaea was held in the spring of 325. Constantine issued an imperial order demanding that all of the bishops of the empire attend the council.

183. Bishop Athanasius of Alexandria (d. 373) was one of the stalwart supporters of the Nicene formulation. For a complete discussion of his career and role in the Arian controversy, see T. D. Barnes, *Athanasius and Constantius* (Cambridge, MA: Harvard University Press, 1993), passim.

184. Marcellus of Ancyra (d. 374) was an opponent of the Arians, but was deemed suspicious because of his modalist views. Photinus (d. 376) had been one of Marcellus's students. His later denial of the incarnation of Christ cast doubt upon his teacher. Marcellus was exiled from his see at the First Council of Constantinople (336) over his refusal to recognize Arius's re-admission into communion. Photinus did not become a bishop until 344 and retained his see until deposed by the Council of Sirmium (351). Sulpicius appears to be recording the decision of the Council of Sirmium here (see Barnes, *Athanasius and Constantius*, 109–110) although this statement is chronologically dislocated.

185. Athanasius was condemned at the Synod of Tyre (335); he fled to Constantinople to appeal to the emperor for support, but was sent into exile in Trier (335); this first exile was not a consequence of his relationship with Marcellus and Photinus (see preceding note and discussion at Barnes, *Athanasius and Constantius*, 22–25).

186. This is Constantine II, who was the oldest of Constantine's surviving sons.

187. The Synod of Serdica was actually convened at the request of Constans, who, in 342, was coruler with his remaining brother Constantius II (see Barnes, *Athanasius and Constantius*, 71).

188.   Constantine II died in 340 after a failed attack on his younger brother, Constans.

189.   In most ecclesiastical accounts of this period, Emperor Constantius II, who ruled 337–361, emerges as one of the Arian villains. Contra other writers, Sulpicius tends to downplay his importance as an active opponent of Nicene Christianity, portraying him rather as an emperor who has been led astray by the Arians who haunt his court (see 2.38.2, 2.39.3).

190.   Photinus claimed that Jesus had not existed before the incarnation.

191.   This occurred at the Council of Sirmium (347).

192.   Modern Belgrade in Serbia.

193.   The usurper Magnentius (350–353) was a Roman general who had grown disaffected under the reign of Constantius's brother and coruler, Constans. He led a revolt in the west in 350 and killed Constans. Constantius II was then forced to march west to confront Magnentius, where the two armies met in Mursa in 351. Magnentius was defeated in this battle but would retain power in the west until 353, when, after having been defeated at the battle of Mons Seleucus, he is said to have killed himself at Lyons (Eutr. *Brev.* 10.12).

194.   The Synod of Milan (354) was convened to secure the condemnation of Athanasius by the western bishops. As Sulpicius indicated, the westerners were more interested in debating the Arian question. Ultimately, the emperor sent several of the western leaders into exile.

195.   As before, Sulpicius shifts responsibility from the emperor to the conniving bishops who clustered around him.

196.   Hilary was the bishop of Poitiers (350–367); a staunch defender of the Nicene formulation, he will play an important role at the Council of Seleucia (see further, 2.41ff.), and his writings were important sources for Sulpicius's version of the Arian controversy (Van Andel, *Concept of History,* 85–97).

197.   Aetius and his disciple Eunomius advanced the proposition that there was no relationship between Christ and God; Christ was of a completely different substance, a created being.

198.   Ossius of Spain (256–357) was the bishop of Cordoba and one of Constantine's leading theological advisors. He had been to Alexandria to investigate the teaching of Arius, and it was his recommendation that led Constantine to convene the Council of Nicaea. A fervent defender of the Nicene formulation and a supporter of Athanasius, he was exiled to Sirmium in 355. At the Synod of Sirmium in 357, he entered into communion with the Arians and was allowed to return to the West.

199.   The Council of Rimini gathered in July 359, in the Italian town of Ariminum (modern Rimini).

200. The parallel Council of Seleucia met in Isauria (modern Turkey) in September 359.

201. Hilary of Poitiers; see above 2.39.4, for his exile. Hilary now emerges as the central figure in Sulpicius's presentation of the Arian controversy (Van Andel, *Concept of History*, 96–97).

202. Sabellianism, or modalism, asserts that God exists in various states or persons at different times.

203. The inexperienced men who had been sent as representatives of the western position to the emperor in Constantinople. According to Sulpicius, they had been forbidden to enter into communion with Arians (2.41.4).

204. To resolve the division between the Councils of Rimini and Seleucia, Emperor Constantius compelled the representatives from both councils to meet together in Constantinople (the First Council of Constantinople, 360). There they were made to sign the creed, which Sulpicius describes in this chapter.

205. By omitting the loaded word *ousia* (nature, being, substance), the framers of this document hoped to produce a creed that all could sign: Jesus was similar to God, and nothing is asserted about whether he shared the same nature with God. The creed states that the Bible makes no positive claims about the *ousia* of Christ, and so the church should follow its lead. As Sulpicius indicates, many bishops believed that a failure to make a positive claim about Christ's nature was the same as asserting that Christ did not share the same nature.

206. The prefect Taurus, who had assembled the bishops in Rimini.

207. Returned from Constantinople to Rimini with the version of the creed that they had signed.

208. Foegadius (or Phoebadius) was the bishop of Agen. Celebrated for his refusal to compromise with the Arians, he would later lead the Council of Saragossa (380) that condemned Priscillianism (see 2.47.1).

209. Sulpicius brings the story of the Arian controversy to a rather hurried conclusion, omitting the later struggle of Athanasius, the Cappadocian fathers, and the role of Emperor Theodosius in containing Arianism.

210. Lucifer (d. 371), bishop of Cagliari on the island of Sardinia, refused to enter into communion with any bishop who had signed the creed of Rimini.

211. Henry Chadwick, *Priscillian of Avila: The Occult and Charismatic in the Early Church* (Oxford: Clarendon, 1976), 8, dates the rise of Priscillianism to the 370s.

212. Chadwick, ibid., 21–22, argues that Sulpicius's account is based on an apologetic text (mentioned at Isid. *Vir.* 15) that had been written by Bishop Ithacius. This (lost) text apparently traced the roots of Priscillianism back to a Mark of Memphis, although Chadwick suspects that this Mark was actually a

second century Gnostic mentioned at Iren. *Haer.* 1.13–22, a connection reinforced by Hier. *Vir. ill.* 121.

213. Possibly of the senatorial rank (Chadwick, *Priscillian*, 8). The description of Priscillian in this chapter draws upon Sallust's description of Catiline at Sal. *Cat.* 5.1–5; see discussion at Van Andel, *Concept of History*, 72–74.

214. Instantius and Salvian were two well-known bishops who, along with Hyginus, did not attend the Council of Saragossa.

215. The Council of Saragossa convened in October 380, under the leadership of twelve bishops, to consider the growing influence of Priscillian. See Chadwick, *Priscillian*, 12–31, for discussion.

216. Ithacius was bishop (379–387) of Ossonoba, modern Faro, Portugal. The earliest manuscript for the *Chronicles* has the misspelling *Sossubensi* here, which should be emended to read *Ossonubensi* (see Chadwick, *Priscillian*, 20–21).

217. Instantius and Salvian consecrated Priscillian as bishop of Avila, without the support of Hydatius, who was the metropolitan bishop of the region, but, apparently, with the support of the people of Avila (Chadwick, *Priscillian*, 33–34).

218. Once again Sulpicius registers his view that the state should not be involved in settling ecclesiastical disputes.

219. Gratian was the older son of Valentinian I; he ruled the western half of the Roman Empire 367–383.

220. See Chadwick, *Priscillian*, 35–36. In response to the consecration of Priscillian, Hydatius appealed to Ambrose of Milan for help. With the assistance of that bishop, a rescript was obtained from Emperor Gratian against pseudobishops and Manichees.

221. Delphinus had been one of the two bishops from Aquitaine present at the Council of Saragossa; he did not permit Priscillian and his party to remain in his diocese.

222. Euchrotia was the wife of Attius Tiro Delphidius, a rhetor who was also a friend of the Roman poet Ausonius. He died while a middle-aged man, possibly around the same time Priscillian arrived (see Chadwick, *Priscillian*, 36–37); this might explain why Euchrotia and Procula joined the party heading for Rome.

223. This well-known rumor was also alluded to by Ausonius (Aus. *Prof.* 5.35).

224. Volentius was proconsul of Lusitania. John Matthews, *Western Aristocracies and Imperial Court: A.D. 364–425* (Oxford: Clarendon, 1975), 164n4, doubts if this was his formal position, suggesting that it may have represented a temporary promotion.

225. Proculus Gregorius was the praetorian prefect of Gaul (383); for a brief outline of his career, see ibid., 71–72. As Matthews suggests (164), the

fact that Ithacius could take refuge with him in Trier demonstrates that the imperial government did not speak with a unified voice.

226. The idea that power is for sale to the highest bidder is another Sallustian theme; see Sal. *Jug.* 8.2; 20.1; 31.25.

227. As praetorian prefect, Gregory was in charge of Spain as well as Gaul. Nevertheless, his ability to overturn the judgment against Ithacius was thwarted when Macedonius appealed to the emperor directly and had the case given to Marinianus, the newly appointed *vicarius* of Spain (Matthews, *Western Aristocracies*, 164–165).

228. Magnus Maximus was the commander of the Roman forces in Britain. Dissatisfied with Emperor Gratian, he revolted in 383 and crossed into Gaul. Near Paris he fought and defeated Gratian's army, forcing the young emperor to flee. Gratian was eventually killed in August 383, leaving Maximus to consolidate his power in Gaul. Since he wanted to be accepted by Theodosius, he actively sought the support of the church and was not inclined to support heretics. For Martin's encounters with Maximus, see Sulp.-Sev. *Mart.* 20, Sulp.-Sev. *Dial.* 2.6; 3.11–13, and further (2.50.2).

229. As Matthews, *Western Aristocracies*, 43, notes, the choice to have the case tried in Bordeaux, the seat of anti-Priscillianist Bishop Delphinus, did not bode well for the Priscillianist cause.

230. Priscillian evidently felt that the bishops were against him, and in view of his past success in capitalizing on his influence in the imperial court, this must have seemed an intelligent ploy. Unfortunately, as Chadwick, *Priscillian*, 120, notes, "In this tense political and religious situation of the years 384–6 nothing would be less likely than an act of generosity by Maximus towards a Spanish bishop known to be regarded as heretical in both Rome and Milan."

231. Martin's struggle with both Maximus and his fellow bishops will be developed at greater length in Sulp.-Sev. *Dial.* 3.11–13.

232. The question of whether disputes that were primarily theological could be heard by a secular court was hotly disputed at this time (see discussion in Chadwick, *Priscillian*, 126–132).

233. As Chadwick, ibid., 140n1, notes, the Manichees were believed to have nocturnal assemblies where men and women prayed naked together.

234. At Sulp.-Sev. *Dial.* 3.11, Sulpicius noted that Maximus wanted the Priscillianists' property; thus a financial agent is brought in as prosecutor when Ithacius stepped aside (Chadwick, *Priscillian*, 144).

235. Since the death of Priscillian, Gallic bishops had been polarized over whether the matter had been handled correctly. This division, asserted Sulpicius, still existed in the Gallic churches.

Dialogues

Book I

1.   Sulpicius has chosen to avoid the normal literary practice of introducing his work with a preface loaded with conventional pleas of authorial inadequacy (see Sulp.-Sev. *Mart.* pref.1–1.9 and Sulp.-Sev. *Chron.* 1.1). He plunges right into this material but, with superb craftsmanship, will insert a deferred preface when Gallus takes over the role of main speaker (see further, 1.27.1).

2.   The inferior quality of Gallic priests and bishops, especially in comparison to Martin, will be a major theme of this work.

3.   Cyprian was bishop of Carthage (249–258). He was executed during the persecution of Valerian.

4.   The sand banks and shoals just off the coast of North Africa.

5.   A possible allusion to Sal. *Jug.* 78: "Between them and the populated Numidia, there are many empty places" (*inter illos et frequentem Numidiam multi vastique loci erant*). Chapters 3—5 of this work will make a number of allusions to Sallust, whose views are then employed as a frame of reference for the critique of clerics found in chapters 6—7 (see Richard Goodrich, "Satan and the Bishops: Origen, *Apokatastasis*, and Ecclesiastical Politics in Sulpicius Severus' *Dialogi*," *Adamantius* 19 [2013]: 88).

6.   Sal. *Jug.* 18.8.

7.   As Jacques Fontaine, *Gallus: Dialogues sur les vertus de Saint Martin* (Paris: Les Éditions du Cerf, 2006), 117n7, noted, this passage parallels the reception accorded Postumianus at 1.1.2 and may have been intended to emphasize the similarity between Sulpicius's monastic practices in Gaul and those of the excellent Cyrenians.

8.   Sulpicius here introduces a subtheme: the gluttony of the Gauls. Just as the introduction of Sallust frames the attack on Gallic clerics, the allusion to gluttony is used to offer a critique of Jerome (see Richard Goodrich, "*Vir Maxime Catholicus:* Sulpicius Severus' Use and Abuse of Jerome in *Dialogi*," *Journal of Ecclesiastical History* 58 [2007]: passim).

9.   The modesty of the Cyrenian priest is designed to serve as a counterpoint to the behavior of the clerics of Alexandria (1.6–7) and Gaul (1.21).

10.   Compare this to the Gallic priests who sit in the church discussing business affairs (2.1.2).

11.   This action must be set against the behavior of the Gallic clergy; at 1.21.2, Sulpicius noted that when a Gallic priest received some money, he viewed it as a sign of God's munificence toward himself. This sentiment also has a strong Sallustian cast: at Sal. *Jug.* 13.5–8, Sallust had noted the corrupting effects of money on government, and repeatedly stated that in Rome,

everything was for sale (Sal. *Jug.* 8.2, 20.1, 31.25; see discussion, Goodrich, "Satan and the Bishops," 89).

12.   For an analysis of this passage, especially its dependence on Sallust, see Goodrich, "Satan and the Bishops," passim. The harmony between the Cyrenian priest and his flock is now contrasted with the discord that tears Alexandria apart after the clerics attempted to impose their will upon the monks and laity of Egypt. This attack on the poor conduct of the clerics shares elements of Sulpicius's critique of the Priscillian controversy, discussed at Sulp.-Sev. *Chron.* 2.46–51, and later in this work at 3.11–13.

13.   This is a position that Rufinus had made famous in his battle with Jerome: Origen had not been a heretic, and any incorrect ideas now found in his works were the product of later heretics who had altered his treatises (Ruf. *Adult.* 7).

14.   See ibid., 9.

15.   Sulpicius now has Postumianus participate in a moment of episcopal disobedience: rather than obeying the bishop's decree that forbade anyone to read these books for fear of corruption (1.6.1), he reads them to reach his own conclusion.

16.   Just as Sulpicius had presented the opinion of Rufinus (that Origen's work had been altered) without crediting it to him, he now commandeers Jerome's opinion (that Origen should be read with discernment, sifting what was good from what was erroneous; see Hier. *Ep.* 85.4 and discussion at Goodrich, "Satan and the Bishops," 93–95). He does not acknowledge Jerome as the source of this position and, in the next chapter, will misrepresent Jerome's opinion.

17.   Sulpicius had a potential problem here: at Sulp.-Sev. *Mart.* 22.5, Sulpicius claimed that Martin had extended an offer of salvation to Satan. As this chapter makes clear, Sulpicius made no attempt to justify his earlier work; see discussion at Goodrich, "Satan and the Bishops," 84–87.

18.   As with the Arian and Priscillianist conflicts, Sulpicius strongly condemns the decision of the bishops to employ secular power to enforce ecclesiastical decisions.

19.   Sulpicius used the Latin word *peritissimus* (highly skilled) to describe Jerome. It is the same word he used previously to describe Origen (1.6.1).

20.   Many modern readers of this work have missed the subtlety of Sulpicius's attack on Jerome. As noted previously (1.6.4), he had placed Jerome's true position on Origen in Postumianus's mouth. In this passage, he reminds his readers of Jerome's stunning *volte-face* on the question of Origen's orthodoxy. Furthermore, he asserts that Jerome now condemned all of Origen's work. This was a charge that Jerome had vigorously denied (see, for instance, Hier. *Ep.* 85.4). For a discussion of Sulpicius's manipulation of Jerome's image, see Goodrich, "*Vir Maxime*," passim).

21. In other words, just as with the Priscillianist controversy, the bishops' attempt to suppress it had simply caused it to spread more widely and grow worse (Sulp.-Sev. *Chron.* 2.51.4).

22. Although ordained, Jerome (according to Epiphanius of Salamis; see Hier. *Ep.* 51.1) refused to exercise his clerical duties in Bethlehem, presumably because this would have required him to submit to one of his enemies, Bishop John of Jerusalem. If Postumianus had visited Bethlehem, then he would have known it; Sulpicius seems to have known about Jerome's intransigence through his letters and took this opportunity to remind his readers of Jerome's poor conduct; see discussion in Goodrich, "*Vir Maxime*," 208–209.

23. Gallus refers here to Jerome's famous letter to Eustochium (Hier. *Ep.* 22).

24. This was undoubtedly intended to raise a red flag in a reader's mind: Sulpicius signals that he is doing something clever, as he will again later (1.27.5).

25. Jerome has been subverted and converted into a critic of the Gauls (see discussion at Goodrich, "*Vir Maxime*," 198–199). Importantly, three of the four faults Gallus lists—avarice, vanity, and pride—are those that are repeatedly named as the faults of the Gallic clerics. Sulpicius will resurrect these charges further, when Postumianus also uses Jerome to offer the same complaints about the clerics (see 1.21.5).

26. Hier. *Ep.* 22.14.

27. Ter. *An.* 68.

28. The division of monks into groups of one hundred is a detail found in Hier. *Ep.* 22.35.

29. See Hier. *Ep.* 22.35: "Their first rule is to obey their elders."

30. Asps were a particularly terrifying creature in desert literature; see *Hist. mon.* 9:1–4 for an encounter with a large asp.

31. The small amount of food eaten by the desert fathers was an Egyptian commonplace; see, for instance, *Apophth. Patr.* Arsenios 17, in which Abba Daniel claims that the brothers would take Abba Arsenios one basket of bread a year, and when they returned in the following year, there would still be bread left over.

32. Bread from heaven is frequently represented as still being miraculously warm in desert literature; see *Hist. mon.* 8.40; 12.4.

33. See ibid., 10.8, for the story of Abba Patermutius, who every Sunday found a loaf from heaven in his cell.

34. This story is also found in Cassian *Inst.* 5.27.

35. Sulpicius is the certain man; his freedman, Pomponius, had abandoned him. An unnamed, former friend had encouraged Pomponius to leave. Pomponius was shipwrecked and died. See 3.18.

36. The *Historia monachorum* contains a very similar story about Abba Macarius's encounter with a hyena. This animal led Macarius to her cave, had

him heal her cubs, and then gave him the skin of a large ram (*Hist. mon.* 21.15–16).

37. Readers of this story might be reminded of Martin's sojourn on the island of Gallinaria, in which the hellebore he was eating was slowly poisoning him. As he drew close to death, however, he perceived the problem and with a quick prayer, drove off the danger (Sulp.-Sev. *Mart.* 6.5–6).

38. This is an interesting claim, as most scholars believe that Paul the Hermit existed only in Jerome's active imagination (J. N. D. Kelly, *Jerome: His Life, Writings, and Controversies* [London: Duckworth, 1975], 60–61). Nevertheless, this reference does allow Sulpicius to make another connection to eastern asceticism and a widely published book (Jerome's *Life of Paul*).

39. A reversal of the consequences of Adam and Eve's decision to eat from the tree of the knowledge of good and evil (Gen 3:1–7).

40. This is a common desert topos: see, for example, the stories about Abba Arsenios, who frequently refused to meet delegations of bishops, monks, and laypeople (*Apophth. Patr.* Arsenios 7, 13, 28, 34, 37). These examples could be profitably compared to the Gallic monks and clerics censured later who are said to be vain and court those who will call them holy (see 1.21).

41. See *Apophth. Patr.* Arsenios 13, where Abba Arsenios defends his refusal to meet people by stating that a person has to choose to live either with God or with humans.

42. Possibly a reference to the Pachomian monasteries, which tended to be larger.

43. See Cassian *Inst.* 4.2–9, for the Egyptian procedures for admitting novices.

44. Dan 3:19–27.

45. A parallel is found in the cold dew that protected Abba Apollonius when he was ordered into a fire by a persecuting Roman magistrate (*Hist. mon.* 19.8); see also Sulp.-Sev. *Ep.* 1.15.

46. The storax (or styrax) is a family of shrubs that produce an aromatic resin used in antiquity.

47. John Cassian offered a different version of this story: although set in a similar context of testing a disciple's obedience, there was no miraculous blossoming, and after a year the abbot was satisfied and threw the stick away (Cassian *Inst.* 4.14).

48. See 1.22.

49. A similar story appears later: a virgin will cure a demoniac with straws from Martin's bed (2.8.8–9).

50. John Cassian suggested that vainglory is one of the most difficult sins to overcome. It is a spiritual sin that becomes stronger the more progress a monk makes toward perfection (see Cassian *Inst.* 11.1–19).

51. This chapter must be read against the story of the simple Cyrenian presbyter that opened this account; that man concealed the fact that he was

a priest, lived in a humble shack of twigs, ate the simplest foods, and refused Postumianus's gift of ten gold coins (see 1.4–5).

52.   The Blemmyes were an Ethiopian people who were renowned for their ferocity.

53.   Possibly John of Lycopolis, one of the most famous of the desert fathers and the subject of the first chapter of the *Historia monachorum* (*Hist. mon.* 1).

54.   Sulpicius seems to have forgotten that Martin had done something similar: at Sulp.-Sev. *Mart.* 5.3–6.3, Martin traveled back to his homeland to preach the gospel to his pagan parents. His mother was converted, but his father was not. Why this was appropriate for Martin and an inappropriate desire for this young monk is not clear.

55.   Sulpicius raises an interesting issue here, one that did trouble the Egyptian desert fathers: How did a person balance the commandment to love one's neighbor (or in this case, family members) with Christ's command to leave family for his sake? Christ said, "Anyone who loves their father or mother more than me is not worthy of me" (Matt 10:37). The monk was supposed to sever all ties with the world, and once he had made the decision to follow Christ, these words would apply: "Whoever puts his hand to the plow and then looks back is not fit for service in the kingdom of God" (Luke 9:62). While many desert fathers simply refused to see their relatives, others would extend care secretly to their relatives. An example of this, according to John Cassian, was Abba Archebius, who, when he learned that his father had died and left his mother in debt, took on extra work to earn enough to repay her debt in secret, without leaving his monastery (Cassian *Inst.* 5.38).

56.   Paulinus of Nola. See pp. 2, 5–6 Sulp.-Sev. *Mart.* 19.3.

57.   This hearty eastern embrace of Martin is intended to be read against the rejection of him in the West and also further cements his identification with the best of eastern asceticism, a point that will be made less subtly in the next chapter.

58.   See Sulp.-Sev. *Mart.* 1.9.

59.   A sentiment that Sulpicius employed at Sulp.-Sev. *Mart.* 27.3–4.

60.   See John 14:12, where Jesus stated that all who believed in him would do the works he did.

61.   Although, as noted above (288n1), Sulpicius has avoided the normal practice of opening a work with a preface, he now inserts a minipreface in which Gallus offers the conventional pleas that would be expected in this sort of work (see discussion at Tore Janson, *Latin Prose Prefaces: Studies in Literary Conventions* [Stockholm: Almquist and Wiksell, 1964], passim, and following page numbers). Sulpicius has subverted his genre by placing a preface in the middle of his work. Here the reader finds the conventions of Latin prose prefaces deployed; Gallus's inadequacy (124–125); his objections overridden because of his obedience to those who demand this material from

him (117–120); the deficiency of his style (125–133); and the privileging of content over form (133–134). For a full treatment of this passage, see ibid., 138–140.

62. See Luke 1:64. This is also a subtle modification of a literary convention: normally an author will solve the problem of his inadequacy to write by pointing to stories where God empowered the subject to do more than he or she normally would have been able to do. Consequently, with God's support, the author might be able to overcome their deficiencies and write something worthy of the subject (Janson, *Latin Prose*, 122–123); Sulpicius alters the conventional approach by placing the solution in Postumianus's mouth.

63. Through the voice of Postumianus, Sulpicius continues to play with the forms and conventions of literary prefaces, and with the word *rhetor*, he signals that he is doing so. See above 1.8.6.

64. Sulpicius's tour de force concludes with Gallus making a conventional claim to be speaking unvarnished truth and limiting himself to relating only what he had witnessed himself.

Book II

1. Gregory of Tours identified Bryce (who became bishop of Tours after Martin's death) as one of Martin's deacons (Greg.-T. *Hist.* 2.1), and noted a history of conflict between the two. Sulpicius will tar Bryce's reputation later (3.15.1–7), which suggests that the unnamed archdeacon here might also have been Bryce.

2. Martin is contrasted with the priests of the church, who, unlike the priest of Cyrenia (1.5) and the monks of Egypt (1.17), are more interested in receiving visitors and discussing their business interests.

3. See further (2.13.3) for the claim that Sulpicius had a special ability to pry information out of Martin about his spiritual experiences.

4. Clare Stancliffe, *St. Martin and His Hagiographer* (Oxford: Oxford University Press, 1983), 60–61, regards this as a verbal allusion to the story of Servius Tullus in Valerius (V. Max. 1.6.1) in which flames were emitted by the sleeping man's head.

5. See also Sulp.-Sev. *Mart.* 12.3, where Martin froze the mourners at a pagan funeral, and further, 2.9.6, where he freezes a pack of dogs. A similar miracle is recorded at *Hist. mon.* 8.25–29.

6. This looks back to 2.1.9, where Gallus said that pious inquirers would be rewarded with information about Martin's deeds, and ahead to 2.13.3, where he asserts that Sulpicius could always get stories out of Martin.

7. See 1.24.2–5, where Sulpicius had argued that Martin's power had been hindered by the fact that he had to live in the world as a bishop.

8. Martin restored a catechumen to life at Sulp.-Sev. *Mart.* 7, and a slave who had hung himself at Sulp.-Sev. *Mart.* 8.

9.   In each of the preceding chapters, Gallus has asserted that he was a witness of what he described; he now shifts the basis for this story to the claim that this is a well-known story, attested by faithful brothers.

10.   The Emperor Valentinian I ruled the western half of the Roman Empire 364–375. One of his great strengths as an emperor, according to Ammianus Marcellinus, was his indifference to religious matters (Amm. *Res.* 30.9.5)—a change from his predecessors Constantius II and Julian.

11.   Here Sulpicius forges a link with the Cyrenian priest of 1.5.6, who had rejected the ten gold pieces that Postumianus had offered. These two examples stand against the Gallic clerics who are said to accept money (1.21.2).

12.   The usurper Magnus Maximus ruled in the West 383–388. He played an important role in the Priscillian controversy (see Sulp.-Sev. *Chron.* 2.49–51, and further, 3.11–13), and Martin had dinner with him on at least one other occasion (Sulp.-Sev. *Mart.* 20).

13.   This paragraph expresses some dangerous sentiments. Maximus was a usurper, and after Theodosius defeated him in 388, most of the sources referred to him as such (see for example, Pacatus, who called Maximus a "bloodthirsty tyrant," *Pan.* 12/2.23–31). To confer legitimacy upon Maximus by calling him an emperor and claiming that his usurpation might have been justified was extremely dangerous. There had been little tolerance extended in the past to Gallic supporters of defeated usurpers (see Amm. *Res.* 14.5.1–5; and further 3.1).

14.   A possible allusion to Acts 24:24–26, in which the Apostle Paul has frequent meetings with the Roman procurator Felix. According to the text, the two had many discussions about faith, justice, self-control, and the coming judgment.

15.   See Luke 7:38.

16.   The queen of Sheba (2 Chr 9:1–9).

17.   See 3.13.4–5, for the story of Martin being forced by necessity to join the communion of Ithacius, which led to a diminution of his spiritual power.

18.   This is problematic. If Martin was in his seventies when he had dinner with Maximus (sometime between 383 and 388), then he would have been older than twenty when discharged from Julian's army in 356. Stancliffe, *St. Martin,* 119–133, has argued that the word *septuagenarian* here should be interpreted as a reference to someone who was old, rather than a literal description of Martin's age.

19.   See Luke 10:38–42.

20.   The reference to unfavorable opinion and the quote "we are Gauls" forms a link between this passage and the critique attributed to Jerome at 1.9.1.

21.   See Acts 19:12, where people are healed by handkerchiefs that have touched Paul, as well as Sulp.-Sev. *Mart.* 18.5, where threads plucked from Martin's robe heal.

22. See Sulp.-Sev. *Ep.* 1.

23. At Hier. *Iou.* 1.3, Jerome uses the biblical parable of the sower (Matt 13:8)—the analogy of the thirty-, sixty-, and one hundredfold return of grain—to schematize the three legitimate Christian states: the married earn a thirtyfold return of grain, the widowed sixty, and virgins earn a hundredfold return on their life. As a result, wrote Jerome, marriage is honored, but virginity is preferred.

24. An allusion back to Jerome's criticism of Gallic gluttony and the improper relationships between the virgins and clerics (see 1.9.2).

25. This type of inquest is hinted at previously (2.1.9) and the assertion suggests that Sulpicius was able to overcome Martin's modest reticence. Consequently, Sulpicius knew stories that others—maybe even the monks of Martin's monastery—did not know.

26. Agnes and Thecla were two famous early martyrs; Mary is presumably the mother of Jesus. All three were virgins, which creates a link back to the material that has just been discussed.

27. For conversations with Mercury and Jupiter, see also Sulp.-Sev. *Mart.* 22.1 and further, 3.6.4.

28. The monks who had lived with Martin at Marmoutier had criticized the version of Martin offered in the *Life of Saint Martin.* Their refusal to believe some of these stories was not necessarily a problem, for, as Sulpicius made clear, not everyone was able to see Martin's works (see 2.2.1–2).

29. Once again, disbelief in the deeds of Martin is equated with doubt about the fundamental Christian message (see 1.26.4 and Sulp.-Sev. *Ep.* 1.7).

30. Presumably, because the light is failing and the discussion can no longer be transcribed. This is a conventional way to close a dialogue, and Sulpicius will use it again at 3.17.1; for a discussion of this literary convention, see Catherine Conybeare, *The Irrational Augustine* (New York: Oxford University Press, 2006), 29.

Book III

1. This is a new approach; to this point, Sulpicius and Gallus had been the witnesses who offered testimony about Martin's life. For an explanation of this change of policy, see Sulpicius's comments at 3.5.

2. Possibly the same Aurelius who was the addressee for *Epistle* II.

3. Sulpicius offers a nod to literary conventions with this plea of oratorical inadequacy (see Tore Janson, *Latin Prose Prefaces: Studies in Literary Conventions* [Stockholm: Almquist and Wiksell, 1964], 125–133).

4. This is the first reference to the fact that these stories were being written down. The literary artifice is a bit thin here: according to the text, only a single night has passed between books II and III of the *Dialogues.* Yet at 3.5.2, Sulpicius wrote that there had been a backlash among readers of those stories

that has required recourse to further witnesses. Most scholars believe that books I and II of the *Dialogues* were published as a unit, and that book III was written later (see Stancliffe, *St. Martin and His Hagiographer* [Oxford: Oxford University Press, 1983], 81–82).

5.   This marks a radical departure from books I and II: these are the first good Gallic bishops mentioned in the *Dialogues*.

6.   The story is similar to the account of Jesus healing the man who was both mute and deaf; see Mark 7:31–37.

7.   Avitianus is described here as an imperial *comes*, a word that in later Latin is translated "count." At this time, *comites* were trusted imperial retainers who had a wide variety of responsibilities. It is possible that this Avitianus is the same man who prosecuted the praetorian prefect Mamertinus during the reign of Valentinian I (Amm. *Res.* 27.7.1). Avitianus's brutal nature is emphasized in two later stories (3.4 and 3.8).

8.   Sulpicius here evokes the miracle of overflowing oil found at 2 Kgs 4:1–7.

9.   This passage reads as an improvement on the story told in Acts 19:13–15, in which some Jewish priests tried to expel a demon by calling upon "the Jesus whom Paul preaches." Their attempt was unsuccessful. See also further (3.14.2), where a storm at sea is calmed by invoking Martin's name.

10.   This scene evokes the activities of the infamous Paul "the Chain," who was sent by Emperor Constantius II to Britain to arrest the supporters of Magnentius. Paul was also legendary for his cruelty, and degraded free men by placing them in chains before executing them (Amm. *Res.* 14.5.6–9).

11.   A possible allusion to the story of the demon that came to wake Mark Antony at Actium (V. Max. 1.7.7; Stancliffe, *St. Martin*, 60–61).

12.   There is another literary slip here: Sulpicius abruptly drops the persona of Gallus and inserts a first person defense of the practice of adducing witnesses for these stories and the choice of literary genre.

13.   Or to put it more accurately, there was disbelief about the stories that had been published and circulated in books I and II of the *Dialogues*. In those books, only three people were present: Sulpicius, Gallus, and Postumianus. It would have taken more than a night for the stories to have been written down and distributed, and for disbelief to have reached such a level as to occasion this change of practice. Obviously, a significant amount of time had elapsed before book III was composed.

14.   Countering the charge that Sulpicius had lied about Martin, stated at 1.26.4.

15.   See 3.1.3.

16.   See Ath. *Vit. Anton.* 31 for the belief that demons are able to foretell the movements of individuals because they are quicker and run ahead of travelers.

17.   See 2.13.6 and Sulp.-Sev. *Mart.* 22.1.

18. See 1 Cor 6:3.

19. See Mark 5:25–34.

20. This story parallels the account in which Jesus instructs the disciples to cast their net on the right side of the boat after a long, unsuccessful night of fishing (John 21:1–6).

21. Stat. *Theb.* 8.750.

22. For Sulpicius's other appraisals of Maximus's character, see 2.6.2, as well as Sulp.-Sev. *Mart.* 20.

23. An important theme in Sulpicius's *Chronicles*, especially those chapters that dealt with the Arian and Priscillianist controversies; see Sulp.-Sev. *Chron.* 2.35–51.

24. Sulpicius's lengthy account of the Priscillianist controversy (including the naming of the participants) forms the last six chapters (2.46–51) of book II of his *Chronicles.*

25. Although Priscillian was executed for political and ecclesiastical reasons, this sentence suggests that Maximus was also motivated by financial considerations: he could add to his war chest by confiscating the assets of the guilty. It was no coincidence that led him to appoint Patricius, a treasury officer, prosecutor for the second trial of Priscillian (see Sulp.-Sev. *Chron.* 2.51.1).

26. Maximus, having defeated Emperor Gratian, was now in a position to deal harshly with those loyalists who had supported the former emperor. Martin traveled to court on their behalf to plead for imperial mercy.

27. Once again, Sulpicius defended the actions of the usurper Maximus (see 294n13). Not only was this dangerous, but it was unnecessary: the story would not be weaker if he had simply asserted that Maximus was avaricious.

28. See Sulp.-Sev. *Chron.* 2.51.1.

29. Ancient Andethanna, now a town in Luxemburg.

30. As the angel noted at 3.13.4, the circumstances (protecting the ascetics of Spain and those for whom he had sought forgiveness) compelled Martin to do something that he did not want to do. A similar justification was offered at 2.7.3, where his desire to win imperial favor for others compelled him to violate his normal rule and have dinner with Maximus's wife.

31. This number poses a chronological problem: Priscillian was executed in 386, so if these events were occurring a year later, this would mean that Martin lived until 403. Jacques Fontaine, *Gallus: Dialogues sur les vertus de Saint Martin* (Paris: Les Éditions du Cerf, 2006), 343n5, suggests that there is a copyist's error in the manuscript and that the word *sedecim* (sixteen) should actually be *sed decem* (but ten), which would mean that Martin died in 397.

32. The portion of the Mediterranean sea that is just off the west coast of Italy.

33. See 3.3.6 for a similar example of the power of Martin's name.

34.   Bryce became bishop of Tours in 397, after Martin's death. According to Gregory of Tours, he would later be driven out of his post when one of his servants became pregnant (Greg.-T. *Hist.* 2.1). After a sojourn in Rome, he eventually returned to Tours and served seven years as bishop before his death.

35.   There is a lacuna in the manuscript at this point.

36.   It is possible that this is the same angry man mentioned earlier at 1.12.2.

37.   Phalaris was the ruler of Agrigentum in Sicily (ca. 570–549 BC). He was notorious for his cruelty, having roasted his enemies alive in a bronze bull.

38.   When Paulinus and Therasia withdrew from the world, they constructed a shrine and monastery in honor of Saint Felix at Nola.

39.   See 1.25.7 for the proposition that a single man, Martin, was greater than all of the eastern ascetics combined.

40.   A city on the west bank of the Nile river in upper Egypt.

41.   Pomponius was one of Sulpicius's ex-slaves and is the fugitive alluded to at 1.12.3–4.

42.   The man who convinced Pomponius to take flight (see also 1.12.3).

LIST OF ABBREVIATIONS
AND BIBLIOGRAPHY

Primary Source Abbreviations

Ambr. *Obit. Th.*	Ambrose of Milan, *Oration on the Death of Theodosius.*
Ambr. *Off.*	Ambrose of Milan, *On the Duties of the Clergy.*
Amm. *Res.*	Ammianus Marcellinus, *Histories.*
Apophth. *Patr.*	*Apophthegmata patrum* (*Sayings of the Desert Fathers*).
App. *Syr.*	Appian, *Syria.*
Ath. *Vit. Anton.*	Athanasius, *Life of Antony.*
Aug. *Ciu.*	Augustine, *The City of God.*
Aug. *Conf.*	Augustine, *Confessions.*
Aus. *Prof.*	Ausonius, *Professors.*
Cassian *Coll.*	Cassian, *Conferences.*
Cassian *Inst.*	Cassian, *Institutes.*
Cic. *N.D.*	Cicero, *On the Nature of the Gods.*
Cic. *Orat.*	Cicero, *On Oratory.*
Cypr. *Ad. Fort.*	Cyprian, *An Exhortation to Martyrdom.*
D.S. *Hist.*	Diodorus Siculus, *Universal History.*
Eus. *Hist. Eccl.*	Eusebius, *Church History.*
Eus. *V. C.*	Eusebius, *Life of Constantine.*
Eutr. *Brev.*	Eutropius, *Breviarium.*
Gennad. *Vir.*	Gennadius, *On Illustrious Men.*
Greg.-T. *Hist.*	Gregory of Tours, *The History of the Franks.*
Hdt. *Hist.*	Herodotus, *Histories.*
Hier. *Chron.*	Jerome, *Eusebius's Chronicle.*
Hier. *Ep.*	Jerome, *Epistles.*
Hier. *Ezech.*	Jerome, *Commentary on Ezekiel.*
Hier. *Iou.*	Jerome, *Against Jovinian.*

299

Hier. *Vigil.*	Jerome, *Against Vigilantius.*
Hier. *Vir. ill.*	Jerome, *On Illustrious Men.*
Hier. *Vit. Hil.*	Jerome, *Life of Saint Hilary the Monk.*
Hilar. *Contra Const.*	Hilary of Poitiers, *Against Constantius.*
Hilar. *Trin.*	Hilary of Poitiers, *On the Trinity.*
Hist. mon.	*History of the Monks in Egypt.*
Iren. *Haer.*	Irenaeus, *Against Heresies.*
Isid. *Vir.*	Isidore, *On Illustrious Men.*
Jos. *A.J.*	Josephus, *Antiquities of the Jews.*
Jos. *B.J.*	Josephus, *The Jewish War.*
Justin *Epit.*	Justin, *Epitome of the Philippic History of Pompeius Trogus.*
Lact. *Inst.*	Lactantius, *The Divine Institutes.*
Lact. *Mort.*	Lactantius, *On the Death of the Persecutors.*
Liv.	Livy, *History of Rome.*
Or. *Princ.*	Origen, *On First Principles.*
Oros. *Hist.*	Orosius, *History against the Pagans.*
Ov. *Met.*	Ovid, *Metamorphoses.*
P.-Nol. *Ep.*	Paulinus of Nola, *Epistles.*
Pan.	*The Latin Panegyrics.*
Pass. Ap. Pet. Paul	*The Passion of the Holy Apostles Peter and Paul.*
Pass. Perp.	*The Passion of Perpetua and Felicity.*
Paulin. *Vit. Ambr.*	Paulinus of Milan, *The Life of Ambrose.*
Plin. *Ep.*	Pliny the Younger, *Epistles.*
Possid. *Vit. Aug.*	Possidius, *The Life of Saint Augustine.*
Ruf. *Adult.*	Rufinus, *On the Adulteration of the Books of Origen.*
Ruf. *Hist.*	Rufinus, *Eusebius's History of the Church, Translated and Continued by Rufinus.*
Rut. Nam. *Red.*	Rutilius Namatianus, *Concerning His Return.*
Sal. *Cat.*	Sallust, *The Catiline Conspiracy.*
Sal. *Jug.*	Sallust, *The Jugurthine War.*
Stat. *Theb.*	Statius, *Thebaid.*
Sulp.-Sev. *Chron.*	Sulpicius Severus, *Chronicles.*
Sulp.-Sev. *Dial.*	Sulpicus Severus, *Dialogues.*
Sulp.-Sev. *Mart.*	Sulpicius Severus, *The Life of Saint Martin.*
Tac. *Ann.*	Tacitus, *Annals.*
Tac. *Hist.*	Tacitus, *Histories.*
Ter. *An.*	Terence, *Andria.*

Tert. *Apol.*	Tertullian, *Apology.*
Tert. *Iud.*	Tertullian, *Against the Jews.*
Tert. *Virg.*	Tertullian, *On Veiling Virgins.*
V. Max.	Valerius Maximus, *Deeds and Memorable Sayings.*
Ver. *Aen.*	Virgil, *Aeneid.*

SECONDARY SOURCES

Barnes, T. D. *Athanasius and Constantius.* Cambridge, MA: Harvard University Press, 1993.

———. "Legislation against the Christians." *Journal of Roman Studies* 58 (1969): 32–50.

Bernheimer, Richard. "The Martyrdom of Isaiah." *The Art Bulletin* 34, no. 1 (1952): 19–34.

Bright, John. *A History of Israel.* 3rd ed. Philadelphia: Westminster Press, 1981.

Bryce, Trevor. *Ancient Syria: A 3,000 Year History.* Oxford: Oxford University Press, 2014.

Chadwick, Henry. *Priscillian of Avila: The Occult and Charismatic in the Early Church.* Oxford: Clarendon, 1976.

Conybeare, Catherine. *The Irrational Augustine.* New York: Oxford University Press, 2006.

Drijvers, Jan. *Helena Augusta: The Mother of Constantine the Great and the Legend of Her Finding of the True Cross.* Leiden: Brill, 1992.

Drinkwater, John. "The Usurpers Constantine III (407–411) and Jovinus (411–413)." *Britannia* 29 (1998): 269–298.

Fontaine, Jacques. *Gallus: Dialogues sur les vertus de Saint Martin.* Paris: Les Éditions du Cerf, 2006.

———. *Sulpice Sévère: Vie de Saint Martin. Tome II: Commentaire.* Paris: Les Éditions du Cerf, 1968.

Goodrich, Richard. "Aristocrats and Slaves: Status in Early Western Monasticism." *Studia Anselmiana* 146 (2009): 151–157.

———. *Contextualising Cassian: Aristocrats, Asceticism, and Reformation in Fifth Century Gaul.* Oxford: Oxford University Press, 2007.

———. "Satan and the Bishops: Origen, *Apokatastasis*, and Ecclesiastical Politics in Sulpicius Severus' *Dialogi.*" *Adamantius* 19 (2013): 84–96.

———. "*Vir Maxime Catholicus:* Sulpicius Severus' Use and Abuse of Jerome in *Dialogi.*" *Journal of Ecclesiastical History* 58 (2007): 189–210.

Janson, Tore. *Latin Prose Prefaces: Studies in Literary Conventions.* Stockholm: Almquist and Wiksell, 1964.

Kelly, J. N. D. *Jerome: His Life, Writings, and Controversies.* London: Duckworth, 1975.

Kuhrt, Amélie. *The Ancient Near East c. 3000–330 BC.* Vol. 2. London: Routledge, 1995.

Matthews, John. *Western Aristocracies and Imperial Court: A.D. 364–425.* Oxford: Clarendon, 1975.

Scolnic, Benjamin. "When Did the Future Antiochus IV Arrive in Athens?" *Journal of the American School of Classical Studies at Athens* 83, no. 1 (2014): 123–142.

Scourfield, J. H. D. *Consoling Heliodorus: A Commentary on Jerome, Letter 60.* Oxford: Clarendon Press, 1993.

Senneville-Grave, Ghislaine de. *Sulpice Sévère: Chroniques.* Sources Chrétiennes 441. Paris: Les Éditions du Cerf, 1999.

Stancliffe, Clare. *St. Martin and His Hagiographer.* Oxford: Oxford University Press, 1983.

Van Andel, G. K. *The Concept of History in the Chronicle of Sulpicius Severus.* Amsterdam: Adolf M. Hakkert, 1976.

VanderKam, James. *From Joshua to Caiaphas: High Priests after the Exile.* Minneapolis: Fortress Press, 2004.

Walsh, Peter. *Letters of St. Paulinus of Nola.* 2 vols. Ancient Christian Writers 35–36. Westminster, Maryland: Newman Press, 1966–67.

Woodman, A. J. *Rhetoric in Classical Historiography.* Kent, England: Croom Helm Ltd., 1988.

INDEX

green
press
INITIATIVE

Paulist Press is committed to preserving ancient forests and natural resources. We elected to print this title on 30% post consumer recycled paper, processed chlorine free. As a result, for this printing, we have saved:

4 Trees (40' tall and 6-8" diameter)
2 Million BTUs of Total Energy
353 Pounds of Greenhouse Gases
1,915 Gallons of Wastewater
129 Pounds of Solid Waste

Paulist Press made this paper choice because our printer, Thomson-Shore, Inc., is a member of Green Press Initiative, a nonprofit program dedicated to supporting authors, publishers, and suppliers in their efforts to reduce their use of fiber obtained from endangered forests.

For more information, visit www.greenpressinitiative.org

Environmental impact estimates were made using the Environmental Defense Paper Calculator. For more information visit: www.papercalculator.org.